Literature and Sensibilities in the Weimar Era

José Porrúa Turanzas, S.A.
EDICIONES

Director General:
JOSÉ PORRÚA VENERO

Sub-Director General:
ENRIQUE PORRÚA VENERO

Director:
CONSTANTINO GARCÍA GARVÍA

Asesor literario:
BRUNO M. DAMIANI

studia humanitatis

Directed by
BRUNO M. DAMIANI
The Catholic University of America

LITERATURE and SENSIBILITIES in the WEIMAR ERA

Short Stories in the *Neue Rundschau*

by Valerie D. Greenberg

Publisher and distributor
José Porrúa Turanzas S.A.
Cea Bermúdez, 10 - Madrid - 3
España

Distributor for the U.S.A.
Studia Humanitatis
1383 Kersey Lane
Potomac, Maryland 20854

I.S.B.N. 0–93–5568–25–5
Library of Congress Catalog Card Number 81–52481

Impreso en Los Estados Unidos
Printed in the United States of America

Cea Bermúdez, 10 - Madrid - 3
Ediciones Jose Porrúa Turanzas, S.A.

---

designed by Richard Kinney

Contents

Preface

Establishing relations between literature and political and economic conditions, or between attitudes and beliefs of society, has been a concern of historical, sociological, and also of literary scholarship. The basic assumption of such scholarship derives from a recognition that literature always presents some reflection of that reality. Moreover, the approach of that kind of scholarship to literature has been dictated primarily by interests and exigencies of the disciplines of history and sociology. Consequently, literary works have been viewed as historical and social documents without too much regard to their constitutive artistic determinants and aesthetic qualities.

Literary scholarship adopted the same stance whenever it ignored the fact that the documentary function of literature depended on what the nature of literature was considered to be. Not every literary work is a literary work of art. When it is a work of art, it may still fulfill the function of reflecting social reality, but it does so in a manner which is different from that of an essay or historical or sociological treatises. The latter reflect that reality by mirroring it in faithful *conformity* to what is objectively given. They proceed from an analysis to a synthesis of materials, which are selected on the basis of their established evidence and in the light of their concrete connections and functions in the objective world. Historical and sociological discourse is constantly mindful of its objective reference. It is "intentionally" bound to the existential qualifications of real persons, occurrences, conditions, and effects, as well as to their actual relations. This discourse fulfills its function when its presentation is a faithful representation of reality.

Roman Ingarden has convincingly shown that the very structure, characteristic of a literary work of art, is subject to exigencies of artistic presentation. The author arranges his materials to fit the system appropriate to the presentation of a world whose parts are linked through various coherences for the purpose of constituting an artistically formed whole that is capable of supporting a unified network of aesthetic (immediately perceptible) qualities, i.e., an aesthetic object. Consequently, the systemic totality which founds the presentation of a literary work of art does not conform to that of objective reality. Although the motifs, i.e., the material elements, such as the setting, the characters and their relations, actions, attitudes, beliefs, views, speech and gestures are normally drawn from real sources, they are assorted and arranged in spatio-temporal coherences intended to support the aesthetic superstructure of the work, which is hardly ever identical to the concrete real structure from which they are drawn. A historical treatise describes them in this, their primary structure, whereas a literary work of art cannot, except perhaps in unusual instances, and then only where small motif clusters happen to fit the whole. Even the selection of materials for artistic purposes is governed by their potentiality to serve as the basis of the aesthetic superstructure, which means that they need to be adjustable to it. This is at least one other reason why the presentation of a literary work of art does not conform to reality; it is merely a material *adaptation* to it. We may conclude, then, that a literary work of art does not reflect reality in the sense of reproducing it; its presentation is a mere semblance of reality.

Because a literary work of art not only presents a world but exhibits it in its manifold aspects for our imaginational experience, we do not merely apprehend cognitively the presented situations, the characters and their actions, thoughts, emotions, and destinies; we are also enabled to intuit their qualitative dimensions. These diverse and correlative qualities endow the presented world with an aura which eludes the tight net of predominantly rational cognition elicited by analytical and synthesizing presentations of the real world. Thus, in historical or sociological writing, it is the presented world itself that becomes thematic, whereas in an artistically exhibited presentation that world's qualities become thematic. By virtue of this qualitative thematic structure, the world does not reveal itself only as it is, for its qualities also allude to its potentialities. For instance, an artistically presented social situation, adapted to reality, may point towards certain trends which we can intuit as implicit in some of its qualities.

In the light of these observations, it appears that artistic literature cannot be considered as a simple reflection of social reality, for it is inadequate as a socio-cultural document and at the same time more than a mere documentary reflection. It may shed a revealing light on that reality on the strength of its qualitative (aesthetic) structure precisely because it does not focus on material conformity. It should also be added that it is important to recognize that artistic literature may, at certain periods, have its own impact on that reality by affecting the intellectual life of some societies. It follows that if we are to ascertain the extent and the degree of accuracy to which literature reflects, and sometimes affects, socio-cultural reality, one must rely both on literary and non-literary sources.

In her highly enlightening study, Dr. Valerie Greenberg examines the basic postures that emerge from short stories which appeared in the *Neue Rundschau* between 1922 and 1933.

Her findings derive from a careful blending of penetrating literary investigations and keen insights into the economic, political, social, and intellectual reality of those portentous years. Her point of view is that of a critic-historian, and my Preface is written in large measure in recognition of what I believe constitutes her set of scholarly assumptions.

Eugene H. Falk

Acknowledgments

I would like to thank the following persons: my husband for his encouragement; Professor Siegfried E. Mews of the Department of Germanic Languages, the University of North Carolina at Chapel Hill, for his advice and criticism; Professor Richard H. Lawson and Professor Christoph E. Schweitzer of the same department for their critical reading of the manuscript; and Stevie Champion for producing a beautiful final copy.

Introduction

One of the most turbulent and interesting of modern cultures was Germany's during the brief Weimar Republic.[1] After fifteen tumultuous years it ended conclusively when Hitler became Chancellor on 30 January 1933. Scholars in various fields are motivated by its disastrous outcome to examine and re-examine the period in an endeavor to ascertain the reasons for the downfall of the Republic and the rise of totalitarian dictatorship.[2] Not merely the catastrophic end of Weimar culture, however, has caused it to capture the imagination, but its variety and richness while it flourished. Historian Walter Laqueur calls it ". . . a fascinating period but not at all easy to come to grips with precisely because it was so rich in content and contradictory in character."[3]

---

[1] Walter Laqueur, in the preface of his balanced and comprehensive study, *Weimar: A Cultural History 1918–1933* (New York: G. P. Putnam's Sons, 1974), calls it ". . . the first truly modern culture."

[2] In his preface to *Die deutsche Literatur in der Weimarer Republik* (Stuttgart: Reclam, 1974), p. 7, editor Wolfgang Rothe sees the question of the fate of the Weimar Republic as the primary motivation for studies of the literature of the period.

[3] *Weimar*, Preface.

One measure of the temper of an era is its literature. The Weimar period, the scene of a kaleidoscope of possibilities in the arts and letters,[4] sustained a body of literature which manifests the tensions and contradictions of the time.[5] Literary and cultural periodicals were a significant vehicle for this literature. There is widespread agreement that periodicals were a dominant force on the Weimar cultural scene.[6] At their height in 1931 there was a total of 7,652 periodicals, of which 96 are classified as literary.[7] In this "flood" of periodicals the non-partisan literary-cultural review affords an insight into "Zeitgeist" which cannot be gained from opposition publications on the right or left.[8] The latter's tendentiousness or

---

[4] Jost Hermand and Frank Trommler emphasize this point in their recent study *Die Kultur der Weimarer Republik* (Munich: Nymphenburg, 1978), p. 110. "Denn die sogenannten Zwanziger Jahre waren nun einmal auch auf ästhetischem Gebiet geradezu ein Schlachtfeld, wo es zwar zu vorübergehenden Siegen, aber nicht zu einem endgültigen Friedensschluss kam."

[5] Rothe, ed., *Die deutsche Literatur in der Weimarer Republik*, p. 7, supports this assertion: "Die zeitgenössische Literatur, . . . [spiegelt] . . . die äusseren Lebensbedingungen, die politischen Verhältnisse und die weltanschaulichen Positionen der Jahre 1918 bis 1932 . . ."

[6] "Das auf Kampf und Breitenwirkung eingestellte kulturelle Leben verlieh der periodischen Presse überragende Bedeutung: trotz der äusserlich bedingten Einschränkungen umfassen allein die hier behandelten und genannten Blätter über eine halbe Million Seiten (z. T. Quartformat). Und während die Buchproducktion mit der Gesamtwirtschaft um 1930 eine Krise durchmachte, erreichte die Zften-Gesamtzahl 1931 ihren höchsten Stand." Fritz Schlawe, *Literarische Zeitschriften 1910–1933*, Sammlung Metzler, 24, 2nd ed. (Stuttgart: Metzler, 1973), p. 1. Further testimony to the importance of periodicals can be found in the following works: Hellmut Diwald, "Literatur und Zeitgeist in der Weimarer Republik," in *Zeitgeist der Weimarer Republik*, ed. by Hans Joachim Schoeps (Stuttgart: Ernst Klett, 1968), pp. 203–260; Harry Pross, *Literatur und Politik. Geschichte und Programme der politisch-literarischen Zeitschriften im deutschen Sprachgebiet seit 1870* (Olten and Freiburg im Breisgau: Walter, 1963); and Susi Stappenbacher, "Die deutschen literarischen Zeitschriften in den Jahren 1918–1925 als Ausdruck geistiger Strömungen der Zeit" (Diss. Erlangen-Nürnberg, 1961).

[7] Schlawe, *Literarische Zeitschriften*, p. 4, quoting Sperlings *Zeitschriftenadressbuch* for 1931.

[8] The term "flood" is from Diwald, "Literatur und Zeitgeist in der Weimarer Republik," p. 209. Diwald stresses the informative value of the

doctrinaire commitments prevent them from including the broad spectrum of prevalent views and cause them to exclude in particular the moderately conservative to liberal/progressive middle ground. A leading liberal and non-partisan cultural review was the *Neue Rundschau*,[9] a monthly published by the S. Fischer Verlag in Berlin from its inception in 1890 until it was suppressed by the Nazis in 1944.[10] After a break of a year the *Neue Rundschau* was published as a quarterly from exile in Stockholm and Amsterdam, and since 1950 it has been published by the S. Fischer Verlag in Frankfurt am Main.[11] As a middle-of-the-road journal, its pages open to a broad spectrum of artistic and political persuasions, the *Neue Rundschau* is a repository of the multiple tendencies of the times.

The heyday of the *Neue Rundschau* coincided with the literary and cultural renaissance which began during the first decade of the twentieth century and ended with the collapse of the Weimar Republic.[12] It is worthy of study both as a literary

---

literary-cultural review, in particular those which occupy the political middle ground.

[9] There is general agreement that the *Neue Rundschau* is to be classified as "liberal." See, for example, Diwald, p. 227, Schlawe, p. 52, and Falk Schwarz, "Die gelenkte Literatur. Die *Neue Rundschau* im Konflikt mit den Kontrollstellen des NS-Staates und der national-sozialistischen 'Bewegung'," in *Die deutsche Literatur im Dritten Reich*, eds. Horst Denkler and Karl Prümm (Stuttgart: Reclam, 1976), p. 66. Only Hermand and Trommler, *Die Kultur der Weimarer Republik*, p. 141, take exception. They call the *Neue Rundschau* in comparison to *Die Weltbühne* a ". . . wesentlich konservativere literarische Zeitschrift. . . ."

[10] The *Neue Rundschau* began as a weekly under the title *Freie Bühne für modernes Leben* whose *raison d'être* was the polemical defense of the Naturalism movement in literature, in particular the plays of Gerhart Hauptmann, which were being sponsored and produced for the first time by a progressive theatre group—the "Freie Bühne"—to which publisher Samuel Fischer belonged. For the history of the *Neue Rundschau*, see Peter de Mendelssohn, *S. Fischer und sein Verlag* (Frankfurt am Main: S. Fischer, 1970).

[11] Schlawe, *Literarische Zeitschriften*, p. 51 summarizes the important dates.

[12] Laqueur, *Weimar*, preface: "In short, 'Weimar Culture' antedates the Weimar Republic by at least a decade."; pp. 110–111: *(continued on page 4)*

standard-bearer (publishing, for example, Fischer authors Gerhart Hauptmann, Thomas Mann, Hermann Hesse, Arthur Schnitzler) and as a journal of political and social commentary. The *Neue Rundschau* has been the subject of dissertations,[13] and has been treated in articles and monographs.[14] Peter de Mendelssohn reviewed its history in his 1347–page tome on the S. Fischer Verlag.[15] These discussions have been primarily historical in orientation. They have not concentrated on the literature *per se*. I propose, by contrast, to examine an entire literary genre in the *Neue Rundschau* intrinsically as well as a voice of the times, whether the authors have become "classics" or are nearly unknown today. The goals of this study are to utilize the results of a close interpretation of the short stories—the genre which appeared most frequently in the *Neue Rundschau*—to comment on the general literary tenor of the periodical during a particularly fascinating epoch and with (the limitations of) that tenor in mind to look for qualities which characterize the sensibilities of the times.

Justifiable time limits can be set by choosing the period from January 1922 to March 1933 when Rudolf Kayser was editor. It is bound on the one side by the almost twenty-eight year editorship of his predecessor, Oskar Bie, during which the *Neue Rundschau*'s literary profile was markedly different,

---

(continued from page 3) "Roughly speaking, the great break with cultural tradition occurred, in Germany as elsewhere, between 1905 and 1914; this decade, incidentally, was also a revolutionary period in the social and natural sciences. The new wave of experimentation manifested itself first and most powerfully in painting, but it was to affect literature and music no less radically."

[13] They are: Wolfgang Grothe, "Die Neue Rundschau des Verlages S. Fischer: Ein Beitrag zur Publizistik und Literaturgeschichte der Jahre von 1890 bis 1925," in *Archiv für Geschichte des Buchwesens*, 4 (1963), cols. 809–996; and Falk Schwarz, "Literarisches Zeitgespräch im Dritten Reich: dargestellt an der Zeitschrift 'Neue Rundschau,' " in *Archiv für Geschichte des Buchwesens*, 12 (1971/72), cols. 1282–1483.

[14] They include those referred to above, nn. 1, 4, 6, and 10, as well as below, nn. 24, 25, 37, and 40.

[15] *S. Fischer und sein Verlag* (Frankfurt am Main: S. Fischer, 1970).

and on the other side by the changes dictated to Kayser's succesor, Peter Suhrkamp, by the post–1933 political pressures and restrictions. Kayser, born in 1889, came to the *Neue Rundschau* as a young man with a background of proven critical acumen and accomplishment.[16] His assumption of the editorship marked the beginning of a new era for the *Neue Rundschau*.[17] The primary change was a noticeably greater preoccupation with the world at large.[18] Under Kayser's aegis the *Neue Rundschau* became a significantly more cosmopolitan journal. Beginning in 1924 Kayser introduced a regular column called the "Europäische Rundschau" which consisted of several sections, each on a separate topic pertaining broadly to culture in Europe, the United States, and sometimes other parts of the world as well.[19] The change was also reflected by a

---

[16] Kayser was born on 28 November 1889 in Parchim/Mecklenburg. His studies at the universities of Berlin, Munich, and Würzburg concluded with the degree of Dr. Phil. He was a teacher before becoming editor of the *Neue Rundschau*. He edited the *Novellen von Achim v. Arnim* (1918) and an anthology of Expressionist poetry entitled *Verkündigung* (1921). He is author of: *Moses Tod (Legende*, 1921), *Die Zeit ohne Mythos* (1923), a biography of Stendhal (1928), a collection of essays entitled *Dichterköpfe* (1930), a biography of Spinoza (1932), and a number of works published after he went into exile. His debut in the *Neue Rundschau* was in 1918 with an essay entitled "Die Intellektuellen und die Geistigen." In 1919 Kayser began to be trained in various departments of the Fischer Verlag. Kayser died in New York on 5 November 1964. (Wilhelm Kosch, ed., *Deutsches Literatur-Lexikon*, 2nd ed. [Berne: Francke, 1949]; Werner Schuder, ed., *Kürschners Deutscher Literatur-Kalender. Nekrolog 1936–1970* [Berlin and New York: Walter de Gruyter, 1973]; and de Mendelssohn, *S. Fischer und sein Verlag*, pp. 857–58.) For further information on Kayser's background see Grothe, "Die Neue Rundschau," cols. 953–56.

[17] de Mendelssohn, p. 858.

[18] *Ibid.*, p. 859.

[19] Kayser wrote the "Europäische Rundschau" from May 1924 to December 1931. De Mendelssohn provides the history of the column: "Er [Kayser] führte 1924 die *Europäische Rundschau* ein, eine regelmässige Sparte kulturpolitischer Betrachtungen, die den Sammelbegriff 'Kulturpolitik' sehr weit fasste und für gewöhnlich ein halbes Dutzend weit gestreuter Themen verklammerte und sich auch nicht auf Europa beschränkte, sondern besonders aufmerksam die Entwicklung Amerikas verfolgte. In den ersten vier Nummern des Jahrgangs 1924 schrieb Willy Haas diese *(continued on page 6)*

change in appearance: Gothic was replaced by Roman typeface, making the *Neue Rundschau* more easily accessible to foreign readers.[20] According to the author of a standard work on the periodicals of this period, the choice of typeface is significant for it is a function of a journal's political standpoint; the Gothic indicated a conservative and the Roman a liberal political orientation.[21]

Kayser was a modest man who put very few of his own writings into the *Neue Rundschau* over the course of his years as editor.[22] His forced departure in 1933 was a sign of the drastically changed times since his assumption of the editorship. Gottfried Bermann Fischer, Samuel Fischer's son-in-law, who by 1933 held the reins in place of the aged and infirm publisher,[23] explains in his memoirs that he let Kayser go because it was time for the *Neue Rundschau* to assume a more aggressive political posture toward the forces of Nazism and its allies on the cultural scene. He believed that Kayser was not sufficiently militant to carry out such a policy.[24] According to de Men-

---

(continued from page 5) Umschau." (p. 859) ". . . und Kayser führte die Sparte vom Mai 1924 bis Dezember 1931 ohne Unterbrechung fort." (p. 860).

[20] de Mendelssohn, p. 859.

[21] Schlawe, *Literarische Zeitschriften*, p. 6.

[22] De Mendelssohn comments as follows: "Er [Kayser] war ein bescheidener Mann, der mit seinem eigenen Namen in der Zeitschrift zurückhielt und ausser seinen regelmässigen Chroniken nur zwei- oder dreimal im Jahr einen grösseren Aufsatz veröffentlichte." (p. 860)

[23] Fischer, who was born in 1859, died in 1934.

[24] In *Bedroht—Bewahrt: Weg eines Verlegers* (Frankfurt am Main: S. Fischer, 1967), p. 81, Bermann Fischer explains his decision: "Mir stand als Kampforgan nur unsere *Neue Rundschau* zur Verfügung, die so hoch über den Wassern schwebte, dass von einem politischen Einfluss keine Rede sein konnte. Ihre Leser waren zumeist Intellektuelle, die sich nicht für Politik interessierten und ahnungslos in das kommende Unheil hineinstolpern sollten. Aber ich wollte es dennoch versuchen, sie zur Gegenwirkung gegen *Die Tat* zu aktivieren. Dazu bedurfte es in erster Linie eines Wechsels in der Redaktion. Dr. Rudolf Kayser, der verdiente langjährige Redakteur der *Neuen Rundschau*—er hatte 1924 Oskar Bie abgelöst—war dieser Aufgabe nicht gewachsen. Ein Mann von ungewöhnlicher Bildung und hohen geistigen Qualitäten, war er in ruhigen Zeiten der ideale Leiter einer literarischen

delssohn, however, co-workers in the publishing house and literary circles in general interpreted the firing of Kayser, a Jew, as a gesture of appeasement to the anti-semitic forces.[25]

Confining the investigation to the tenure of a single editor means that the influence of his style and opinions can be regarded as a consistent determining factor. In addition publisher Samuel Fischer himself, according to all evidence, maintained a strong and continuing influence over the selection of pieces to be published in the *Neue Rundschau*. His tastes and convictions determined its format and tone.[26] It is important to keep in mind that the *Neue Rundschau* was, among other things, the "house publication" of the S. Fischer Verlag and intended, at least indirectly, to encourage sales in part by creating its own market, that is a taste among readers for literature of the range and quality which Fischer published.[27] The *Neue Rundschau* reviewed important Fischer books and

---

Zeitschrift. Eine Kämpfernatur, insbesondere gegenüber der pseudowissenschaftlichen Aggression der *Tat*, war er nicht." One can easily dispute several of Bermann Fischer's points, including the incorrect date for the beginning of Kayser's editorship. De Mendelssohn implies skepticism about the advisability of the decision to try to turn the *Neue Rundschau* into a political organ. (*S. Fischer und sein Verlag*, p. 1247.)

[25] de Mendelssohn, pp. 1245–46. Falk Schwarz provides yet another interpretation in "Die gelenkte Literatur. Die *Neue Rundschau* im Konflikt mit den Kontrollstellen des NS-Staates und der nationalsozialistischen 'Bewegung'," p. 66: "Dass die Nationalsozialisten wirklich einmal Deutschland regieren würden, daran hatte in der Zeitschrift niemand ernsthaft geglaubt. So herrschten nach dem 30. Januar 1933 in Redaktion und Verlag Verwirrung und Ohnmacht. Man war sich zunächst einig, für den bisherigen jüdischen Redakteur der *Neuen Rundschau*, Rudolf Kayser, einen Nachfolger zu suchen. Kaysers Name war in den elf Jahren seiner Redaktionsarbeit so sehr mit der Literatur, die im Hause S. Fischer verlegt wurde, verknüpft, dass er den neuen Machthabern direkte Angriffsflächen bieten musste. Ausserdem erhoffte sich der Verlag von einem Wechsel in der Redaktion der Zeitschrift auch neue Akzente und Impulse."

[26] There is evidence for this fact in Grothe, "Die Neue Rundschau . . . ," cols. 816–24, as well as throughout de Mendelssohn, *S. Fischer und sein Verlag*, especially pp. 136, 451, 463, 1002 and 1319.

[27] Grothe, cols. 815–17, and de Mendelssohn, throughout.

Fischer authors were well represented.[28] The *Neue Rundschau* was also a product of Samuel Fischer's insistence upon maintaining consistently high stylistic standards.[29] In truth, of course, like any other long-lived journal, it published over the years contributions of varying stylistic quality, despite S. Fischer's strictures on excellence. In fact, among the short stories there are a surprising number which fall short of the quality one would expect from the *Neue Rundschau*'s reputation.

According to reputation and its publisher's and editor's intention, the *Neue Rundschau* was a progressive journal which maintained high literary standards while critically welcoming the new, and changing and developing along with the changing and developing culture. At the same time it remained very much attuned to traditional literary values.[30] Gradually over the course of the post-World War I years the *Neue Rundschau* broadened its original literary scope to include more essays on philosophy, politics, economics, the sciences, history, sociology and the like. Contributors included leading scholars and practitioners in these fields. Albert Einstein (whose daughter married Kayser in 1924),[31] Bertrand Russell, José Ortega y

---

[28] de Mendelssohn, p. 473, and throughout.

[29] de Mendelssohn, pp. 469–70, and throughout.

[30] This assessment finds support in Grothe, cols. 945–46; Schlawe, *Literarische Zeitschriften*, p. 52; Schwarz, "Die gelenkte Literatur," p. 66; de Mendelssohn throughout, and in particular de Mendelssohn's quote from a statement by Rudolf Kayser which appeared in the 1926 fortieth anniversary almanac of the S. Fischer Verlag: "Produktive Geistigkeit: das ist der Sinn unserer Arbeit. Damit ist auch die verfängliche Frage nach Alter und Generation beantwortet. So sicher die Formen des Geistes im Verlauf des geschichtlichen Prozesses sich wandeln, so sicher bleibt seine Mission dieselbe. Im Negativen bedeutet das, dass eine Zeitschrift ungeistig ist, sobald sie reaktionär wird und bei bestimmten Ausdrucksformen stehen bleibt. Allerdings ist die *Neue Rundschau* nicht mehr wie zu ihren Anfängen die Kampfzeitschrift einer bestimmten Weltanschauung. Ihr Radikalismus liegt nicht in der Erfüllung bestimmter Thesen, aber in der des Geistes und seiner aktuellen Lebendigkeit." (de Mendelssohn, p. 1036.)

[31] Grothe, col. 955.

Gasset are representative names. The political area in particular grew in importance through the contributions of political editor Samuel Saenger, an experienced diplomat and one of the most astute political commentators of the time.[32] The *Neue Rundschau*'s relatively modest circulation figures—8,000 in 1920 and 10,000 in 1930–33—belie its influence.[33] Its readership is thought to have included influential circles at home and abroad.[34] Every one of the five founding members of the Section for Literature of the Prussian Academy of Arts (Gerhart Hauptmann, Thomas Mann, Hermann Stehr, Ludwig Fulda and Arno Holz) was a Fischer author or early contributor to the *Neue Rundschau* (when it was called the *Freie Bühne für modernes Leben*).[35] Of the twenty-one members whom they elected at their first meeting (1926), two-thirds were Fischer authors and all the others, with the exception of two, were *Neue Rundschau* contributors.[36] In addition to leading German authors, foreign writers are heavily represented in the *New Rundschau*. The following authors, among others appeared there: Joseph Conrad, Dos Passos, Dostoevsky, Flaubert, Gide, Gorki, Eugene O'Neill, Priandello, Proust, Rolland, G. B. Shaw, Strindberg, Tolstoy, Trotsky, Unamuno,

---

[32] All sources agree on the caliber of Saenger's political commentary. Examples are Schlawe, p. 52: ". . . vor allem S. Saenger lieferte hochstehende politische Übersichten." Diwald, "Literatur und Zeitgeist in der Weimarer Republik," p. 229, writes: "Samuel Saenger, dessen politische Übersichten in der *Neuen Rundschau* heute als klassisch bezeichnet werden dürfen, . . ."

[33] Schlawe, p. 51.

[34] Grothe, cols. 967–87.

[35] de Mendelssohn, p. 1039.

[36] The twenty one members were: Hermann Bahr, Max Halbe, Hermann Hesse, Ricarda Huch, Georg Kaiser, Bernhard Kellermann, Erwin Guido Kolbenheyer, Oskar Loerke, Heinrich Mann, Walter von Molo, Josef Ponten, Wilhelm Schäfer, René Schickele, Wilhelm Schmidtbonn, Arthur Schnitzler, Karl Schönherr, Wilhelm von Scholz, Emil Strauss, Eduard Stucken, Jakob Wassermann and Franz Werfel. The two who were not connected with the S. Fischer Verlag or the *Neue Rundschau* were Kolbenheyer and Molo. (de Mendelssohn, p. 1040.)

Valéry, Virginia Woolf, W. B. Yeats. Clearly the *Neue Rundschau* was a representative journal of considerable significance beyond its function as the "house publication" of the S. Fischer Verlag.[37]

In addition to the editor's and publisher's selection procedure, the exigencies of literary production and availability of stories, there are several broader limitations which I have borne in mind and potential pitfalls which I tried to avoid in the study and conclusions presented here. They have to do with problems of dealing with literature and society in general and the Weimar period in particular. One significant limitation to drawing conclusions about the temper of an era from a body of literature is the fact that the source is a circumscribed group—writers as part of the larger category of intellectuals. Although writers above all can and ought to be able to transcend, through imagination and empathy, the limits of their own caste, the fact remains that literature is not produced by a sociological cross-section of a populace and therefore is filtered by the consciousness and experience of a particular group. Laqueur as well as Hermand and Trommler make the point that intellectual and cultural circles were more conservative than presumed in the conventional view of the Weimar era.[38] Laqueur shows that generalizations based on the view-

---

[37] There is general agreement on the significance and the representative nature of the *Neue Rundschau*. An example is Peter Gay's description of it as ". . . the Fischer Verlag's highly esteemed monthly, . . ." (*Weimar Culture: The Outsider as Insider* [New York: Harper & Row, 1968], p. 35). In three different contexts Gay refers to articles or quotes from the *Neue Rundschau* to exemplify major trends in Weimar culture. The only dissenting voice is that of Laqueur, *Weimar*, p. 125: "The literary periodicals expressed the views of small groups or political parties, or (such as Fischer's *Neue Rundschau*) featured the authors of a certain publishing house. There was no great representative journal in which literary figures would appear irrespective of style and orientation." Needless to say, I disagree with Laqueur's judgment on this matter.

[38] Laqueur, p. 4: "The intelligentsia was by and large conservative, . . ."; Hermand and Trommler, *Die Kultur der Weimarer Republik*, p. 153: "Ohne

points of the intellectuals must always be qualified generalizations:

> If it is difficult to generalize about the German *Intelligenz* before 1914, it is almost impossible to do so for the period after the First World War. For within the German intelligentsia there were various groups representing totally different attitudes, policies, points of view, political and unpolitical, left and right, and some who defied classification altogether. The limelight shifted from time to time. The liberal intelligentsia had set the tone roughly speaking up to the 1860s and were followed by the national liberals, who held the position up to the end of the war, whereas the left-liberal intelligentsia predominated during the 1920s. But none of these ever had the scene all to itself; various factions coexisted in time without speaking the same language.[39]

This is a point of considerable importance which has sometimes been disregarded in works on Weimar culture.[40]

One must also beware of accepting the concept of the Berlin-centered culture—that whatever was said and done, performed and published in Berlin stood for Weimar Germany as a whole.[41] "The liberal Berlin intellectuals tended to overrate their impact on the country at large."; ". . . there was a Berlin literature and a regional literature, and each little coterie was deeply absorbed in its own affairs. There was no spiritual

---

Zweifel orientierte sich ein Grossteil der kulturellen Medien an den traditionellen literarischen Überzeugungen und Werken, wie man überhaupt davon gesprochen hat, dass die kulturelle Szene der zwanziger Jahre weitaus konservativer war, als es angesichts der Fülle progressiver Künstler und Schriftsteller im Rückblick scheinen mag. Diese Seite soll nicht unterschlagen werden, insofern zahlreiche Autoren den Blick über die neuen Erfahrungen mit Technik, Grosstadt, Massenunterhaltung und sozialen Kämpfen hinweg auf 'Bleibendes' richteten, besonders im Bereich der Natur und des Mythischen."

[39] Laqueur, p. 30.

[40] Examples are Jenö Kurucz, *Struktur und Funktion der Intelligenz während der Weimarer Republik* (Spich Bez. Cologne: Grote, 1967), and John Willett, *Art and Politics in the Weimar Period. The New Sobriety, 1917–1933* (New York: Pantheon Books, 1978).

[41] An example of this point of view is Otto Friedrich's *Before the Deluge: A Portrait of Berlin in the 1920's* (New York: Harper & Row, 1972).

or geographical centre."[42] Writers tended—a truism at any time—to be more skeptical than the man in the street, and more subject to pessimism.[43] Laqueur makes the useful, though somewhat overstated point that writers were isolated from the mainstream of concerns: ". . . the Weimar writers did not know their own country well, and their world was a very small one, poles apart from the rest of the people."[44] Although I do not completely accept Laqueur's portrait of the writers in an ivory tower, I believe it is important to keep this reservation in view when drawing conclusions from a body of literature. This study is intended to show that within these qualifying boundaries literature may yet yield unique and valid insights into society.

An approach to Weimar culture which I regard as misleading is to concentrate primarily, if not exclusively, upon the avant-garde—those individuals, groups, movements, publications and works which seem to mark a complete break with the past. While these are perhaps the most intriguing to our time and are, in retrospect, seminal areas, they do not stand for the broad spectrum of Weimar culture as contemporaries experienced it. As mentioned above, the mainstream was more conservative and remained attached to traditions. I take issue in particular with the kind of exclusive preoccupation with the avant-garde represented by John Willett's *Art and Politics in the Weimar Period*,[45] and by Hermand and Trommler's insistence that totally new standards must be used to assess the art of the period. According to Hermand and Trommler, these are to be applied to the only significant forces, that is, those whose art is committed to overcoming "das Erbe des Wilhelminismus"—reactionary pre-World War

---

[42] Laqueur, p. 30 and p. 125.
[43] Laqueur, pp. 36–38.
[44] Laqueur, p. 134.
[45] See above, n. 40.

I society under the Kaiser.[46] These views neglect the forces of continuity in society and culture which not only endured but played a larger role for the Weimar audience than did the relatively esoteric avant-garde.[47] I find Laqueur's comprehensive approach more convincing:

> It would no doubt be easier for the historian if the cultural history of Weimar were identical with the plays and theories of Brecht, the creations of the Bauhaus and the articles published by the *Weltbühne*. But there were a great many other individuals and groups at work, and whether the historian likes them or not, he cannot afford to ignore them, or their ideas and activities.[48]

If any generalization at all can be made without reservation about Weimar culture it is that its essence was contradiction:

> Many of the old taboos had disappeared; there was much greater openness towards new ideas. But at the same time the upholders of the old order and its values had by no means disappeared. The

[46] "Wenn man überhaupt bestimmte Trends konstatieren will, muss man zwangsläufig von den gewandelten produktions- und rezeptionsästhetischen Bedingungen für Kunst ausgehen, um nicht von vornherein in überholte Stilkonzepte zurückzufallen, die auf die neue Massen- und Mediengesellschaft dieser Ära überhaupt nicht mehr zutreffen. Doch nicht nur das. Man muss zugleich eine gewisse ideologische Vorentscheidung treffen und sich die Aufgabe stellen, im Laufe der Darstellung vor allem jene Kräfte zu akzentuieren, die sich—wie im Bereich der Ideologiebildung—'nach vorn' entscheiden. Es wird daher im folgenden weitgehend von der Frage ausgegangen: Welches sind die Kräfte, die das Erbe des Wilhelminismus auch ästhetisch überwinden wollten, indem sie etwas zur Förderung des Demokratischen, Republikanischen oder gar Sozialistischen beizutragen versuchten?" (Hermand and Trommler, pp. 110–11.) Aside from the fact that their argument is weakened by use of jargon ("produktions- und rezeptionsästhetischen Bedingungen"), Hemand and Trommler's narrowly dogmatic approach must inevitably exclude and distort to meet their criteria.

[47] This point is supported by an interview with Lilo and Friedrich Solmsen (Chapel Hill, N.C., May 1979), whose memories of Weimar (Mrs. Solmsen was a student at the University of Berlin, and Prof. Solmsen was a student and *Dozent* there from 1922 to 1933) show them to have been astute and informed observers of the Weimar cultural scene.

[48] Laqueur, Preface.

> clash between tradition and modernism continued with a vengeance, . . .[49]

An example is the role of women and men's attitudes toward women. On the one hand a range of new social roles had become available to women in the working world and in their relations with men. The new freedom was reflected in clothes and behavior. On the other hand, as a number of *Neue Rundschau* stories reveal, this new freedom was largely superficial. Patriarchal attitudes persisted and even some men otherwise modern in outlook continued to view women in terms of the old stereotypes. In the eyes of many people women retained their primary function as appendages of the male ego.[50] The example of the role of women supports the validity of looking at Weimar through literature in the *Neue Rundschau*. Because the *Neue Rundschau* was not an organ of the avant-garde it had the scope to encompass the tensions of the period. This study, consequently, may serve as a corrective of some widely-held assumptions.[51]

---

[49] Laqueur, p. 26.

[50] Hermand and Trommler, p. 81, state the case for the continuing dominance of traditional clichés about women. They expose the contradictions behind the facade of emancipation and point out that contrary to the usual assumptions about women in the 1920's, the number of emancipated women remained small. Laqueur, pp. 31–32, by contrast, gives scant attention to the contradictions.

[51] Several of these can be found in the preface (p. xiii) to Gay's *Weimar Culture*, a pioneering and sensitive study which otherwise is extremely useful. Here, I believe, Gay romanticizes the period (although he distances himself from "the legend of 'the golden twenties.' " p. xiv): "The Weimar Republic died only thirty-five years ago, in 1933, yet it is already a legend. Its tormented brief life with its memorable artifacts, and its tragic death—part murder, part wasting sickness, part suicide—have left their imprint on men's minds, often vague perhaps, but always splendid. When we think of Weimar, we think of modernity in art, literature, and thought; we think of the rebellion of sons against fathers, Dadaists against art, Berliners against beefy philistinism, libertines against old-fashioned moralists; we think of *The Threepenny Opera, The Cabinet of Dr. Caligari, The Magic Mountain,* the *Bauhaus,* Marlene Dietrich. And we think, above all, of the exiles who exported Weimar culture all over the world."

A pitfall which I have tried to avoid is the facile linkage of art to politics. It is exemplified in Gay's statement: "The parallel course of Weimar culture and Weimar politics is too obvious to have gone unnoticed."[52] This linkage is based on the conventional division of the Weimar era into three distinct periods. Gay sees this periodization mirrored in one avant-garde institution—the Bauhaus—as well as in the arts in general:

> The three lives of the Bauhaus—venturesome trials at the beginning, secure accomplishment in the middle years, and frantic pessimism at the end—are expressive of the three periods of the Republic itself. The time from November 1918 to 1924, with its revolution, civil war, foreign occupation, political murder, and fantastic inflation, was a time of experimentation in the arts; Expressionism dominated politics as much as painting or the stage. Between 1924 and 1929, when Germany enjoyed fiscal stabilization, relaxation of political violence, renewed prestige abroad, and widespread prosperity, the arts moved into the phase of *Neue Sachlichkeit*—of objectivity, matter-of-factness, sobriety. And then, between 1929 and 1933, the years of disastrously rising unemployment, government by decree, decay of middle-class parties, and resumption of violence, culture became less the critic than the mirror of events; . . .[53]

Actually the period of greatest experimentation in the arts and the dominance of Expressionism occurred prior to World War I; subsuming politics as well as the arts under the rubric of Expressionism can only distort both.[54] These parallels give the impression of being forced because they are based on simplifications which limit and reduce the culture of the period. In another example, Grimm and Hermand, despite the skeptical title—*Die sogenannten zwanziger Jahre*—of the workshop whose results they edited, and despite their rejection of standard assumptions, present the usual tripartite division based on

---

[52] Gay, p. 119.
[53] Gay, p. 120.
[54] Laqueur, above n. 12.

political and economic developments coinciding with developments in the arts: " 'Vom Zusammenbruch bis zur Inflation' (1918–1923), 'Die Stabilisierungsepoche' (1923–1929) und 'Die zunehmende Radikalisierung angesichts der Weltwirtschaftskrise' (1929–1933)."[55]

There is no doubt about the dates of critical political and economic events during the time period encompassed by this study: 11 January 1923—the French occupation of the Ruhr; 1923—the extremities of inflation; 15 November 1923—the currency reform; the year 1929—the death of Gustav Stresemann and the beginning of the Great Depression; 14 September 1930—the Nazis increase their number of seats in the Reichstag from 12 to 107; 30 January 1933—Hitler is named Chancellor. These are a few dates which stand out. However, the relationship of these and other events and trends to attitudes, moods and trends in the arts can by no means be as certain. Historians Theodor Eschenburg and Gerhard Schulz, for example, show that the so-called period of optimism and stability (1923/24–1929, post-inflation and pre-depression) rested on shaky economic foundations and on major social

---

[55] Reinhold Grimm and Jost Hermand, eds., *Die sogenannten zwanziger Jahre. First Wisconsin Workshop* (Bad Homburg: Gehlen, 1970), p. 8. How forced such parallels may become is illustrated by the list of disparate characteristics which Grimm and Hermand include in their cultural periodization: "Der ersten Teilstrecke dieser chronologischen Abfolge entsprechen Stil- und Kulturphänomene wie Spätexpressionismus, Dada, Proletkult und Werke wie Golls *Methusalem* und Brechts *Baal*, in denen sich der eigentliche Epochenumbruch vollzieht und deren innere Gemeinsamkeit hauptsächlich in der offen zur Schau getragenen Radikalität zum Ausdruck kommt, gleichgültig ob sich diese nun politisch-aktivistisch, zynisch-grotesk oder sonstwie äussert. Dagegen herrscht in den Jahren zwischen 1923 und 1929 die eigentliche 'Sachlichkeit,' die mehr zum Objektivistischen, Bieder- Republikverpflichteten oder Zynisch-Neutralistischen neigt, aber auch einige Ausflüge ins Schlicht-Volkstümliche und Brutal-Amerikanistische unternimmt. Seit 1929 schliesslich lässt sich ein bedrohliches Anwachsen des Mythos auf der rechten und der radikalisierten Kollektivität auf der linken Seite beobachten, . . ." (p. 8) The same quality characterizes their polemical discussion of the concept "Neue Sachlichkeit."

dislocations.[56] There may have been widespread moods very different from those presumed by the chronologies which Gay and Grimm/Hermand propose. By assembling a different group of exemplary works one could presumably come to different conclusions about the arts of the period. Laqueur treats this problem as well with appropriate skepticism:

> The periods of cultural history hardly ever coincide with those of political history. It is as pointless to investigate diplomacy in the period of Impressionism as it is to write on the history of art in the era of Stresemann.[57]

There is certainly a relationship between artistic expression and its time, but it is a complex, multifaceted, even amorphous relationship which defies easy parallels.

As a result of a close reading of seventy-three stories which appeared in the *Neue Rundschau* from 1922 to 1933 I have found, not a division into a chronology of types whose characteristics coincide with political and economic change, but rather a series of contradictions which, however, over time produce the picture of broad but distinctive trends in fundamental postures. Starting from the literary text rather than from history avoids forcing the interpretation of artistic expression into a straitjacket of certainly related but not necessarily parallel outside events.

The major question raised by this study is that of the relationship between literature and society. The results, I believe, point in the direction of possible answers. The approach followed here is obviously not that of the over-all study of Weimar literature or culture (or even, for that matter, of literature as represented in the *Neue Rundschau*) which others

---

[56] Theodor Eschenburg, *Die improvisierte Demokratie. Gesammelte Aufsätze zur Weimarer Republik* (Munich: R. Piper, 1963), p. 67; Gerhard Schulz, *Deutschland seit dem Ersten Weltkrieg 1918–1945* (Göttingen: Vandenhoeck & Ruprecht, 1976), pp. 79–82, and pp. 87–88.

[57] Laqueur, p. 110.

The Stories According to Category

	Vol.	*Affirm.*	*Neg.*	*Non-Judg.*	*Satir.*	*Nihil.*	*Totals*
1922	1	XX		X			3
	2			XX	X		3
1923	1	XXX		X			4
	2	XX	X	X			4
1924	1	XX					2
	2	XX	X		X		4
1925	1	X	X	XX	X		5
	2	X		X			2
1926	1		XXX				3
	2	X	X				2
1927	1	XX	X	X			4
	2		X		X	X	3
1928	1	XX	X	XX			5
	2	XX				X	3
1929	1		XXX				3
	2	X				X	2
1930	1	XX	X			X	4
	2		XXX			X	4
1931	1		X	XX			3
	2		XX	X		X	4
1932	1					XX	2
	2		X		X		2
1933 (thru March)	1					XX	2
Totals		23	21	14	5	10	73

have undertaken, but rather of a close and detailed look at a segment from which (within the above-mentioned limitations) certain conclusions may be drawn as to the nature of the larger context.

The stories examined are all those by German-language authors which appeared in the *Neue Rundschau* during Rudolf Kayser's editorship and which are neither manifestly excerpts from larger works nor samples of an author's much earlier work. The term short story is used to encompass the nomenclatures—"Erzählung" or "Novelle"—used by some authors, as well as the stories which have no such heading. All may appropriately be called short stories in English; any further distinction is of no significance in the context of this study. The forty-eight authors range from those generally held in the highest esteem today—such as Franz Kafka, Robert Musil, or Heinrich and Thomas Mann—to those less highly regarded as well as those who are nearly unknown, in some cases because circumstances cut short their literary careers. I have deliberately de-emphasized the "classic" authors because there seems to be no need for yet another interpretation, for example, of Kafka's "Ein Hungerkünstler," Thomas Mann's "Unordnung und frühes Leid," Arthur Schnitzler's "Fräulein Else" or stories by Heinrich Mann and Hermann Hesse. From the stories about which shelves of interpretation already exist and from—at the other extreme—stories so slight that they do not lend themselves to productive scrutiny, I have culled merely the points which are pertinent to this study. By contrast there are several intriguing discoveries among the lesser-known writers—stories executed with extraordinary skill, even brilliance, which demand a close, detailed interpretation. Biographical data on authors have not been included in the text of this study, as they are not relevant to its main concerns. Authors' dates appear in the appendix where the authors are listed in alphabetical order with their stories and the year when each story appeared.

The order of the stories is determined by categories which have been established as a result of close analysis of the texts. The seventy-three stories appear to group themselves into several categories according to a fundamental posture or sensibility. I call these sensibilities affirmative, negative, nonjudgmental, satirical, and nihilistic. The chronological relationship between categories (see chart, p. 18) shows a development over the years which provides an insight (subject to the above-mentioned limitations) into changing states of mind which accompanied political and social change. A signal function is borne by language, style and structure, and by the treatment of central themes. Examples of such themes are nature, women, love, death, the role of "Geist" in society. The evolution from 1922 to 1933 of these and other aspects of the stories in relation to Kayser's writings (and other pertinent articles and essays) in the *Neue Rundschau* is an indication of the evolution in attitudes and values.

To examine literature intrinsically as well as attempt to draw conclusions about an era may be a problematic undertaking. There is no doubt that the aesthetic imagination filters and shapes the moods and attitudes, collective memories and trauma, illusions and ideals, doubts and anxieties which permeate a culture. But the role of a body of literature as a voice of its time is predicated upon examination and assessment of the literature in its own terms—as a product of aesthetic imagination realized in literary discourse. Wolfgang Rothe, a representative critic of Weimar literature in the social/political context, states that the historical and ideological perspective of his book on Weimar literature necessarily excludes "mere" structural and formal analysis as well as the intrinsic approach to interpretation.[58] I believe, on the contrary, that only attention to intrinsic qualities—an approach which need not be exclusive however—will yield insights which are not distorted by having had to pass through an ideological grid.[59] To reach

---

[58] Rothe, ed., *Die deutsche Literatur in der Weimarer Republik*, p. 8.

[59] The following are main sources for this approach: Eugene Falk, lectures on Kafka and Camus (University of North Carolina, Chapel Hill, 1974); Roman Ingarden, *The Literary Work of Art* [1931], trans., with an introduction by George G. Grabowicz (Evanston: Northwestern Univ. Press, 1973); Lee T. Lemon and Marion Reis, trans., *Russian Formalist Criticism: Four Essays*, Regents Critics Series (Lincoln: Univ. of Nebraska Press, 1965); René Wellek, *Concepts of Criticism* (New Haven and London: Yale University Press, 1963); René Wellek and Austin Warren, *Theory of Literature*, 3rd ed. (New York: Harcourt, Brace & World, 1956).

this end a work must be treated as an integral whole. Style and structure in themselves—since they are the essential foundation of a work—ought to be, whenever possible, a guide to fundamental premises and therefore to the posture which the work reflects. The author, after all, has chosen the language of literature as opposed to any other in which to express himself. The choice of mode itself signifies that something other than mere sociological documentation is intended. The interpreter must, I believe, respect this choice and be cognizant of its peculiar properties. Only if we are attentive to the language of literature—in the broadest sense—are we justified in asking that literature assume a role in an expanded context.

Chapter I

Stories in the Affirmative Category: The Early Phase 1922–25

The broad category of affirmative stories—stories which mark a victory for life itself or a set of values, which reach a positive resolution of conflict, which confirm or uphold ideals—constitutes the largest category during the years under consideration. Generally, the twenty-three stories which are so categorized achieve their positive resolution by means of something approximating an epiphany and rebirth of the hero (an epithet appropriate to the protagonists of stories in the affirmative category). Like the negative posture, the affirmative is to be determined by the resolution of a story. Prior to 1929 the affirmative is the dominant sensibility.

In view of editor Rudolf Kayser's introductory message "An die Leser"[1] in the March 1923 *Neue Rundschau (NR)* (I, 193–94) and the general tenor of those years of crisis, the

[1] References to the *NR* will be given in the following form: month, year, volume number (each year's issues are collected in two volumes), and page numbers. Succeeding quotations from the same story or article will be followed by page number only unless further information is required for the sake of clarity.

frequency of the affirmative disposition in the *NR* stories of the early twenties is notable. Kayser writes of the "darkness of these times" when "German life" has been "robbed of all joy and nobility." (193) He speaks in the language of idealistic nationalism:

> Bleibt unser Leben weiter unter die Brutalität der äusseren Tatsachen gebeugt? Und Wesen und Sinn und Schicksal unseres deutschen Seins, soll es bis in alle Zukunft verzerrt, entstellt, geschändet werden durch diesen neuen Zivilisationsjargon, der Leben und Charakter eines grossen Volkes zu umschreiben meint, wenn er von finanziellem Zusammenbruch, von Tributzahlungen an die Siegerstaaten, von Valuta und von Geschäften spricht? Es will uns nicht in den Sinn. (193) . . .
>
> Hinter all den Schrecknissen des Tages, die uns das Leben fast verekeln, hinter den sinnlosen Brutalitäten, die Stunde für Stunde uns quälen und uns zu vernichten drohen, verbirgt sich das andere, das eigentliche Deutschland, verbirgt sich und - schweigt. Deutscher Staat und deutscher Geist waren wohl nie ein und dasselbe. Mag man es für Schwäche oder Stärke halten: die Greuel der Eroberungen wie die Greuel der Not reichten nie zu jener Tiefe hinab, wo die grossen Schöpfungen deutscher Art sich vollzogen. (194)

In these attitudes lies one possible explanation for the affirmative stories in those years. Kayser is expressing a traditional contempt of German intellectuals for political and economic realities. Human endeavor is divided, in this view, into tainted political reality and the pristine, uncompromised world of ideals.[2] "Deutscher Staat" and "deutscher Geist" are incompatible and there is no doubt which is the superior. This is the

---

[2] Peter Gay, in *Weimar Culture: The Outsider as Insider* (New York: Harper & Row, 1968), p. 71, describes this outlook as ". . . the aversion to politics, not to this or that policy, this or that party, but to politics as such." He goes on to explain the viewpoint which Kayser's statement illustrates: "The world of the Germans—and here the poets helped, as models and spokesmen—came to be separated into the higher realm of self-perfection, *Bildung*, the achievement of *Kultur* for its own sake and free of politics, and the lower realm of human affairs, sordid with practical matters and compromised." (p. 72)

fateful distinction which had plagued German thinking and theory—that there is an "essence" of the "German character" which is distinct from and uncorrupted by mundane considerations. Kayser, a liberal and a Jew who had to flee Germany in 1933, could hardly be accused of being a right-wing extremist.[3] Yet here, even in his vocabulary, is that irrational,[4] almost mystical, nationalistic terminology whose implications were to be so dangerous: "Wesen und Sinn und Schicksal unseres deutschen Seins," "geschändet . . . durch . . . Zivilisationsjargon," "Schöpfungen deutscher Art."[5]

The idealistic distinction between "dirty" politics and a higher German essence allows hope for the future. Kayser's intention is for the *NR* to provide a beacon in evil times: "Wir wollen die deutsche Heimat von ihrer bösen Gegenwart befreien: die Landschaften ihrer Seele und ihrer Musik wieder auferstehen lassen und ihre Kräfte fruchtbar machen in der fiebernden Zeit." (194) These intentions would be reflected in

---

[3] Kayser, as a supporter of the "Rat geistiger Arbeiter," could be considered—at last in 1918–19—as belonging to the "independent left." (Jenö Kurucz, *Struktur und Funktion der Intelligenz während der Weimarer Republik* [Spich Bez. Köln: Gröte, 1967], p. 93.)

[4] Kurt Sontheimer (*Antidemokratisches Denken in der Weimarer Republik* [Munich: Nymphenburg, 1962], note, p. 58) reasons that the irrational mood is a product of crisis: "Ein gut Teil der antirationalistischen Reaktion geht auf das Konto einer verzweifelten Krisenstimmung. Man sah in plötzlicher Klarheit, dass man mit dem Rationalismus nicht mehr weiter kam."

[5] Kayser's thinking at this time was representative, as the following analyses by two leading German historians indicate: "Nur eine Minderheit von Politikern und Publizisten war nicht von der kriegsbedingten Überspannung der alten antiwestlichen Ressentiments und von der nationalistisch ausgeweiteten romantischen Ideologie von der deutschen Eigenwüchsigkeit und Einzigartigkeit erfasst." (Karl Dietrich Bracher, *Die Auflösung der Weimarer Republik* [5th ed.; Villingen/Schwarzwald: Ring, 1971], p. 15.) "Der Mehrheit der Patrioten war der Gedanke eines Gegensatzes der deutschen Kultur zum Zivilisationsgeist des Westens seit Generationen eingeimpft. Ein antiwestlicher Affekt des deutschen Kulturbürgers, der längst bestand, war im Kriege noch gesteigert worden. Nur in den breiteren Volksschichten war dieser Affekt unbekannt." (Karl Buchheim, *Die Weimarer Republik. Das Deutsche Reich ohne Kaiser* [3rd ed.; Munich: Kösel, 1970], p. 35.)

editorial policy including the choice of fiction. The brave, illusory belief that the *NR* (or any journal for that matter) might contribute to "liberating the homeland from the evil present," that it might be able to cause the "resurrection of the landscapes of its soul" testifies to profound idealism. In later years such illusions must cave in before reality. Certainly at this time the tendency was to hope despite crisis. Stories whose conflicts are resolved in the affirmative, against all odds, by a higher synthesis, a mystical vision and rebirth, or a new understanding and affirmation of life would fit well into this idealistic tendency.

A prototype is the brief story Kayser himself wrote—"Die Begegnung in Padua"—which was published in the May 1924 (I, 445–57) issue. It is also significant as an illustration of several stereotypes in style and theme. One is the introductory statement of the moral of the story—in this case that coincidence can be the occasion of a major turning point in life. The life which arrives at a turning point is that of a dry, youngish German scholar who is visiting Padua in April 1923 in order to do research on Giotto. Almost from the beginning of his stay, the disturbingly evocative environment prevents him from concentrating on his scholarship. The cool blond German so out of place against the warm southern background, tempted by dark and (it seems to him) exotic Italian sensuality, loses his inhibitions and is swept away. This romantic stereotype has always depended, of course, on a misunderstanding of Italian society and morés.[6] In this case the German is invited to the home of an Italian man who struck up a late night conversation with him in a café. Before leaving his hotel the northerner suddenly becomes aware of his own unfulfilled need for tenderness, warmth, a "du" relationship.

[6] There are more realistic treatments of the Italian setting in the stories by Hans Reisiger, "Stehe auf und wandle" (below, Ch. III, p. 143), and Ludwig Strauss, "Gertrud und Bianca" (below, Ch. IV, p. 176).

Fortunately for the visitor, the host's twenty-four-year-old adopted daughter is present at dinner. In a cliché of feminine beauty which appears again and again in the *NR* stories, the girl is pale-skinned, her face white, her eyes large and dark. When his host is called away unexpectedly, the scholar experiences a sudden loss of his usual shyness and well-mannered self-control. His body seems to take over. He develops an uncontrollable desire for the girl across the table from him, grabs her when she approaches him, tears off her clothes, and rapes her. The girl herself remains completely passive. He then departs immediately, before the father returns—presumably the girl is left lying naked on the carpet—returns to his hotel, and finds that he has been transformed. He is now freed of those inhibitions which had limited and controlled his life. Up to now, for example, he had never been able to express tenderness in a sexual relationship; his relations with women consisted of "one night stands" or visits to brothels. Exactly what the difference was between those former encounters and this one with a girl to whom he had not spoken a word before attacking her, is not clear to the reader. She seems to have been no less a distant sex object than the previous women. Nevertheless one must take at face value the narrator-hero's assertion that this was a profound experience which changed his life:

> Es scheint mir nur, dass etwas in mir zerbricht und ein anderes aufzublühen beginnt. Das Leben, bisher nicht von mir gemieden, sondern ich von ihm, hat mich angerührt, meinen Körper gepackt, mich hineingerissen in das Gefühl der Welt. Mit Taten durchdrungen ist dieses Gefühl. Es spannt alle Sehnen und Entschlüsse und wirft Brücken hinüber zu jedem wartenden Du. (457)

Despite the glaring discrepancy between the rhapsodic resolution and the crude event which stimulated it, we must accept the seriousness of the narrator's statement of his inner metamorphosis. He concludes with an affirmation of life, of the world of feeling, and of the need for emotional involvement with other human beings.

The "southern" mood of this issue of *NR* is maintained by an installment of a Spanish travel essay which immediately follows "Die Begegnung in Padua," by a lead essay on Mussolini, and by a central segment on Italy in an installment of Arthur Holitscher's memoirs. Two other essays have a philosophical bent, one by Max Brod, another by Karl Vossler. Werner Bergengruen examines "Die russischen Kommunisten und der bäuerliche Mythos." (496–503) Otto Flake tours the occupied Rhineland with an insightful essay which is at the same time impressionistic landscape and sober political/social analysis. The issue includes letters from Gustav Mahler to Franz Steiner, and the regular "Politische Chronik" (511–19) by "Junius" (Samuel Saenger)[7]—cogent, dispassionate examinations of the contemporary German political scene which have not lost their validity in more than half a century. It closes with brief reviews by Kayser (in the regular section "Europäische Rundschau"[8] [520–26]) entitled: "Stendhal und Europa," "Intelligenz und Demokratie," "Der Balzac-Preis," "Zum Thema: Lenin," "Henry Ford," "Epilog auf Wilson," and finally, a longer review by Ernst Blass of Alfred Döblin's new novel "Berge, Meere, Giganten." The non-fiction is a high quality mix—typical in its variety, non-tendentiousness, and progressive, cosmopolitan nature. Of one hundred and twelve pages, only eleven and a half are devoted to fiction, namely the Kayser story which seems reactionary in sentiment compared to the rest of the issue.

---

[7] Saenger, the *NR*'s political editor, wrote the "Politische Chronik" under the pseudonym "Junius" from 1908 to 1928 and from 1925 to 1933 also under his own name. (Peter de Mendelssohn, *S. Fischer und sein Verlag* [Frankfurt am Main: S. Fischer, 1970], pp. 461–62.)

[8] Kayser wrote the "Europäische Rundschau" from May 1924 to December 1931. (de Mendelssohn, p. 860.)

The last line in Kayser's story reads: "Mein Buch über Giotto werde ich nie schreiben." (457) Intellectual endeavor no longer will play a pre-eminent role for the narrator. It has been replaced by his new-found preoccupation with an amorphous entity called "Leben" or "das Gefühl der Welt." (456) The resolution of the Kayser tale is an example of attitudes which Kurt Sontheimer, in *Antidemokratisches Denken in der Weimarer Republik,* calls "modern irrationalism."[9] "Nicht mehr das Denken wurde als die vornehmste menschliche Bestimmung ausgegeben, sondern das Erleben, das Fühlen, das Schauen, die mystische Einswerdung mit dem Gegenstand, die Vergegenwärtigung des Mythos."[10] Sontheimer finds the source of the anti-intellectual trend in the rejection of outworn nineteenth century values and ideals—holdovers from the Enlightenment—in favor of a new consciousness which began to develop among thinkers around the turn of the century and gradually spread to the general populace.

> Seit dem Beginn des Jahrhunderts war unter den wacheren Geistern des Landes eine Suche nach neuen Masstäben, vertieften Gesichtspunkten, neuen zukunftsweisenden Utopien angebrochen, die sich bald dem öffentlichen Bewusstsein mitteilte. Es war der Versuch, den Schablonen des 19. Jahrhunderts zu entrinnen, den Menschen tiefer zu begreifen als bisher und ihm auch politisch-gesellschaftlich ein neues Bewusstsein zu geben. Das antidemokratische Denken der zwanziger Jahre ist eine Frucht dieses geistigen Wandlungs-Prozesses, den man in der Kunst, wie in der Wissenschaft, aber auch in der Publizistik wahrnehmen kann.[11]

Kayser's narrator-hero finds that his life as a scholar has been emotionally impoverished. The cure is a dramatic endorsement of "life," a term which seems to have encompassed a variety of aspects:

---

[9] Sontheimer, *Antidemokratisches Denken in der Weimarer Republik*, p. 43.
[10] *Ibid.*, p. 51.
[11] *Ibid.*, pp. 42–43.

> Das Leben, das nun in die Mitte des geistigen Daseins trat, wurde mit mancherlei Namen versehen. Es erschien als das Organische im Gegensatz zum Mechanischen, als das Universalistische im Gegensatz zum Individualistischen, als Dynamik gegen Statik, als Seele gegen Geist.[12]

These artificial dichotomies are products of naive oversimplification. Kayser is guilty of viewing public affairs in these terms as well. In the July 1924 (II, 748–51) issue his "Europäische Rundschau" is devoted primarily to French culture and politics. Beginning with defensible premises about the short-sighted rigidity of French politicians (Poincaré) who regarded the Versailles Treaty as immutable and above criticism, and advocating the necessity rather of flexibility and compromise, Kayser justifies his case as follows:

> Worin besteht Politik? In Ideen, dem Widerspruch der Erde gegen sie und der Kunst, dieses Ja und Nein auszubalanzieren. Die konsequente Politik sieht nur das Ja und folgt ihm blindlings. Sie ist deshalb abstrakt und letzten Endes unfruchtbar. Das Nein der Erde, die natürlichen Widerstände des Lebens gegen das Abstrakte, das organische Sein der Staaten und Völker: mit diesen Unbekannten muss gerechnet werden. (748)

A reasonable, practical and specific political commentary grows by this train of thought (or better—feeling) into a grandiloquent, global simplification which pits the "abstract" against the "organic."

In Stefan Zweig's story "Phantastische Nacht"[13] (which appeared in May [513–28] and June [590–627] of 1922 [Vol. I]), the contradictions are resolved without qualification in favor of the "life" alternatives. "Phantastische Nacht" is a paean to non-rational life forces. Its effusive style is marked by vocabulary which illustrates Sontheimer's thesis: "Die Einseitigkeit des Intellekts gilt als entlarvt; um so mehr betont man die

---

[12] *Ibid.*, p. 49.

[13] Zweig also contributed a second story during this time period—"Rahel rechtet mit Gott" (1927); see below Ch. V, p. 203.

Notwendigkeit einfühlenden Verstehens, das mystische Eintauchen in eine von übersinnlichen Kräften durchflutete Welt, die Versenkung in das von allen Äusserlichkeiten befreite Wesen der Dinge, die schöpferische Kraft des Erlebnisses." (48) In the first three pages of "Phantastische Nacht" the word "Erlebnis" occurs six times. The same event is also referred to in those three pages as "das Gelebte," "das Erlebte," "der Vorgang," "die Begebenheit," "das Geschehnis," and "die Angelegenheit." All refer to the most profound experience in the life of the narrator-hero—his epiphany.

A thirty-six-year-old Viennese "gentleman and reserve officer" of independent means tells the story of his inner metamorphosis which occurred during six hours beginning in the afternoon of June 7, 1913. Since receiving his inheritance at the age of twenty, the narrator has led what appears from the outside to be an enviable existence. He is able to pursue his interests and pleasures in unlimited luxury and freedom, and to enjoy the benefits of moving in the highest circles of Viennese society. Gradually, however, after some years spent in unhampered fulfillment of his every desire, he begins to notice a condition in himself which disturbs him. It is a coldness, an inability to feel strong emotions even under the greatest provocation. He calls it a "Trägheit," "Kälte des Gefühls" (518), "grausam-kalte Fühllosigkeit," "Gefühlsstarre," "Gleichgültigkeit," (519) and is frightened by the condition which he likens to being dead. Nevertheless the coldness remains and overshadows all formerly keenly-felt enjoyments. Until one day in aimless revisiting of old pleasure haunts he inadvertently cheats a stranger of his winnings at the horse races. The stranger, portrayed as a despicable type, accidentally drops his tickets for the races. He finds all but one of them which the narrator, exploiting the opportunity to play a roguish trick, has concealed under his shoe. That very ticket turns out to be a winning one and the narrator collects the profits. In order to rid himself of the annoying ill-gotten gains he bets them on a sure loser. The horse comes in first and the narrator is handed extravagant winnings. Riding home in a hansom cab with his unlawful profit, the narrator experiences a thrill of emotion, an awakening of his feelings as a result of having committed an offense against the legal and social code which up to now had governed his life.

The process which will transform him has begun. The influence of Nietzsche's *Beyond Good and Evil* is apparent in the revivifying effects of shedding conventional morality. The influence of Freud[14] is apparent in the process of self-discovery by descent into the realm of the id.

> Eine Tür war aufgerissen vom Sturm dieser Leidenschaft, eine Tiefe aufgetan in mich hinein, und ich starrte in wollüstigem Schwindel hinab in dies Unbekannte in mir, das mich erschreckte und beseligte zugleich. Und langsam—während der Wagen lässig meinen träumenden Körper durch die bürgerlich-gesellschaftliche Welt hinrollte—stieg ich, Stufe um Stufe hinab in die Tiefe des Menschlichen in mir, unsäglich allein in diesem schweigenden Gang, nur überhöht von der aufgehobenen grellen Fackel meines jäh entzündeten Bewusstseins. Und indess tausend Menschen um mich lachend und schwätzend wogten, suchte ich mich, den verlorenen Menschen in mir, tastete ich Jahre ab in dem magischen Lauf des Besinnens. Ganz verschollene Dinge tauchten plötzlich aus den verstaubten und erblindeten Spiegeln meines Lebens auf, . . . (601)

The process of liberation and discovery leads to "life": "Oh, ich hatte ja immer gelebt, nur nicht gewagt zu leben, ich hatte mich verschnürt und verborgen vor mir selbst, nun aber war die gepresste Kraft aufgebrochen, das Leben, das reiche, das unsäglich gewaltsame hatte mich überwältigt." (602) The violence of this encounter parallels the experience of Kayser's hero and is reminiscent of the accounts which mystics give of their encounters with God. This "life" seems to be an active

---

[14] Gay, *Weimar Culture*, p. 36, quotes Felix Gilbert: "Freud as an intellectual event had certainly permeated the entire intellectual scene."

and powerful force which overcomes the individual and is beyond his control. The descent into the sphere of repressed drives is accompanied by release of social inhibitions and a craving for community with the masses of humanity. The hero does successfully break through to a common humanity by means of munificent charity, tolerance and kindness toward the disreputable and downtrodden souls he encounters in the Prater park late that same night. He has become a new man and a happier man who has uncovered meaning in life. For him, as for Kayser's hero, that meaning, paradoxically, is "life" itself: ". . . ich weiss nur, dass ich ein glücklicherer bin, weil ich irgend einen heissen Sinn für mein ganz ausgekühltes Leben gefunden habe, einen Sinn, für den ich kein Wort finde als eben das Wort Leben selbst." (625–26) He has become sensitive to people and nature and to other creatures and is moved by his empathy with them. Nature itself seems to be in consonance with the new life within him. "Alles empfand ich, als lebte es nur für mich allein und mich wieder mit allem strömend verbunden. Schwarz umstanden mich die Bäume, sie rauschten mir zu, und ich liebte sie. Sterne glänzten von oben zu, und ich atmete ihren weissen Gruss." ". . . man braucht sich nur aufzutun und schon fliesst von Mensch zu Menschen der lebendige Strom." (623)

From being primarily calculating, Zweig's hero has become primarily a feeling person. The resolution of the story lies in the hero's acceptance of life in all its manifestations, and his shedding of his old "gentleman's conscience" in favor of the new conviction that the only possible crime is to be indifferent to life:

> Seitdem verbiete ich mir nichts mehr, weil ich die Normen und Formen meiner Gesellschaft als wesenlos empfinde, ich schäme mich weder vor andern noch vor mir selbst. Worte, wie Ehre, Verbrechen, Laster haben plötzlich einen kalten blechernen Klangton bekommen, ich vermag sie ohne Grauen gar nicht auszusprechen. (626)

The influence of Nietzsche is obvious, as is the parallel to the emancipation, in particular from traditional sexual morality, evident in the Kayser story.

The style reflects the embrace of the irrational. It is marked by often-repeated words such as "Hingabe," "dumpf," "Wollust," "Schlamm." Typical of its seemingly uncontrolled effusions is a single paragraph of sixteen lines which alone contain the following vocabulary of the irrational: the verbs fühlen (4 times), rauschen, herausschreien, quälen, gären, spüren, leben, atmen, empfinden (twice), zusammenschmelzen; the nouns Tumult, Gefühl (twice), Schwall, Herz, Erstickender, Schmerz, Lust, Erschrecken, Entsetzen, Schwebe; and the modifiers taumelnd, tosend, urhaft, inner, gewaltsam, schmerzhaft, trunken, ekstatisch, lebendig. They are combined into such phrases as: "von diesem tosenden Tumult," "dieser innere Schwall," "das Herz [gärte] schmerzhaft," "dieses urhafte Gefühl." (603) The language reflects the hero's new morality.

Conspicuous by their absence are terms from the realm of ratio. This realm provides the dialectic of the story—those concepts which the hero condemns and rejects on his way to his new higher synthesis. They include social conventions and the city as a symbol of modern alienation. The example of the latter is Manchester, England, "eine jener stählernen Städte, die in einen lichtlosen Himmel von Lärm brausen wie eine Untergrundbahn, und die doch gleichzeitig eine Frost von Einsamkeit haben, der durch die Poren bis ins Blut dringt." (613) In this "stählernen Kerker" (613) his medicine against loneliness was sex. As in other stories women's role is primarily to provide a vehicle for the hero's escape from alienation to life. He rejects the machine *per se*—" . . . heute nachmittags habe ich mich herausgestürzt aus eurer kalten knöchernen Welt, wo ich ein Rad war, ein lautlos funktionierendes in der grossen Maschine . . ." (603)—a metaphor not without inadvertent irony in view of the opulently privileged life which the hero has led and continues to lead. He rejects the culture of the intellect, illustrating his change for the better by remarking that he was recently more moved by a sad story of real life than by the tragedies of Shakespeare. He is critical even of the tools of intellectual activity: ". . . ich verstehe wohl die eigene Anmassung, eine kalte Feder in die warme lebendige Hand zu nehmen und auf einem trockenen Papier sich hinzuschreiben, man lebe wirklich." (627)

The absurdity and the risks of dividing the human experience into mutually exclusive, contradictory realms such as feeling versus reason, mind versus soul, or "life" versus "science" are pointed out by historian Ernst Troeltsch in his essay "Die Krise des Historismus" which appeared in the June 1922 *NR* (I, 572–90) juxtaposed to the second installment of "Phantastische Nacht" and which serves as a direct counterpoint to the story. In his introductory remarks explaining the erroneously pejorative use of the term "historicism," Troeltsch also elucidates the contemporary rejection of science in favor of a neoromanticisim and mysticism:

> Es gehört in diesem Sinne in die allgemeine heutige Rebellion gegen die Wissenschaft überhaupt hinein, in der sich die Enttäuschung einer leidenden, dem intellektuellen Fortschritt nicht mehr trauenden Menschheit Luft macht. Man zerstört die Mittel der Lebenserhaltung, weil das Leben mit ihrer Hilfe, freilich auch unter Mitwirkung von hundert ganz anderen Umständen, nicht erfreulicher geworden ist. Ähnlich haben die Handwerker die Maschinen bei ihrem Aufkommen in ihrer blinden Wut zerstört. Wie freilich das Leben ungeheurer Massen ohne die Mittel der Wissenschaft sich gestalten soll, darüber macht man sich keine Gedanken. Da gibt es prachtvolle poetische Bilder neuer Ursprünglichkeit und Lebensfrische oder mystischen Erkenntnisersatzes, indessen die Lehrer und Diener der "alten" Wissenschaften durch ihre fortgesetzte Arbeit dafür sorgen, dass die Welt an dieser Romantik und Mystik nicht allzusehr leidet und ihren mühseligen Gang weiter geht. (573)[15]

These remarks represent one direction in the 1922 *NR*. It

---

[15] In his wholesale rejection of what he conceives to be the "American way of life," Kayser himself comes very close to the attitudes Troeltsch is

appears most consistently in the contributions of the *NR*'s political editor Samuel Saenger and in other political essays. Another direction is represented in Rudolf Kayser's essay "Zur Soziologie der modernen Kultur" which appeared in January 1922 (I, 4–15). It is important to examine Kayser's thinking because of its inevitable influence on the range of stories in the *NR* during his tenure.

In this his maiden essay as editor-in-chief Kayser is setting a tone for the future while deliberately avoiding establishing guidelines. The statement is a spirited condemnation of a concept which he calls "legalism." According to Kayser this sterile and restrictive principle dominates the modern world. A product of "Renaissance individualism," it has taken the place of religion, God and the myths of former times. Consequences are an overemphasis on formal categories in art and on methodology in science. At this time Kayser is definitely to be reckoned in the camp of "life" as opposed to "science." The individual, he believes, is subject in the modern world to a network of restrictions based on purely utilitarian considerations. "Er [modern man] kommt nicht los vom zeiträumlichen Alltag, von den Erfahrungen im Beruf, von einer Systematik der Menschenwelt, die aus keinerlei Wertmasstäben, sondern allein aus Technik und Nützlichkeit geschaffen ist." (4–5) Kayser is horrified at the loss of self-determination for the individual, at the pervasiveness of materialism, the preeminence of the "Empiriker und Methodiker" (9), and the accompanying absence of values and ideals. Metaphysical

---

condemning. Kayser made the following comments in an article entitled "Amerikanischer Journalismus" (750–51) in his July 1924 (I, 740–51) "Europäische Rundschau": "Innerhalb des mechanisierten amerikanischen Daseins ist auch die Zeitung eine Maschine. Sie produziert das Bild der grösseren Maschine: das amerikanische Leben, aber sie produziert nur Einzelheiten. Deshalb bleibt die Orientierung immer noch schwer. Wir beherrschen diese Maschine noch nicht so gut, wie sie uns beherrscht. Noch muss an ihrer Vervollkommnung weiter gearbeitet werden. Vielleicht kommt sonst der Tag,—wo die Wut über sie die Maschine zerschlägt." (751)

needs, according to Kayser, cannot be permanently repressed. People need religion or myths to provide them with a transcendental reality.[16] There were in the past "universalistic ages" when faith and myths created a community of mankind and this community represented political and cultural power.[17] Today, in a fragmented and legalistic age, culture has suffered. The parallel in art to "legalism" in society is the form principle. Laws and principles govern art according to rational concepts borrowed from the "legalistic system." Kayser rejects the idea of a normative aesthetic: "Gibt es aber Gesetze für die Kunst, so sind sie allein in der Kunst selbst, nicht aber ausserhalb ihrer zu suchen." (13) Like Zweig, Kayser relies heavily on Nietzschean and Freudian concepts:

> Der Dualismus zwischen dem natürlichen Ich und der künstlichen Legalität greift sogar in das Innere des Ich hinein und spaltet es. So kommt der Kampf in uns selbst, zwischen dem was uns natürlich und dem was legal ist. Es kommt der grauenvolle Passionsweg zur Einsamkeit, der in Werken gipfelt, die die schmerzliche Befreiung

---

[16] Jost Hermand and Frank Trommler, in *Die Kultur der Weimarer Republik* (Munich: Nymphenburg, 1978), p. 155, use Kayser's work as an example of the contemporary craving for myth: "Die Klage über die mythoslose Gegenwart, wie sie Rudolf Kayser, lange Zeit Chefredakteur der *Neuen Rundschau*, 1923 in der Schrift *Die Zeit ohne Mythos* vorbrachte, hatte sich inzwischen intensiviert."

[17] Gay, *Weimar Culture*, treats this widespread illusion in a chapter titled "The Hunger for Wholeness." He uses the example of Hugo von Hofmannsthal's 1927 speech at the University of Munich—"Das Schrifttum als geistiger Raum der Nation"—which Gay paraphrases as follows: "Indeed, only where there is 'believed wholeness of existence—*geglaubte Ganzheit des Daseins*'—*there* is reality. And now, in the 1920s, there are some seekers and prophets in Germany who are groping for this reality, and in two ways. They 'seek, not freedom, but connection,' and they have achieved the insight 'that it is impossible to live without believed wholeness,' that 'life becomes livable only through valid connections,' that 'scattered worthless individuals' must become 'the core of the nation'—that, in a word, 'all partitions into which mind has polarized life, must be overcome in the mind, and transformed into spiritual unity.' Hofmannsthal was fortunate; he died in 1929, before he saw the consequences to which fatigue with freedom and the denigration of individuality would lead." (85)

von der von aussen nach innen vorgeschrittenen Legalität bedeuten: jedes Genie der Neuzeit musste sich ja erst von der Formgesinnung der ästhetischen, moralischen, politischen Schulen und Parteien loslösen, eine Loslösung, die selbst aber viel mehr als nur Formales bedeutet. (11)[18]

Die Wirkung der Legalität im sozialen Leben ist so stark, dass sie uns den Weg zu den eigentlich moralischen Entscheidungen fast versperrt. Der Apparat der Gesetze, Verordnungen, Konventionen ist so durchorganisiert, dass er nur wenige Möglichkeiten in den zwischenmenschlichen Beziehungen freigibt und seinen Instanzen entzieht. Die angeblich zum Schutze des Individuums geschaffenen Einrichtungen dringen bis in die heimlichsten Provinzen unseres Lebens vor und machen sich zum Vormund unserer sämtlichen Entschlüsse. Man möchte fast sagen: moralische Entscheidungen kann man erst gewinnen, wenn man die Legalität hinter sich gelassen hat. (11–12)

Kayser is advocating for the superior individual the same liberation from laws and conventions which served to transform Zweig's hero. (The liberation is not for everyman; it is definitely not a democratic concept but an elitist one.) According to Kayser the freeing of the natural self from proscriptions and laws is the key to artistic excellence.

A chief weakness is the essay's global approach to human experience. Kayser proposes a theory which is meant to encompass all social, historical and cultural phenomena and consequently rests on serious distortions of history and the present. While some of his particular dissatisfactions with developments as he sees them and some of his conclusions are convincing, the whole is not. His approach seems to rest on a response of anxiety and wholesale rejection. It is as Sontheimer suggests with some irony: "In Verbitterung über den als Verhängnis empfundenen Charakter einer von der ratio

---

[18] Kayser apparently failed to recognize the contradiction between, on the one hand his condemnation of "Renaissance individualism" and its latter-day consequences, and on the other hand his glorification of the individual genius.

geprägten Zivilisation, strebte man in die Tiefen neuen Welterlebens."[19] The striving for sweeping truths is characterized by lack of concreteness, mystification, and internal contradictions in the essay. In spite of his discouraged point of view Kayser does not advocate resignation. He concludes that "salvation" (again a transcendental concept) is possible: "Es wäre Selbstmord, jetzt zu resignieren, die Ohnmacht des Augenblicks zum Schicksal der Zukunft zu machen. Wir haben zwar die Erkenntnis dessen was stirbt, aber auch den Willen und das Gerüstetsein zu dem, was uns erlösen wird, was uns erlösen muss." (15)

On the basis of Kayser's convictions as expressed in this essay, we ought not to expect to find that formal experimentation plays a significant role in *NR* stories during the years of his editorship. While not all stories will correspond to his thinking as closely as "Phantastische Nacht," it would not be surprising to find idealism, belief in individual self-determination, indifference to or rejection of social conventions and bourgeois moral codes, and focus on the creative and self-regenerative possibilities of the individual who has broken through restrictive norms. Transcendentalism can be expected to play a role, as well as an inner relationship between man and nature (as opposed to the superficial one which Kayser laments: "Er [modern man] sieht die Landschaft als Gegenstand der Sonntage und Urlaubsreisen, und Berg, Ebene, Meer sind in ihrem Rhythmus und Atem kaum anders unterschieden, als durch die veränderten äusseren Lebensverhältnisse, die sie bedingen." [5]). Stylistically, there might be a tendency toward the unstructured, the rhapsodic. On the negative side modern science and technology, the city, concrete economic and social problems, politics and public policy will probably not be major concerns. The emphasis is likely to be on the

[19] Sontheimer, *Antidemokratisches Denken in der Weimarer Republik*, p. 52.

inner self (individual psychology) to the detriment of a larger, external (social) reality.

Having been directed by the stories by Kayser and Zweig to the characteristic sensibilities of the affirmative category and presumptions on which they are based, it remains to examine the other stories which make up this category. They follow in chronological order within the category.

Albrecht Schaeffer contributed four stories to the *NR* between January 1922 and March 1933. The first two—"Das Gitter" (March 1922, I, 265–304) and "Meleagros und Atalante" (November 1928, II, 562–78)—belong to the affirmative category; the third—"Die silberne Saite" (October 1930, II, 525–41) to the negative; and the fourth—"Der Major" (June 1931, I, 786–804) to the nonjudgmental. This chronology also happens to illustrate the change in sensibilities which the order of categories represents.

"Das Gitter" is, in its fundamental premises, a reflection of Kayser's theories. It is a romantic tale in a style which is frequently rhapsodic, touching on pathos and marked by archaisms and elaborate periods. The underlying theme is art itself and the qualities which make an artist and exceptional individual. It advocates that such persons break through the barriers of convention in order to release their creative powers. Superior individuals are exhorted to know and be true to themselves. It treats the inevitable striving of such people for a transcendental ideal, and presumes an essential kinship between the exceptional individual and nature.

The hero's name is Bruno Galba—a combination which points to the author's concern with contrasts between north and south,[20] Germanic and Italianate (also connected in the story to blond/dark and flatland/mountains). Bruno grows up

[20] This is true also of Kayser's and other stories set in Italy.

on an isolated Alpine farm with his Italianate father, a sensitive would-be intellectual farmer and failed artist. The boy's direction is determined by his isolation with his father and by the pervasive mountain landscape. Bruno is at home in the natural world around him. His father has taken sole responsibility for Bruno's education in order that his son's talent and imagination not be hampered and eventually inhibited as the father's had been by being exposed to an unattainable ideal. The high point of the father's life and permanent dampening of his creativity occurred when—on a visit to Spain—he experienced the works of El Greco. It is the father's joy to discover his hopes being fulfilled for a true, natural artist in his son: "Dass er plante, wirkte, und ausführte *von innen her*, aus *Phantasie*, aus *selbsterzeugten Gesichten*, denen *die äussere Welt als Gestalt* zu dienen hatte, die ihr *Wesen* jedoch nicht von jener entlehnten." (271) (Italics mine.) Again, in the language of idealism, this sentence reads as if it came from Kayser's essay.

When Bruno is eighteen, his father dies and the young man suddenly becomes aware of the narrowness of his life up to then. He decides to set off on foot, to "descend" to northern Germany to find the sister he had never known because she was born after their (blond, northern German) mother had been estranged from their father.

Schaeffer is concerned with the psychology of his characters as he builds a case for the conflicts which develop. He emphasizes, for example, Bruno's isolation from women, the fact that he had "only theoretical" knowledge of the female body. The hero's descent from the mountains into the flatlands is at the same time an entry into the wide world and exposure to its unfamiliar space, freedom, and temptations. There are so many new sensations and impressions that Bruno is overwhelmed and no longer able to create his art. This experience precedes the central event of the story—from which it takes its title—Bruno's arrival at the castle-like estate of his sister's guardian to discover, beyond a tall gate, an almost mystical vision of a lovely girl in white, seated at the edge of a fountain in a garden where she is feeding a variety of beautiful birds. Bruno has the impression that many are the same birds which were his friends at home in the mountains. Though he knows it is the place he is seeking, Bruno instinctively and almost unconsciously passes and continues his journey for a quarter of an hour before turning back to the house. Schaeffer has strewn these clues about for the reader who up to now has been led to believe, as has Bruno, by a letter from the guardian that only the guardian's housekeeper, Helke, is at home. The vision in the garden turns out to be Helke. She and Bruno are alone for several days before the unsavory, middle-aged guardian, who lusts after Helke, returns from a business trip. During that time they kiss, and fall into an uncontrollable, overpowering, erotic and almost mystical passion for each other. Overcome with desire, Bruno tiptoes to Helke's bedroom door at night, but the sense of her purity prevents him from opening it. The next day the guardian returns and reveals the "little joke" he has played on the two young people: Helke is really Bruno's sister.

The news destroys Bruno. He departs immediately for Munich where he languishes as an art student. He masters his craft but proves to be totally ungifted. Robbed of its spiritual sustenance, his art is no longer meaningful. Bruno's talent disappeared when he had to deny the needs of his soul and thereby lost the ability to communicate with his innermost self (the subconscious); like his father, Bruno has become inhibited. He has lost the prerequisite of the great artist: the ability to comprehend the whole;[21] Bruno can only compre-

---

[21] See n. 17 for Gay's chapter on this theme. He quotes historian Friedrich Meinecke's *Die Idee der Staatsräson in der neueren Geschichte* (1924), p. 490: "Meinecke saw it precisely in 1924: 'The deep yearning for the inner unity and harmony of all laws of life and events in life remains a powerful force in the German spirit.'" (Gay, *Weimar Culture*, p. 81.)

hend segments: ". . . soweit die Geschwächtheit seiner Augen gestattete, die ihn stets nur ein Einzelnes sehn liess, niemals ein Ganzes; will sagen eigentlich Teile nur, . . ." (290) Like Icarus, Bruno thinks, he too flew too high and was burned:

> Scheinbar von den Bergen hinab in die Ebene gestiegen, hatte er in Wirklichkeit Schwingen ins Morgenrot erhoben; hatte immer höheren, leichteren Flugs Gottes Gestirn überflogen, hatte die Kammer im Azur offen gefunden und vor der Jungfräulichen gekniet, der ewigen Schwester, dem höchsten Idol der Unerreichbaren. Vielleicht war dieses der einfache Sinn; den Menschen trennt, wer er auch sei, Unmöglichkeit von der reinen Idee; . . . (288)

This characteristic moralizing the Schaeffer stories share with the Kayser and the Zweig stories. Definitive interpretation is provided for the reader. At intervals the deeper significance of what has transpired is explained, thereby relieving the reader of the effort of thinking. By this token there is to be only one admissible interpretation. It is a structural and stylistic device which reveals a peculiar sensibility—already noted in Kayser's thinking—the tendency toward moralizing idealism, absolutes, the psychological/introspective and the mystical/transcendental. It is distinguished from the other, modern sensibility represented in the affirmative category by the Süskind stories (below, p. 77). They are multi-leveled and ambiguous. Missing is the "message" which is to be found on nearly every other page of the idealistic stories. The latter are concerned with "timeless" values and ideals which are taken as givens, neither questioned nor examined. The conclusion of "Das Gitter," in particular, reveals the dark pathways which unfettered and uncorrected irrationalism may follow.

In his misery, Bruno speculates a great deal about Germanic, Greek, Egyptian high personages of myth and history, for whom aberrant sexual behavior, namely brother/sister incest, was condoned. His thoughts center on the superior individuals and the extraordinary privileges to which their station entitled them. He and Helke ought to have such privileges and be entitled to rise above the ancient taboos. Related thoughts are continued years later when Bruno, having returned to his farm, is watching his little daughter being taught by a narrowminded teacher who imposes conventional restrictive moral codes on the world of nature and instinct:

> Und Bruno begann die dritte Veränderung seines Lebens mit einer Berichtigung der menschlichen Irrlehre, welche der Elster, einem schönen und sinnvollen Vogel, weil er dasselbe tut und denkt wie der Mensch, dass ihm nämlich wohlgefällt, was glänzt, und er sichs verschafft, wenn er es sieht, einen Schandnamen machte aus seiner, des Vogels, Unkenntnis der Gesetze. (293)

Like Zweig's hero, he arrives at the conclusion that laws, conventions, codes and social norms are to be defied if they deny natural instincts.

The ideal is realized in Bruno's daughter, Dorothee, born of his marriage to an actress. She is a child of nature: "Die Natur selber schien in das zärtliche Zeltlein der Menschenhaftigkeit eingezogen und reichte sich selber von drinnen nach draussen die lebendige Hand." (293) Dorothee has that wonderful congruence between inner self—soul— and outer world—nature—which Bruno once had but lost. She is all intuition, no sterile rational words, and therefore she is able to comprehend the universe as a whole:

> Sie liebte das Ganze, liebte es mit dem Wesen, kaum mit ihrem Bewusstsein, und Worte machte sie nie daraus, ausgenommen die Kosenamen für ihre Hühner und Gänse und die erworbenen Freundschaften der Elstern, mit denen sie endlose Kindsgeschwätze vollführte. Bäume und Büsche und selber die strengen Felsen waren ihr freundlich gesinnt, öffneten sich der liebevollen Vernunft, redeten verständliche Sprache. (294)

Her language is the language of nature, of "liebevoller Vernunft," as distinct from cold reason.

Despite its emphatic advocacy positions, "Das Gitter" finds a surprisingly undefiant and artificially neat resolution.

Many years later, the middle-aged Bruno, now estranged from his wife, is visiting Munich with Dorothee and accidentally runs into Helke, who also happens to be there on a visit with her son, Hans Wilke (again, the Germanic name is symbolic). The four immediately find one another compatible and become inseparable companions. In the meantime their two spouses meet coincidentally and conveniently decide to run off together. Helke and her son are free to move onto the farm with Bruno and Dorothee where, despite several near misses, Helke and Bruno never commit incest—not, however, for want of trying. Finally, in the ultimate happy end and submission, after all, to the taboo, they observe the blossoming love between the two offspring and find their own fulfillment through this union by proxy of their "blood," which results in stilling their own ardor for each other.

Schaeffer is preoccupied in this tale with theories of "blood" and inheritance. When Bruno first learned that Helke was his sister, he wondered whether the "mistakes" of their father and mother—Hans Galba had seen his wife, who at that time was pregnant with Helke, kiss another man, had locked her out of his house and never relented though she begged forgiveness—and of many earlier fathers and mothers were not passed on in his and Helke's "mistake." It is the Old Testament imperative that the sins of the fathers shall be visited upon generations of children. The two grandchildren are the reincarnations of their grandparents—Dorothee is dark, sensitive and artistic like grandfather Hans Galba, and Hans Wilke is blond and outgoing like his grandmother, the northern girl who had been Hans Galba's wife. In the concluding paragraphs of "Das Gitter," Bruno and Helke see—as if in a vision—the young people's embrace as a substitute for their own embrace and become content:

> Die Gegend oben entrückte sich; das weisse Haus begann ei Gold aus sich zu strahlen, das nicht irdisch war, und so gross und deutlich es blieb, war es nun in wolkiger Höhe gelegen. Die

> Umschlungenen [Dorothee and Hans Wilke] vor ihm verwandelten sich; ihre Kleider fielen nicht ab, und doch schimmerten sie wie klare Nackte, schimmerten sie wie beglückte Befreite, reine Geschöpfe der Natur, und als wäre der *Dämon Geist ein Fluch* und eine Wolke gewesen und von ihnen genommen.
>
> Die beiden unten [Bruno and Helke] jedoch, die dieses Gesicht erzeugten, spürten im Gefühl einer beseligenden Entkräftung ihr Blut von sich gehn und in diese so sehr Geliebten hineinschwinden. Das Gitter war gefallen. Sie, befreit und geklärt, er befreit und zu allen Aufgaben gekräftet, vollendete Geschwister: sie sahen, sie hörten über sich auf dem festen Berg ihr lange getrenntes Blut zu einem grossen und dauernden Brausen zusammenfliessen. (304) (Italics mine.)

This turgid nonsense—simplistic genetic theorizing and irrational ("Dämon Geist") speculations about mystical blood ties—foreshadows the obscurant theories which in later years were realized in political terms. In Schaeffer's case, however, these views stem from preoccupation with mysticism and romanticized mythology. An exile from 1939 to 1950, Schaeffer in later life abjured these aspects of his early works.[22]

Georg Hirschfeld's "Die Insel des Verbrennens" (February 1923, I, 127–45) is the simple tale of a famous British physician to lepers, John Turner, who himself contracts leprosy and, to protect others, banishes himself to an uninhabited, almost inaccessible northern island where he plans to live out his remaining days—accompanied only by his faithful German shepherd "Bill," a herd of sheep, and the island's wild animals—in the pursuit of a cure for leprosy which might be his legacy for mankind. After many trials and the gruesome deterioration of his body, Turner is visited by his young and beautiful, socially prominent fiancée, with the (unlikely and

[22] Gero von Wilpert, *Deutsches Dichterlexikon* (Stuttgart: Alfred Kröner, 1963), p. 506; and Hermann Kunisch, ed., *Handbuch der deutschen Gegenwartsliteratur*, II (2nd ed.; Munich: Nymphenburg, 1970), p. 157.

inadvertently humorous) name of "Fennimore." Fennimore willingly exposes herself to the disease in order to be with Turner and help him with his work. As their last act before their planned joint suicide by poison, the saintly pair leaves the bundle of sheep's wool, which encloses the record of Turner's successful experiments, on the beach where it will be retrieved by the Faeroe island fishermen who at regular intervals leave supplies in exchange for wool, and whose last visit brings notice from the King of Turner's having been knighted in absentia. The noble doctor's final good deed before he and Fennimore walk off into the sunset together, is to shoot his faithful dog so that he may not survive his master to suffer loneliness and attack the sheep. It is, in short, a maudlin tale, marked by a plethora of stereotypes and easy sentimentalities. Noteworthy, however, are some rhapsodic descriptions of the landscape and wild creatures. The hero encounters the animals as a friend, and wholeheartedly embraces the magnificient natural setting, whether it be engulfed in violent winter storms or the sun in summer. Rudolf Kayser comments as follows on "Die Insel des Verbrennens": "Visionär verdichtet sich in ihr das Schicksal menschlicher Einsamkeit. Landschaft und Leben durchdringen sich." (192) It is the shared vocabulary of the irrational, of romantic, high-minded idealism.

Regina Ullmann's "Die Barockkirche" (May 1923, I, 439–49)—the one story in our time period which is truly in keeping with religious orthodoxy—does not fall into the trap of heavy-handed moralizing. It is the tale of a humble soul in whose person a miracle is realized. A forty-seven-year-old pious Catholic maiden devotes herself, at great personal sacrifice, to the service of God. In childhood she had taken an oath to show her love of God and the Church by attending Mass every day. Arriving in the dead of winter in an Alpine village to carry out a charitable errand, the modest little woman proceeds to set out to her distant destination although it is perilously late in the day for a trek through the snowbound forest. Contrary to the instructions she received to stay overnight, she has decided to go on in order to reach her destination in time for morning Mass the next day. The lonely trudge through the forest becomes a struggle with the cold, wind and snow, a trial, and then a martyrdom—her epiphany—which mystically leads her in a circle to the Baroque church from which she had originally departed. Her transfigured self—to the awe of the assembled congregation—appears walking down the aisle toward the Communion rail to receive her last Communion before dying. She had, by her singular dedication to the will of God, become a saint. The story is masterly in its communication of the transcendental world of the soul and succeeds entirely in presenting the qualities of sainthood.

Unexpectedly, Franz Werfel in "Cabrinowitsch. Ein Tagebuch aus dem Jahre 1915" (June 1923, I, 552–81) achieves the same effect. Cabrinowitsch, perpetrator of a heinous crime, is mystically transformed into a saintly figure as a result of his own intense suffering and his innocent soul. The character who achieves this unlikely transfiguration is the young assassin of the Archduke Franz Ferdinand at Sarajevo (and indirect perpetrator of the first world war). In the eyes of the narrator Cabrinowitsch is too young—the idealistic, impressionable tool of sinister forces—to bear the guilt for his deed. The narrator happens to visit the twenty-year-old in a military hospital where he has been held temporarily because he is—twice doomed—the victim of advanced, incurable tuberculosis. The narrator watches Cabrinowitsch roughly moved from hospital to prison again and observes the almost paralyzing effect—as if an apparition—which the sight of the wasted, ethereal figure has upon onlookers. In a spiritual sense Cabrinowitsch has triumphed over his persecutors and the claims of the world upon him.

The two stories which deal with a transcendental realm have elements in common with René Schickele's "Tulpen"

(July 1923, II, 623–38). They share a preoccupation with the internal world, the life of the mind or soul. In Schickele's case, however, structure is provided the story not by sequential events but by the techniques of psychoanalysis transposed into literary form. One of the seven stories in our time period which are (at least largely) set in Italy, "Tulpen" is a complex composition. Form is paramount. This separates it somewhat from Kayser's strictures, but it shares his emphasis on individual development. It is a story about memory and introspection. The *Leitmotiv* of tulips provides the structural principle and also bears a number of symbolic functions. They stand, for example, for the decadent quality of Venice, to which the narrator's memories return in order to relive in a dream his love affair with Maria Capponi. Night dreams, day dreams, waking reality, reality as a symbol, past, and present are intermingled, sometimes hardly distinguishable, and all of equal importance.

In the beginning the narrator suffers from insomnia and fear of the night. He can find no peace of mind. The tulips in his garden are his comfort and gateway to the subconscious. Their colors, their brilliance, their different moods and appearances according to time of day and weather are intoxicating and lead to saving dreams of the past.

The style is lyrical, marked by personifications of nature and objects, by striking imagery and unusual metaphors, for example: "Der Honigregen fiel, verfiel, und den glücklichen Abend frass wolfshungrig eine Nacht, in deren Gewölk der Mond voll umhertorkelte." (624) Above all, color is prevalent as a device which not only creates mood, but itself becomes experience: ". . . und die Farbe selbst des Erlebnisses geworden war." (633) Associations between dream and reality, past and present, one experience and another are stimulated by imagery. There is a joy in words, in the rhythm of a single sentence, apart from its meaning: "Stück um Stück wiederhole ich immer denselben Satz, nehme ihn auseinander, um ihn von neuem zusammenzusetzen mit der Freude eines Kindes, das zwischen den Steinen seines Baukastens zu regieren vermeint, weil es gelernt hat, dem Gesetz zu gehorchen, das die Steine zum Bau fügt." (629) There are tones of ironic humor reminiscent of Heinrich Heine's prose, for example: "In den engen Gassen um den Markusplatz, die ich zu meiden pflegte, wie eine unverdorbene Herzogin den Fischmarkt, . . ." (634) There are references to the transcendental in the wonders of nature and a religiosity in the narrator's awe before its beauty.

The process of introspection, following the colors and images of memory and impression, guided and accompanied by the brilliant flowers in their many symbolic and aesthetic functions, has led the narrator to review his last meeting with Maria and the end of their love affair. This process of review of the past in a half-dream, half-waking state has brought him to terms with the past and with himself and has given him consolation. It is this happy resolution of the narrator's initial emotional turmoil which places this story in the affirmative category even though it tells of a bygone love:

> Heute war ein glasheller Tag, man sah, über die Ebene, in die Vogesentäler hinein, jetzt am Abend färbt die Sonne die Wipfel des Waldes ganz blond. Im Garten stehn die Tulpen wie besondere Wesen über der Erde versammelt, atmende Siegel von Träumen, die Seelen von zärtlichen, von tapferen Studen, die gewesen, die Seelen von Gefühlen und Gedanken, die einmal so mächtig in uns gelebt, dass sie eine Art Persönlichkeit erworben haben.
>
> Heute werde ich schlafen. Ich lächle der Gefürchteten, der Nacht entgegen, ich lächle, nicke ihr zu. Eine Tanzweise gibt das Signal zum Löschen des Lichtes. Die Tulpen haben kein Geheimnis mehr vor mir. (638)

The tulips were the realm of his subconscious. The narrator has plumbed its secrets and as a result they hold no more fear for him. In real and symbolic nature he has gained peace of mind from the sense that the past can have life and meaning in memory.

An epiphany in a different sense is experienced by young Hugo Bandler, *Gymnasium* student and Jew, who survives and learns from the trauma of adolescence in Ludwig Winder's "Turnlehrer Pravda" (August 1923, II, 698–716). It is another story which shows a strong Freudian influence. Stories of adolescence were common during the Weimar period.[23] In our group there are three; "Turnlehrer Pravda" is one of two affirmative ones. From about 1929 on the typical school boy tale more commonly includes suicides.[24]

The title "Turnlehrer Pravda" refers to a new gym teacher in the "tschechisches Gymnasium" who mesmerizes the eleven- to thirteen-year-old boys. A brutal, proto-Nazi type, he combines unpredictability with sadism, and an attractive, effeminate appearance. Soon the teacher has selected six favorites on the basis of their appearance. Others, including Hugo, are brutalized or ignored. Despite the teacher's anti-semitism, Hugo becomes infatuated with Pravda and tries desperately to make an impression. Finally, as a result of the teacher's gross insults, these feelings are crushed. Only when he discovers, by observing Pravda's house, that the

---

[23] Gay, *Weimar Culture*, p. 79: ". . . there was a certain fixation on the experience of youth itself; novels about schools and youth groups exemplified and strengthened this fixation."

[24] *Ibid.*, p. 140: "There was a whole genre of novels dealing with the suicides of young high school students—*Schülerselbstmordromane*—and its popularity reflected widespread interest in a grave phenomenon. In early 1929 Friedrich Torberg [cf. his story on a different subject, below, p. 167] published a characteristic suicide novel, *Der Schüler Gerber*, and prefaced his story with the laconic comment that in a single week—January 27 to February 3, 1929—he had read in the newspapers of ten such suicides." For an example of such a story, see Arnold Ulitz' "Boykott" below, p. 162. This is one of the several contexts in which Gay refers to the *NR* as exemplary for major trends: "To judge from the literature, by 1932 this concern had deepened into alarm. In the first six months of that year, to give only one instance, the monthly *Neue Rundschau* published no fewer than six long articles, all worried, all intelligent, all understanding of the problems of youth, all exhorting to reason and patience." (p. 142)

teacher's relationship with the favorites is a homosexual one, does Hugo become aware of his own homoerotic feelings. His shock and disgust with the others and with his own body bring on a severe emotional crisis, expressed in the metaphor familiar from Kafka's "Metamorphosis": "Dann lag er im Bett und warf sich in grossen Schwüngen von links nach rechts, von rechts nach links, wie einen riesigen Mistkäfer warf er seinen Körper hin und her." (712)[25]

In sober, brief, factual sentences, Winder examines perceptively and convincingly the psychology of the adolescent, and in particular the effects of the double burden of adolescence and anti-semitism on a sensitive and intelligent boy. Hugo is shown grappling with the emotional turmoil caused by erotic drives for which the only outlet was a seductive and corrupt male teacher. Hugo suffers from dreams which have obvious Freudian symbolism. Though isolated from his peers by anti-semitism and from his parents by an education gap, dependent solely upon his own resources, the boy manages almost instinctively to cope with the problem, proving himself

[25] Winder was very likely acquainted with Kafka's work. Winder was born in 1889 in a small town (Schaffa) in southern Moravia. (publisher's biographical note in: Ludwig Winder, *Hugo, Tragödie eines Knaben* [Vienna: Rikola, 1924]. This work consists of three parts, the first of which is "Turnlehrer Pravda.") Winder, who lived in Prague, emigrated to England in 1939. He died in London on 16 June 1946. (Wilhelm Kosch, ed. *Deutsches Literatur-Lexikon*, 2nd ed. [Berne and Munich: Francke, 1949].) Ernst Alker sees a similarity between Winder and Kafka: "(*Die jüdische Orgel* [novel by Winder]—Roman eines jungen Menschen, der, ohne Gelingen, aus engstickiger, halb glaubens-fanatischer, halb betont händlerischer Welt eines mährischen Gettos ausbricht—bietet, nebenbei gesagt, vorzügliche Unterlagen für die Erkenntnis der bloss zwei oder drei Generationen zurückliegenden seelischen Voraussetzungen, die Franz Kafka zu eine ganze Welt erschütternden Geständnissen seiner plasmatisch bedingten Ängste, Bedrängnisse und seines letzthin, bei aller geschliffenen Dialektik, noch rabbinisch-talmudistischen Empfindens gegenüber dem Sündigen, d.h. nicht mehr entsprechend dem jüdischen Orthodoxismus gelebten Dasein dichterisch gestaltet hat.)" (Ernst Alker, *Profile und Gestalten der deutschen Literatur nach 1914*, ed. by Eugen Thurnher [Stuttgart: Alfred Kröner, 1977], p. 208.)

by the way and quite inadvertently, to be brave, mature and competent. Until the very end it appears that Hugo might be the victim, but by a series of desperate, unpremeditated actions, he succeeds in trapping Pravda. Hugo cows the teacher by convincing him that the transgressions have been revealed. In a *coup de grace*, Hugo gives him one hour's time to escape and Pravda takes an abrupt exit through the window and out of town.

Although not directly expressed, it is apparent that Hugo's problems are the consequence of a repressive society. In an apparently unintentional, almost dreamlike sequence of actions, the boy triumphs over his difficulty, but no exposure of the context of repression has occurred. It is a private moral victory over an individual external enemy and the "enemy" within. There are no broader consequences or implications. In the emphasis on the Freudian psychology of the individual, and in its unrealistically positive outcome, "Turnlehrer Pravda" coincides with the directions in Kayser's thinking and with previous stories in the affirmative category. By contrast the May 1930 (I, 641–63) story about adolescence and anti-semitism, Arnold Ulitz' "Boykott" (in the negative category), directly implicates society, in that case corruption in political and financial circles, tying the fate of the individual to this larger context. In the later story anti-semitism has taken on a deadly virulence; a student commits suicide, and the persecuted, deserving young hero does not triumph over his enemies.

The larger world—politics, the direction which German society seems to be taking in the early twenties—is of very direct concern to the hero of Otto Flake's "Die zweite Jugend" (April 1924, I, 322–52). Flake's second story during our time period—"Der Selfmademan"—appeared in July 1931 (II, 103–20) and belongs to the non-judgmental category. "Die zweite Jugend" is affirmative because, as the title indicates, it portrays an individual renewal and new beginning of life. Flake, a fine essayist, considered leftist in his political sympathies, was a favorite contributor to the *NR* over many years.[26] His fiction too is essay-like in character. The stories tend overly toward theoretical commentary; they explain rather than depict. Unfortunately they are characterized by trite expressions and derivative ideas. Sentences are choppy and clumsy, lacking rhythm, consistency, and control. Breathless, incomplete sentences reflect the same quality in the composition as a whole. In fact there is little which could rightly be called style.

"Die zweite Jugend" rests upon a heavy-handed organizational scheme. It is divided into an introduction and day one, two, three, and four of the hero's stay in Garmisch. Each day marks the next higher stage in the hero's climb (and return) of one mountain (the "Kramer") until, on the last day, he decides to go over the top. Each day's climb is meant to represent a parallel spiritual progress in the hero as a consequence of his examination of self and the past. The substitution of a "tell" technique for "show" is illustrated at the very beginning by guidelines for the reader which belabor the obvious: "Mit jedem Tag wurde er etwas vertrauter mit den Bergen, und ohne dass er des Schemas bewusst wurde, schuf er sich ein Gleichnis für diese wachsende Befreiung: die Etappen, in denen er den Kramer bestieg." (322) On each of the four days, he selects the next higher point which will be his goal for the day: "Diese vier Punkte steckten die Spaziergänge ab, die am Morgen nach seiner Ankunft begannen und am vierten Tag zu einem Ereignis führten, das ihn vor eine Entscheidung stellte, durch die sein Leben bestimmt wurde." (323) Neither subtlety nor ambiguity are virtues of the author. Each day and stage is accompanied by reminiscences of crucial periods in the hero's life. They mark those times when, as a

[26] Supposedly, S. Fischer at one point considered asking Flake to be editor of the *NR*. (de Mendelssohn, *S. Fischer und sein Verlag*, p. 860.)

consequence of being deeply moved, he produced an important work of art. A sculptor by profession, the hero bears the conspicuously symbolic name of Wahrmut. From their description, however, these works show a striking lack of imagination as well as ignorance of what might be considered important or original in art. They are busts of two people Wahrmut admired and an eagle modeled after one in a zoo. Nevertheless Wahrmut engages in sweeping speculations about the nature of art and the creative process. Unfortunately, they amount only to shallow platitudes.

The subject of the story appears to be the exceptional individual whose gifts raise him above the common herd (cf. "Phantastische Nacht" and "Das Gitter") and entitle him to be unencumbered by normal constraints. However, there is a contradiction between the hero's obvious feeling that he is a representative of enlightened modernism, and his unenlightened attitudes and behavior,[27] between his tone of superiority and self-conscious elitism, and the reality of his talents and conduct. We must take the hero and these contradictions at face value because the author has not used any devices which create distance from the hero. There is neither irony nor any other stylistic means of viewing the hero from a critical perspective. Next to Wahrmut all other characters suffer a shadowy existence. They offer the hero no competition. In neither of his stories is Flake able to breath life into a character other than his hero.

The tone is male chauvinist—conveyed by hair-raising clichés about women. A favorite description of a woman uses

---

[27] For one view of this Flake quality see Wolfgang Wendler's "Die Einschätzung der Gegenwart im deutschen Zeitroman," in *Die deutsche Literatur in der Weimarer Republik*, ed. by Wolfgang Rothe (Stuttgart: Reclam, 1974), p. 176: "Flake [in his novel *Villa U.S.A.*, 1926] versucht noch einmal, mit Vorstellungen des 18. und 19. Jahrhunderts, Selbstverwirklichung vorzuführen . . ."

"Rasse" or "rassig"—a term which is charitably described by contemporary *NR* author Hans Reisiger (in his story "Stehe auf und wandle," August 1926, II, p. 133) as "trivial." It is a stale attribute, already in Flake's time so overused that it no longer had meaning. A good example are the platitudes with which the hero describes a woman musician whom he is watching: "Das war Rasse, und wer Rasse hat, erlebt nicht obenhin, er erlebt ganz." (323–24)—a comment more suited to a horse show. Flake's devotion to this usage culminates in the hero's list, in borderline racist terminology, of most desirable qualities in a woman—any woman: above all "Rasse," and "gutes Blut." (343) This would be his "benennbares Ideal der Frau, mit der er sich hätte messen mögen." (343) Of course in practice there is no real woman who can measure up to Wahrmut.

From his superior vantage point Wahrmut encourages women in their sexual emancipation: "Er war Weltmann genug, um die Geringschätzung, die er empfand, zu verbergen und keine Frau, die sich gab, zu missachten." (343) He does not mind patronizing a house of school girl prostitutes in Berlin where the girl intended for him—as he discovers in the nick of time—turns out to be his own daughter whom he had not seen for years.[28] On the other hand Wahrmut refers to his own sexual needs with prissy victorian euphemisms: "Um

[28] The same incident—with other characters—is portrayed by Erich Kästner in his 1931 novel *Fabian*. The character Fabian relates it: "In another street not far from here, there's a boardinghouse where young schoolgirls sell themselves, to earn pocket-money. Just six months ago, there was a scandal, which wasn't easy to keep quiet. An elderly gentleman, who had rented a room for his pleasure, and who expected to find a naked sixteen-year-old girl waiting for him, found that the waiting girl was unfortunately his daughter, which he hadn't expected." Otto Friedrich, in *Before the Deluge: A Portrait of Berlin in the 1920's* (New York: Harper & Row, 1972), p. 348, quotes these remarks in a longer passage from *Fabian* which he uses to convey the state of moral decay in late Weimar Berlin.

alles in einem Wort zu sagen, die Frauen denen er hier begegnete, machten wenig Schwierigkeiten. Er war wieder allein, es galt das zu regeln, wovon man nicht spricht. (342) "Er . . . stand wieder der Not dessen, wovon man nicht spricht, gegenüber . . ." (343) Wahrmut's affair with a Russian girl, Marja (she is of course "rassig") who falls in love with him, is limited on his side by his patronizing attitudes and basically adversary position toward women. It seems as if Flake collected every cliché about women which he could find and put them together into one story. The effect would be humorous if there were any indication that the author meant it to be so. The sculptor comments on his plan to sculpt a bust of Marja: "Es ist nicht genug, sagte er; bei einem Mann der Kopf, bei einer Frau der Körper, und begann sie ganz zu modellieren." (333) He describes her sexual behavior in terms such as: "unersättlich," "Tartarenmädchen . . . das biss, wenn es entflammte." (334) Man has a mind, and woman a body. That body is an object which behaves according to the imaginary ideal of everyman's erotic dreams—descriptions so clichéd that they fall into the emotionally deprived category of pornography. According to the hero, all women think alike, all revel in self-abnegation and submission: "Er machte die Entdeckung, dass der Künstler in ihm den Menschen begleitet hatte, wie eine Frau einen Mann begleitet, obwohl er ihr weh tut, sie missachtet." (328) ". . . er hatte eine weibliche Empfindung, Schoss zu sein, der willig trägt." (350) The goal of all women is to snare a man who will take care of them: ". . . und [er] stiess auf die geheimen, stets geleugneten Wünsche, denen sich Frauen überlassen, wenn sie den gefunden haben, der für sie denken, ordnen, alles einfach machen könnte." (336) Wahrmut prides himself, ". . . dass er sich nicht wie jener Graf und Bankier doch noch fangen lässt." (338)

To Marja's confession of love, Wahrmut reacts with the immature devices of rationalization, self-righteousness, deceit and flight. Like a spoiled child, he refuses to accept the fact that someone has a legitimate claim on him, and that the claim results from his own conduct:

> Er schwieg, was sie sagte, erschütterte ihn. In die Erschütterung mischte sich die Auflehnung, sich vergewaltigt zu wissen, dafür dass man natürlich und vielleicht gut gewesen war, verantwortlich gemacht zu werden. Was konnte unheimlicher sein, als dass der freien Verabredung der Zwang entsprang, dem Idyll die Tragödie—in gerader Linie entsprang, ohne dass irgendein neuer Umstand dazugekommen wäre? Als er zwei Tage darauf ein Telegramm erhielt, das ihn nach Wien rief, sah sie ihn fragend an, erwartend, dass er sie einlud, ihn zu begleiten, und begriff, als er sagte, dass er sie in Berlin treffen werde, dass die Depesche bestellt war. (337)

Of course, ". . . in dieser Lage werden Frauen hysterisch." (338) A beautiful, tempestuous woman is, according to the hackneyed image, especially beautiful when she is angry: "Sie schrie auf, war schön, leidenschaftlich, echt." (338) In order to remark another person's pain in such a fashion, that person must be an object to the observer.

The hero is egocentric, an old-fashioned snob. His ideal woman must have enjoyed "beste Erziehung." (343) "Er konnte um Mädchen aus anderen Kreisen als dem, worin Marja lebte, werben—" (336) (Noteworthy here is the use of the term "Mädchen" when serious marital prospects and "higher" social circles are involved.) "In jenem Winter, in dem er sich von Marja trennte, begann er in Gesellschaft zu gehn. Die Geselligkeit war eingeschränkt, die guten Familien sparten, er sah sich in die von Ausländern und neuen Reichen gedrängt." (342) Two standard German prejudices appear here: against foreigners and the "new rich." The two groups were particularly prominent during the inflation—which is the period Wahrmut is speaking of here—when speculators became rich overnight, and foreigners exploited the advantage of having hard currency which bought valuable properties Germans could no longer afford. This situation is portrayed by

W. E. Süskind in "Raymund."[29] Above all, Wahrmut seeks to lead a life uncomplicated by the claims of others on him. His reaction to news of Marja's suicide attempt illustrates his customary childish and self-serving avoidance reaction whenever trouble threatens:

> Vom Telephon ging er zum Diwan—das zu tun, was sich immer bewährt hatte: ausgestreckt liegen und schweigen. Stehen war die Haltung dessen, der umtobt, angegriffen, erreicht wird, dessen, der sich erreichen lässt. Wer lag, war in die Ströme gebettet, die über ihn hinweg gingen, ganz indem sie ihn zu überfluten schienen; wer lag, ruhte parallel zu ihnen, sie verflossen, er blieb zurück. (340)

Wahrmut shows no awareness of the incongruity between this pseudo-buddhism and his egotism.

The episode with his daughter the prostitute leaves Wahrmut with emotional distress which complicates the life he had tried so hard to keep clear and simple. The two shocks—Marja and his daughter—lead to Wahrmut's decision to leave these troubles behind:

> . . . zuletzt blieb ein schwer zu umschreibendes Gefühl übrig: die Auflehnung dagegen, dass es ihm nicht gelungen war, seinen Weg zu gehn, ohne dass er beschmutzt wurde, ohne dass das Hässliche nach ihm griff, ohne dass er den Tribut zahlte. Die Auflehnung blieb, und ihre Ohnmacht. Damals kam ihm zuerst der Gedanke, dass es ein Mittel geben sollte, um solche Belastungen auszuscheiden, abzuwerfen, hinter sich zu bringen. Das Mittel hätte darin bestanden, von neuem anzufangen, den Strich unter einen Lebensabschnitt zu setzen, die Vergangenheit auszulöschen, . . . (346)

This thinking harks back to Kayser's remarks in his March 1923 essay:[30] there is a pure, an untainted, an ideal realm and there is everyday reality, whether it be politics, as for Kayser, or also the everyday reality of his private affairs, as for the character

[29] See below, p. 86.
[30] See above, pp. 22–24.

Wahrmut. For Wahrmut that reality is too disturbing, contradictory, morally ambiguous, and burdensome. He regards himself as belonging to the ideal realm. "Ugly" reality has contaminated him. The only cure is amputation of the past as if, like a gangrenous limb, it could be separated from the continuum of life. On the personal level such thinking would be called lack of maturity. As a symptom of the times in a general populace its inherent dangers should be obvious. Wahrmut makes it clear that he believes his mood reflects the mood of the times: "Es war die Zeit, in der das Reich zu zerbrechen schien, man schrieb September 1923. Jeder ungefähr im Land wünschte, in neue Verhältnisse zu flüchten; wer konnte, ging ins Ausland." (347) Apathy and the desire to escape have been the widespread reaction to political troubles.

Wahrmut experiences an epiphany as a result of his (structurally totally unmotivated) chance encounter with an ascetic and self-disciplined writer who lives in isolation on the mountain. Consequently Wahrmut is able to view his own desire to start life over again in a more profound context than mere escape: "Es war der Buddhawunsch, nicht eingefangen zu werden in das, was zeitlich ist. Immer war in jedem, der das Grosse fühlte, der gleiche, ein Drang am Werk, sich um des Ewigen willen vom Zeitlichen zu lösen." (349) According to Wahrmut's pompous self-evaluation, casting off all ties and obligations, past guilt and troubles for a "second youth" signifies a feeling for greatness, a striving for eternity. In actuality Wahrmut goes only as far as familiar, sunny Italy. He denies that he is trying to escape: "Flucht aus der Welt? Nein, diese Frage war entschieden." (350) "Nicht aus dem Leben fliehen . . ." (350)—which would, after all, mean sacrificing the pleasures of the senses. Flight—if only to his first stop in comfortable Lugano—is the only alternative when one's world view is based in the dualism of unattainable ideal and irremediable reality. It is the fateful dichotomy which characterized so much of German thinking, and is based on simplistic, reductionist views of politics. An example is Wahrmut's political judgments (which also happen to be extensions of his ability to find rationalizations for his egocentric behavior): "Das Land zerfleischte sich, instinktlos, er [Wahrmut] gestand keine Treue zu, wo er nicht mehr achten konnte. Sie zerfleischten sich—nicht seine Sache wurde da geführt." (350) "O Deutschland, dachte er, wie gut tut es, aus deiner vergrämten Luft in die Welt, die ihren Gang weiter geht, zu ziehn." (352) It amounts—in Wahrmut's case in the private as well as the public sphere—to irresponsibility, turning one's back on reality because it is unattractive and means compromise. It is the equivalent of putting his head in the sand to search for that eternal ideal which is always presumed to be in some other time or place or realm, and is just as likely to be found in that ostrich posture in the sand.

Josef Ponten's "Das grosse Asien oder: Wiedersehen mit Charlotte" (July 1924, II, 714–31) is an exposé of romantic illusion—of the hope of returning home, recapturing childhood, of fantasies being fulfilled. Ponten is represented during our time period with four stories in the *NR*: "Unterredung im Grase" (February 1922, I, 182–94), "Das Autodafé" (September 1922, II, 902–12), "Frau im Süden" (November 1925, II, 1145–56), and "Das grosse Asien." All are masterly investigations of the soul—timeless in their concerns. The three earlier ones belong to the non-judgmental category which represents a more characteristic posture for Ponten. "Das grosse Asien" fits into the affirmative category because its conflicts are resolved with a victory for the ethic of selflessness and self-sacrifice for the sake of others.

Ponten's story is everything which the Flake story is not. The style is clear and controlled, characterized by economy of means and sensitivity to aesthetic effects. Structural devices are subtle and effective. The stories by Ponten are marked by internal consistency on all levels—language as well as structure and character development. The language is alive with strong rhythms, sensual sounds and vibrant imagery. An example is the scene of the blacksmith at work:

> Fritz sah Ludwig nicht. Denn er trieb eben mit dem schweren Zuschlaghammer einen glühenden Eisenreifen, den Gesellen mit langen Greifzangen hielten, auf das neue künstliche Gesperre eines eichenen Rades, der hölzerne Radkranz rauchte heftig unter der Berührung des glühenden Reifens. Alle Männer im heiligen Dampf der Arbeit banden Augen und Hände an ihr Werk, und niemand sah den Fremdling, der mit bewundernden Blicken draussen lehnte; an dem Bocke lehnte er, der den noch dreibeinigen Gatterwagen an Stelle des vierten fehlenden Rades unterstüzt hielt, vom Wagen waren bereits alle fahrenden Stücke, die Räder, die Achsen, das Gestelle zinnoberrot, die gefahrenen Teile, der Gatterkasten, himmelblau gemalt. Laut klangen Merkrufe und Hammertöne aus der Schmiede, schwarzer Rauch verbrannten Holzes und weisser Dampf von Wasser, von den noch zwischen den Beinen der Männer tätigen Lehrlingen auf die schon angepassten Reifenstrecken gegossen, wälzten sich aus dem Tore. Mit tiefem Vergnügen sah Ludwig das gediegene und gefährliche Werk, die Sammlung und Aufmerksamkeit der Gesellen und die spielenden Muskeln des stolzen Meisters inmitten. Wie würde er ihm nachher die schwielige ehrenreiche Hand drücken, dem prächtigen Vulkan! (717)

The colors, the movement, the evocative word sounds, the running sentences, the shifting perspective from smithy to observation point and back, the denouement with return to observer and view toward the future—all create a carefully structured scene which is rich, sensual and full of life, which depends for its effects upon the full sense of the possibilities of each word and their combinations into images. Yet by means of irony distance from the idyll is maintained, for Ludwig's anticipation is illusory; he will never shake the hand of the "magnificent Vulcan." The story has multiple strata. Its several messages are illustrated in characters' thought and behavior rather than explained in comments interjected by the narrative voice. They form an integral part of the narrative in contrast to the obtrusive philosophizing which characterized the Flake story and others (Kayser, Zweig, Hirschfeld,

Schaeffer). The psychology of the characters is credible. Characters other than the hero have independent stature and convincing individuality. Ponten is a master of the ironic perspective, thereby providing the distance from the hero which art requires. One of Ponten's strengths in this and the three other stories is a unique empathy with women's emotions and sympathetic grasp of their conflicts. His woman characters are multi-faceted human beings in their own right rather than one-dimensional appendages of the hero's needs. In two of his stories the central characters are women; one is told from the woman's point of view. All four stories take their impetus from a fundamental contradiction between the standpoint of a man and a woman character. The stories deal with timeless problems of interpersonal relations; there is no direct reference to the social context, no mention of contemporary events.

The first sentence establishes theme and direction of the tale. The thought and the mood which it expresses are repeated later, varied in form to suit the new context, when the hero Ludwig Rotmüller is about to take the selfless step which will resolve the central conflict. The opening sentence's structure and rhythm are characteristic:

> In Afrika, in Asien weit verloren, um die vom Körper durchreiste und sozusagen in ihn aufgenommene Landbreite auch seelisch erweitert und mit einem ungeheuren zugewachsenen Spielraum der Entschlüsse vergrössert, fühlte Ludwig an einem Weihnachtstage beim rauchenden Lagerfeuer den jähen Wunsch in sich aufkommen, das kleine Dorf seiner Heimat wiederzusehen. (714)

The complexity of the imagined concept—the dialectic between the self having absorbed and been expanded by vast distances, and its sudden craving for the circumscribed and the intimate—is reflected in the complexity of the sentence. Ludwig will return home full of hopes, imagining scenes of triumph as he is welcomed as a hero for his fame and achievements as an explorer and receives the recognition which was denied to him in his youth. Having won acclaim in the larger world, Ludwig now needs and expects that sweetest acknowledgment of all—from the folks at home. Of course it all turns out to be illusory. There is no welcome. Ludwig is not even recognized after his fifteen-year absence. The little village does not stir upon his arrival. Once he has realized that he remains the outsider he always was, Ludwig does not even try to look up those people who still might mean something to him. Childhood cannot be recaptured and those satisfactions which were missing in childhood are lost forever. One person's approval would mean more to Ludwig than any other—that of Charlotte Hörsing, the sensitive and devoted friend of his youth. Ludwig is convinced that he will find Charlotte in the midst of an idyllic family life with the blacksmith Fritz who always loved her.

But when they meet accidentally in the empty church, Ludwig learns that Charlotte has remained single all these years in the hope that he, Ludwig, would return to claim her. Deprived of his last lovely illusion, he perpetrates a small deception in order to deprive Charlotte of the illusion which is destroying her life. Ludwig is able to marshal his strength to help Charlotte although it means dismissing forever the fantasies and hope for her approval which his soul had nourished. Impersonating the priest in the confessional, he tells Charlotte that Ludwig Rotmüller has spoken disparagingly of her in public. The disappointment kills her hopeless love and her illusions: "—ihr argloses Herz war getäuscht. Ein Glaube zerbrach." (730) Despite the initial pain, disillusionment will in the long run be liberating. It gives the freedom to begin life anew, on a firmer, more realistic, if more sober basis. Ludwig returns to his duty in the deserts of central Asia.

The July 1924 issue of the *NR* closes with Rudolf Kayser's eulogy to Franz Kafka, who died the month before. It is worth noting because Kayser maintains that he considers Kafka's prose to be among the best in contemporary German literature. The qualities which he singles out for praise are its clarity, objectivity and simplicity. Kayser has an ear for these virtues even though they may not necessarily have been reflected up to now in his selection of stories.

One story whose style does meet standards of precision and clarity is Hermann von Boetticher's "Die aussätzige Magd" (December 1924, II, 1248–75), one of the most powerful and enigmatic stories during our time period. It is the epitome of the affirmative type because the important conflict in the story is a spiritual one which is resolved by epiphany (in the literal sense) and resultant catharsis for two characters. The opening paragraphs indicate that the spiritual condition which the story describes is also meant to be an allegory of the larger world—material, social and spiritual disintegration in postwar Europe:

> Es war im Herbst des Jahres 1921, in dem alle Dinge in Europa noch flüssig waren von der mächtigen Erschütterung, welche den Erdteil zerrissen hatte, als ein Wanderer mit bleichem Gesicht den Aufstieg durch eines der Gebirgstäler unternahm, die das Wiener Tiefland von den Kalkalpen trennen.
>
> In der Frühdämmerung war er noch vom Nord- zum Südbahnhof durch die Häuserreihen der Stadt geeilt, die grau, kalt und gespenstisch auf ihn aus ihren erblindeten Fensteraugen heruntersahen. Feuchter Schmutz machte das Pflaster glitschig; die Armut und Hungrigkeit der Bewohner blickte aus den leeren Läden, den schief sitzenden unausgebesserten Türen und Fensterläden. Selbst die wenigen Hunde und Katzen, die bei dem hallenden Schritt von den Kehrrichteimern und düstren Torbogen flüchteten, zeigten in ihren mageren Gestalten und struppigen Fellen die Atmosphäre eines von menschlichen Selbstmorden angefüllten, zerfallenden Kosmos. (1248)

The pale wanderer contains in himself the contradictions of the times between disintegration and resistance to it: "Das Aussehen der Stadt hatte auch auf den Wanderer seinen Eindruck ausgeübt; in seinem Gesicht kämpften deutlich die Dämonen der Auflösung mit den Kräften des standhaltenden Geistes." (1248) A second level of meaning appears to be the struggle of a mind against personal demons in the form of mental illness.[31] The other-worldly expression on the wanderer's face—his smile which is the "anonymous smile of God" (1249)—has an extraordinary effect upon the strangers who notice him as he passes by—some cross themselves, others cry out in fright. The imagery which describes the landscape he traverses is dark and threatening, marked by associations with death in the midst of beauty. The wanderer talks to himself in scattered bits of incomprehensible conversation. It is apparent that he has reached a crisis point which seems to be a consequence of a lost love. While no reasons are gven for his pilgrimage to the mountains, it becomes apparent that it is a kind of trial or ordeal to which he has exposed himself in the hope that God will cure his mind or let him die. He takes a daring climb late in the day and arrives only after dark at a mountain hut, his thoughts in a turmoil bordering on madness. The workings of his mind during the journey are reminiscent of another unbalanced mind of a wanderer—the title hero of Georg Büchner's prose fragment "Lenz." Through the eyes of von Boetticher's wanderer the mountain landscape takes on an evocative, mysterious and threatening, mystical beauty.

At the hut the wanderer encounters its caretakers—an aged woman and a young woman who has been banned by her family to the mountain hut because she suffers from ad-

[31] Von Boetticher was himself a victim of mental illness. He was born on 13 August 1887 in Eldingen/Lüneburger Heide. In 1914 he emigrated to the U.S.A. After returning to Europe he was captured by the French and while in captivity (1915) wrote a major drama, *Friedrich der Grosse*, which was published by the S. Fischer Verlag in 1917. The *NR* published poems, an account of his captivity, a novella, and a drama. "Die aussätzige Magd" was von Boetticher's last work. He had been living as a transient in various European cities and finally was confined, after 1925, to a mental institution. In May 1941 von Boetticher's mother received an urn with his ashes and was notified that he had died of a "stroke" in an asylum in Saxony. (de Mendelssohn, *S. Fischer und sein Verlag*, pp. 757–58.)

vanced syphilis. The young woman offers her body to the visitor—before he is aware of her illness—as she has done to every traveler. Her folk superstition has led her to believe that her disease can be gotten rid of by being passed on to another victim. However, when she creeps to his room late at night—as they had agreed—she finds him gone. The wanderer has gone to climb yet further, all the way to the peak. There he experiences his epiphany as he watches a brilliant sunrise over the peaks. The experience brings on a catharsis and his ultimate salvation.

Meanwhile the suffering girl—who had sought salvation through him—is bitterly disappointed and carries murderous thoughts in her heart. The returning stranger begs her forgiveness, tells her to have faith, and kisses her disfigured face. She is shocked to the essence of her being, experiences an epiphany of great spiritual violence, and believes she is cured of her illness. She believes that she has been kissed by Christ. Perhaps she has—the possibility is not excluded. As a consequence, in the ecstasy of a soul on fire, she sets the hut on fire and is consumed in a catharsis of body and soul:

> Die Glut des Hauses hatte längst die letzten Zerstörungszeichen der Krankheit von ihren Körper gefressen, alle Geschwüre und Narben waren von den Flammen weggezehrt und nur die im tiefsten Herzen Gottes gedachte Gestalt des Menschen wuchs in den Farben der mächtigen weissen Lilie eines weiblichen Leibes auf, um immer dunkler in der Gestalt der feuerfarbenen Gebirgslilie zu sterben. (1275)

High above, the wanderer, who has continued his pilgrimage over the mountains, looks back at the distant smoke and flames, his now peaceful spirit undisturbed: ". . . liess er nach kurzem tiefen Besinnen das Feuer als ein Ereignis, dessen er nicht mehr Herr war, vorüberziehen an seinem ruhiggewordenen Geiste." (1275) Both characters had sought redemption and cure—he from spiritual (mental or emotional) anguish, she from physical anguish and disgrace. Both were misfits, outcasts, exceptional individuals raised high above their fellow men for a trial which went far beyond what ordinary people experience. (For example the truck driver who had infected the girl with syphilis went about his everyday routine of work in the village below, accepted by villagers, not ostracized as the girl was.) Both were rewarded by a searing mystical vision and rebirth.

Annette Kolb's "Spitzbögen" (April 1925, I, 351–90) concludes with an epiphany on a considerably more modest scale. Told in the first person, it is the diary-like record of a young girl's thoughts, emotions, and experiences on three separate trips to Italy. Again, Italy plays a prominent role. It provides the girl with a series of disappointments, reveals decay beneath its beauty, robs the protagonist of her romantic illusions. In poetic language the story captures youth's impetuousness, intolerance of age, hunger for experience, frivolity, foolhardy courage, charm, and capacity for fanatical commitment to temporary idols (in her case it is Richard Wagner). It is the chronicle of one version of growing up in pre-war upper class Europe. The teenaged girl learns to leave childhood behind and to cope with life. In the end she moves beyond disillusionment to a new, affirmative outlook on the future.

The epiphany which marks her ultimate affirmative stance is brought on by a dream which—when she reviews it upon awakening—leaves her with a joyous feeling which seems, in part, to be a sense of *unio mystica*. The story closes with the young woman's words of encouragement to herself: "Mut, sagte ich zu mur, Mut, Mut." (390)

Schickele's second story, "Die Gletscherspalte" (July 1925, II, 702–13), is told by the same narrator as "Tulpen." As in "Tulpen," the name Maria Capponi and the narrator's affair with her are mentioned, but this time the tale is a straightforward, realistic one. The narrator Claus and his wife Fanny are vacationing in the Alps. While hiking across a glacier they break through the snow covering and fall into a fifteen-meter deep crevasse. They are not found for two days and during that time alone they experience a new closeness and a renewed passion for each other. For the adoring wife it is the fulfillment of her dream to have her husband once all to herself. They reminisce, discuss their marriage, and discover again how deeply they love one another. Having come to appreciate each other more than ever, they resolve to live together in greater harmony than before. But it is too late. By the time they are rescued Fanny has frozen to death.

There is a symbolic aspect to the events. It is indicated early: ". . . der Schnee sank unter uns, um uns, so fuhren wir in die Tiefe." (702) Like "Tulpen" and "Phantastische Nacht" it represents a process, resembling psychoanalysis, of coming to terms with the inner self and the past. In this process nature plays an important role. Trapped in an eerie frozen world, each partner conjures up the seasons of the year, the weather and landscape, and what these meant to him at different times during their relationship. Again nature, real and in its role as symbol, is catalyst for the salvation of the soul. Although Fanny does not survive, she has fulfilled her innermost desire for union with Claus. Both were truthful. They salvaged the integrity of their relationship. "Die Gletscherspalte" is undoubtedly an affirmative story. What husband and wife experienced in their icy prison was an epiphany.

Chapter II

Stories in the Affirmative Category: The Later Phase 1926–30

In the November 1926 issue where the next story in the affirmative category—Max Brod's "Beschneite Spinnweben. Eine Ehegeschichte" (II, 476–98)—appears, Kayser's "Europäische Rundschau" (556–60) begins with "Die Rückkehr zum Westen," a review of French books and articles on "the East-West problem," i.e., the fascination which the Eastern cultures and religions had exercised over Western intellectuals.[1] Kayser, in agreement with the French writers, notes a trend away from Eastern mysticism and toward "Western rationalism": "Wir erlebten, gerade in Deutschland, während der expressionistischen Jahre ein weites, sehr weites Vordringen zum Osten, über Russland bis Indien hin: die westliche Ratio wurde östlicher Mystik geopfert. Jetzt beginnen wir, uns dem Westen wieder zu nähren und uns den Geboten von Form und Wirklichkeit wieder zu fügen." (556) The fact that Kayser includes himself in the turn toward "form and reality" ought

[1] For example, see the references to Buddhism in the Flake story, above p. 59.

to mean that the caliber of stories published in the *NR* will benefit. These concepts were alien to the view of art which he had presented in his major essay of January 1922 (above, pp. 35–38).

But the conclusion of his review shows that Kayser unfortunately has not abandoned the old dualistic view of human experience, though it sounds considerably moderated since 1922. He recognizes a "Dualismus" between "der erfinderischen und ordnenden Intelligenz" and "der gefühlsmässigen Arten der menschlichen Produktion, was es auch immer sei." (557) The burden of this distinction is maintained by Kayser to the detriment of an integral perspective.

The Brod story in some ways represents a transition in the above-mentioned trend toward "Western rationalism" and the "requirements of form and reality." For a number of reasons the Brod story is an important one. It shows a change of direction on several fronts. The style is formal, though in much of the story it encompasses emotional turmoil. It begins: "Das junge Ehepaar Hopfner hatte den Brauch eingeführt, bei Missverständnissen den schriftlichen Gedankenaustausch an Stelle des mündlichen zu bemühen. In Briefen begrenzt man sich, schon wegen der Schreibarbeit, und hält damit auch den Streitfall in den engsten Grenzen." (476) It is as if the author too is accomplishing by means of style the restraint which writing letters imposes upon the characters. The formal, restrained tone, tempered by gentle irony, is also indicative of the personality of the hero, Stephan Hopfner, a person who continually monitors his intense emotions and tries to keep a tight rein on them of civilized courtesy and restraint.

The title refers to an image at the conclusion which is a metaphor for the wife's personality and approach to life. Stephan and Mathilde (Mirl) have been very happily married for two years. They live in the city of Eger, Czechoslovakia, where Stephan had to take over the family factory upon his father's death. In the opening scene they have reached a crisis when the factory is in financial trouble and Mirl offers to resume her successful stage career in Berlin. Stephan resists her leaving, and resorts even to deception. The occasion becomes a test of their relationship, but is happily resolved when Stephan achieves a new level of understanding.

For the first time in the category of stories which I call affirmative, concern for immediate social problems is expressed. (Up to now if they existed at all in the stories—as, for example, the prostitute in Zweig's "Phantastische Nacht"—they were accepted as givens, representative of inevitable human suffering; Flake merely says a few words here and there about political crisis.) Stephan Hopfner, more philosopher than hard-nosed capitalist, is distressed by the lot of assembly-line workers in his factory; his conscience is troubled by his helplessness to change it. Although his sympathies are socialist, Stephan does not believe that socialism would alleviate the deadening monotony of the work, for the problem is a manifestation not of a particular system, but of modern technology *per se*. We learn of the economic crisis in Europe and consequent drop in exports which has led to the crisis at Stephan's factory, where he does everything he can, even at financial sacrifice, to avoid firing workers.

Stephan is troubled by the materialism of the times: "Das Furchtbare unserer Zeit, . . .—es kann alles in Geld ausgedrückt werden!" (479) and protests against the coldness of a machine-like world. This burden of *Weltschmerz* makes of him a melancholy man whose motto is "Taedium vitae." (483) He tends to dark, "heavy" thoughts: ". . . —schwer, schwer, ich möchte das Wort hundertmal hintereinander hinschreiben—Schwere ist geradezu die Prägung, die unserem ganzen Dasein aufgedrückt ist." (480) The only counterweight for Stephan is Mirl and their love for each other. Her outlook is the opposite of his " 'Die leichten Schneeflocken,' sagte die Frau. 'Sieh' nur, was für leichte Dinge es gibt.' 'Leicht?' seufzte er. 'Du solltest den Schnee auf den Kohlenhalden sehen—oder im Fabrikshof. Wie mit Keulen hingeschmettert, wie niemals mehr wegzuwälzen sieht er da aus.' " (488) By her high spirits, charm and beauty, Mirl provides the essential contrast in Stephan's life—the light, the happiness, his only comfort, his only defense against harsh reality, his only reason for living. Consequently he resists her emancipation with all his might. " 'Geh' nicht weg—bleib' bei mir, Mirl,' schmeichelte er." (481) The narrative voice interjects: "Die Frau sollte und durfte seiner Macht nicht entzogen werden." (491) This admission of the truth of Stephan's position—his dependence and his needs—in relation to the woman is remarkable, unique in fact, and sets Stephan apart from the "male chauvinist" heroes of previous stories. The problematic nature of Stephan's attitude is clearly outlined in his response to his wife's plea to be permitted to help him by resuming her successful acting career: " 'ich will aber keine Kameradin. Keine Nora Nummer zwei. Ich will dich, Mirl. Du bist mein Engel. Das ist mehr als Kameradschaft. Etwas ganz anderes. Dieses Wort von der 'Frau als Kameradin' haben genau dieselben nüchternen Leute erfunden, die 'Zeit ist Geld' sagen—' " (487) There are several levels of irony in the remark about "Nora." Stephan is referring to the Heroine of *A Doll's House* after she has liberated herself. What he really wants is "Nora" prior to her emancipation (who could also be called "Nora Nummer eins").

Stephan is a disappointed romantic. Made distraught by the fear that Mirl might take a job in Berlin, Stephan rushes out into the fresh air and finds there—nothing, not the solace which the Kayser-type hero inevitably sought and found in nature, not that communion, that healing effect of an integral bond between the self and nature:

> Frische Luft! Er lief abends in die Schneefelder hinaus. Aber auch die blieben ihm tot und langweilig. Die Natur tröstet nicht. Nach diesen oder jenen Gesetzen wird der Schnee in einigen Monaten auftaun, zwangsläufig—es ist wie bei den Menschen das Geld, man kann es vorausberechnen, und es ist immer dasselbe Einerlei.

Die Natur schafft nichts Neues. Es ist immer derselbe Lauf. Dabei drang ihm Nässe durch die Schuhsohlen, was seine gute Laune nicht eben erhöhte. (486)

This disenchantment separates Brod's hero even from the "young moderns" about whom W. E. Süskind writes.[2] Although Süskind's heroes are representative types of the twenties, they still resort to nature for comfort. They find in her the means of communion with a higher harmony which resolves conflict and provides a universal perspective.

Stephan's self-defense against Mirl's intentions is to resort to deception and thereby put himself morally in the wrong. He conceals a letter and contract ready for signature which was sent to Mirl by Max Reinhardt, the most famous director in Berlin. By subterfuge, Stephan persuades Mirl to audition before a local director in the hope that she will be offered a job nearer to home which would keep her closer to her husband. Stephan's epiphany—the typical metamorphosis of heroes in the affirmative stories—takes place while, for the first time, he watches Mirl audition and becomes aware of her extraordinary gifts. For the first time Stephan appreciates that art can also be an achievement deserving of respect, an example of the highest accomplishment, and a manifestation of the "Geist" which he has always revered: "Ist etwa auch dies Geist—meinte er zagend—schaffender Segen, wie er ihn bisher nur in Erfindungen, in seinem guten Studium hatte sehen wollen?" (495) This epiphany entails (under the impression of the erotic effect which Mirl creates on stage) the realization that "nature" and "Geist" are not separate entities, mutually exclusive, but are intertwined, integral to one another: "O Geist, nimmermüder, schöpferischer, unerschöpflich in neuer Form und Lust—die dumpfe Natur bliebt dir

[2] See below, beginning p. 77; cf. the comparable scene in "Raymund," below p. 86.

nicht stumm und unveränderlich—sie jauchzt dir entgegen, gar nicht mehr langweilig, und ergibt sich deiner glutvollen Bewegung. Da kehrte ihm mit einemmal die Zuversicht zurück, die ihm so lange fern geblieben war." (495) With this realization there comes to Stephan new insight, renewed confidence, a balanced *Weltanschauung*. He has learned to dispense with the old dualism (which still marked Kayser's thinking at the time this story appeared). Aided by his wife's strength and understanding (she had known all along about the Reinhardt letter and reacted with her own appropriate strategy), Stephan has achieved a mature view of the world and human relations. He is no longer insecure in his relationship to Mirl. He is no longer an inveterate melancholic. He has found a measure of composure and ability to enjoy the moment:

> Es gab für eine Weile diese scharfen Trennungen nicht, die uns beängstigen und schuldig oder unschuldig sprechen. Sondern die Stunde war da, in der man ganz plötzlich erkennt, wie die Dinge aus sich selbst sich neu erschaffen und mischen und wiedererschaffen—die Stunde, in der kein Unglück aufkommt, nicht einmal das des Geldes und der Arbeitshöllen im Hintergrund. Ja, auch dass man nicht weiss, warum jetzt diese Glücksstunde, warum sie da ist und morgen vielleicht nicht und niemals mehr—nicht einmal dieser Gedanke raubt ihr etwas von ihrer Süsssigkeit. (498)

The culmination of this insight is the stroll of the now happy couple in a dark pine forest where they see the image which symbolizes Stephan's new approach to life and which gives the story its title:

> Immerhin stapften sie noch etwas tiefer in den Wald hinein, einer in den Fusstapfen des andern. Dann standen sie still. Es roch, freundlicher noch als in den Gassen, nach Schneenässe, dazu nach Erde, feuchtem Holz, altem Laub. Und verstärkt, wie Reifen um die Stirn, diese Ruhe, glatt und kühl. Da zeigte ihm Mathilde frische Schneeflocken, die scheinbar ganz frei in der Luft hingen. Aber wenn man näher hinsah, merkte man, dass noch vom Sommer her feine Spinnweben genügten, um den Schnee zu tragen. In Spinnweben—Leichtes, vom Leichtesten gehalten—

hatten sich die Flocken verfangen und schaukelten leise, wenn man anstiess. (498)

With this closing paragraph the story returns to Kayser's way of thinking in the sense of finding romantic nature where solace and inspiration wait to serve the purposes of human beings who are in emotional need. A cool, peaceful, soothing atmosphere is created which is startlingly reminiscent of the closing paragraphs of W. E. Süskind's "Raymund" (below, pp. 91–92)—in particular the images of trees, earth, dampness, coolness on the forehead, and walking in each other's footsteps—and alike in the message that recovery and rejuvenation are to be found in submission to the healing embrace of nature. It is a *Leitmotiv* throughout most of the affirmative category.

In this same issue of *NR* there is an essay on Joseph Conrad (536–48) by Süskind, who is author of three stories in the *NR* during our time period.[3] The essay is likely intended to

---

[3] They are: "Raymund" (April 1927, I, 369–88), and "Beginn einer Liebe" (March 1930, I, 370–89) in the affirmative category, and "Das Leben zu dritt" (March 1931, I, 366–90) in the non-judgmental category. The three stories, in particular "Raymund," play an important role in this study. In his essay "Jugend als Lebensform," which appeared in the June 1929 (I, 816–28) *NR*, and in his stories Süskind concerns himself with the generation born around 1900 to 1905. Süskind himself was born in 1901. Lennartz says of Süskind's early stories: "In seinen ersten Prosawerken spiegelte er die Gefühlswelt junger, sensibler Menschen der Zeit, . . ." (Franz Lennartz, *Deutsche Dichter und Schriftsteller unserer Zeit*, 10th ed. [Stuttgart: Alfred Kröner, 1969], p. 680.) "Raymund" appeared in a collection of five short stories entitled *Tordis* (1927). Süskind wrote the novels *Jugend* (1930) and *Mary und ihr Knecht* (1932). Süskind, like other representatives of his generation such as Kurt Heuser, Hans Meisel, and Herbert Schlüter (of the authors represented in this study), ceased early to write fiction. Political developments put an end to their story-writing careers (Schlüter alone published fiction again after World War II). De Mendelssohn says of that generation of Fischer authors: "Hier musste eine Generation verwelken, noch ehe sie hatte recht aufblühen können." (Peter de Mendelssohn, *S. Fischer und sein Verlag* [Frankfurt am Main: S. Fischer, 1970], p. 1102.) Süskind, however, pursued a successful career in journalism. From 1933 to 1942 he was editor of the journal *Die Literatur*. Over the course of many years he did a series of translations from works, for *(continued on page 76)*

whet the appetite of *NR* readers for the Conrad story and letters which appear in February and June 1927 issues (and for the collected works in translation published by S. Fischer). It also serves, incidentally, as introduction to Süskind's own style and themes. At some points he could be commenting as much on his own works as on Conrad's. The remarks most relevant to our focus concern Conrad's heroes and his women characters. The heroes are modern—flawed in character and introspective:

> Sie sind samt und sonders keine "ganzen Kerle," sondern problematische Helden—allesamt leben sie unter der Gefahr, in ihrem Wesen eine wurmstichige Stelle zu haben, "the soft spot," wie Conrad das mit einem knappen Wort nennt. Sie haben, so sehr sie Träger einer abenteuerlichen Geschichte sind, die Eigenschaft, die dem tüchtigen Abenteuerhelden vor allem fehlt: sie besinnen sich über ihren Charakter. (544)

These are qualities also of Süskind's (anti-) heroes who can be introspective to the point of inaction. At least two of them can be described with the terms "Unsicherheit und Heimatlosigkeit" (544) which Süskind applies to the Conrad characters.

Süskind's view of Conrad's women characters as elusive, mysterious, intuitive creatures who have a secret wellspring in the forces of nature could well be a description of Süskind's treatment of women characters:

(continued from page 75) example, by Herman Melville, D. H. Lawrence, and E. M. Forster. After World War II he turned to political reporting, first covering the Nuremberg Trials. Beginning in 1949 he served as editor-in-chief of the *Süddeutsche Zeitung* in Munich. He published several works on the German language, including the wellknown *Aus dem Wörterbuch des Unmenschen* (1957, in collaboration with Dolf Sternberger and Gerhard Storz). Süskind died in 1970. Thomas Koebner, who wrote the piece on Süskind in Herman Kunisch, ed., *Handbuch der deutschen Gegenwartsliteratur*, 2nd ed. [Munich: Nymphenburg, 1970] assesses Süskind's point of view as conservative, ". . . , soweit die Tradition sich als wertvoller erwies; . . ." (p. 237), a point of view which is already apparent in the three *NR* stories dealt with in this study.

> . . . die Chance, das Leben, die Naturkraft: . . . der wortlose Einfluss einer Frau, von dem es in dem Buche heisst, dass der "eine verborgene, geheimnisvolle Tatkraft in sich schliesst, der nicht ganz zu trauen ist, wie anderen Naturkräften auch." (546)

Süskind's comments on the importance of Conrad's women characters apply to his own women characters as well: "Denn auch Frauen stehen gross unter seinen Gestalten, gering an der Zahl freilich und ins Feierliche sehr erhöht, als gierigste Hexen und Gegnerinnen (wie Almayers Frauen [in the novel *Almayer's Folly*]) oder als Kameraden von verschleierter Heldischkeit." (548) In Süskind's three stories we shall see examples of these character types and of the same sober style.

Five months after his essay, Süskind's "Raymund" (I, 369–88) appeared in the April 1927 issue. Along with his second story, "Beginn einer Liebe" (March 1930, I), it belongs to the affirmative group. Süskind's third contribution—"Das Leben zu dritt" (March 1931, I) belongs to the non-judgmental category. "Raymund" is a key story for several reasons. Although the resolution is decidely affirmative, it marks a significant departure in style from the previous stories in this category. In the context of the *NR* it seems to fulfill Kayser's new sense of "accommodation to the requirements of form and reality." (Above, p. 69.) In the larger literary context it might be considered an initial example in the *NR* of that amorphous classification "Neue Sachlichkeit."[4]

In "Raymund" Süskind has captured the plight of a

[4] This term will not be discussed here as its definition is not relevant to the concerns of this study. The problematic nature of the concept is discussed by Jost Hermand, "Unity Within Diversity? The History of the Concept 'Neue Sachlichkeit'," trans. Peter and Margaret Lincoln, in *Culture and Society in the Weimar Republic*, ed. by Keith Bullivant (Manchester: Manchester Univ. Press, 1977), pp. 166–81; and by Jost Hermand and Frank Trommler, *Die Kultur der Weimarer Republik* (Munich: Nymphenburg, 1978), esp. pp. 118–19 and 132–33.

generation of young men, born around 1900 or shortly thereafter, and cast adrift in the chaotic early 1920's. "Raymund" has also been placed into this broader context by being directly preceded in the April 1927 issue by the first installment of an essay by François Mauriac, "Der junge Mensch," (350–69) which examines what it is like to be a young man, and in particular seeks to explain the contemporary generation of young men.

Süskind's style is a means of access to understanding the "hero" Raymund and his version of the external world. A modified style—though events in the story might remain the same—would have produced a different "hero" and a different picture of the times. This interdependence is revealed in a close examination of the introductory paragraphs:

> Als Raymund vierzehn Jahre alt wurde, *begann* eine *unordentliche* Zeit *für ihn*. Seine Mutter wurde sehr krank, sie lag zu Bett, aber das war nicht genug, und *man* brachte sie fort, weit weg, in ein Sanatorium. Es *könne* sehr lange dauern, sagte *man* zu Raymund, und ab und zu *las man ihm* aus Briefen *vor*, es *ginge* ihr besser oder schlechter und *man habe* wieder operieren müssen, damit sie gesund werden *könne*. Er *hörte* das aber nur, empfand *keinen Schmerz* und fühlte *Tag für Tag an sich herankommen*, auch ohne seine Mutter, stärker sogar und mit mehr *Freiheit*.
>
> *Es hatten sich* nämlich *verschiedene* weibliche Verwandte bereit gefunden, das Haus so lange zu verwalten. Tanten von *irgendwoher*, ältere und jüngere, *vielleicht* auch Freundinnen seiner Mutter oder jüngere Schwestern aus befreundeten Familien. *Keine von ihnen* blieb sehr lange. Geschäfte zu Hause riefen sie bald wieder ab, und so wurde dies eine *undeutliche* und *raschlebige Zeit* für Raymund, eine Tantenzeit immerhin, denn immer war ein weibliches Wesen im Hause, sehr bedacht, einen neuen Takt anzugeben. Raymund aber ward darüber fast übersehen. Er ass und trank und bekam Unterschriften unter seine Zeugnisse, sonst aber schlüpfte er wenig beachtet untendurch und genoss viel *Freiheit*, lange Stunden in fremden Häusern, auf der Strasse und in den Wäldern ringsum. Meistens *schien* Sommer *zu sein*: alle Erlebnisse *spielten sich* im Garten *ab* und in den Nachbargärten, und Obstbaüme und Plünderung fremder Blumenbeete, das war wichtig in dieser Zeit.
>
> Damals war Krieg, aber das war nur *nebenbei*, *Schatten* und Wichtigkeit im *Hintergrunde*, . . .

Sonst nämlich war das eine *unordentliche Zeit*, eine *zweifelhafte* und *zuchtlose Kriegszeit* oder eine *Tantenzeit* vielmehr: *man wurde ausgelassen in ihr*, vorlaut und neugierig. Vieles war weggeblasen, ganze Jahre und Schulklassen: wenn *man* achtzehn war, würde *man* Soldat werden, mit neunzehn Offizier. Viel mehr Frauen waren mit einmal da, und dann gleich ältere Männer. Die sahen einen an, als müssten sie schon die Vierzehnjährigen ernst nehmen, und wenn sie überlegen taten, kam's ihnen nicht von Herzen; wurde man frech, so schnurrten sie ängstlich ein. (369–70) (Italics mine.)

The style is sober, economical. The tone is distant, unemotional. Raymund's state is indicated in the opening sentence with the predicate "begann" . . . "für ihn." He is the receiver of action rather than an actor. The outside world happens to him. A theme of the story is established with the words "eine unordentliche Zeit." "Zeit" and "unordentlich" (or similar epithets) will be frequently repeated, and in various combinations. Raymund, in other words, is the passive object, the victim, of the disordered times.

The people or the forces which manage the outside world are anonymous—referred to as "man"—and beyond Raymund's control. That world presents itself to him in the non-committal subjunctive and is accepted by Raymund without pain. Raymund receives the world by means of the most passive sense—hearing. He does not approach each day of his life, but rather is approached by the days, and takes pleasure in the lack of something, namely restriction, though he refers to this pleasure by its positive name, "freedom." The various female relatives who take charge of the household during the absence of parents—Raymund's father is at the front—remain faceless and interchangeable with one exception mentioned below. Impressions are indeterminate rather than definitive, possibilities rather than absolutes—"Meistens *schien* Sommer zu sein . . ." Even the First World War itself remains shadowy background for the boy. The only certainty is that Raymund is on his own in disorderly and equivocal times.

There is no causal connection—at least in the mind of the "hero"—between occurrences. Things merely happen, one after another, without reason, analysis, or attempts at explanation on his part. This posture of acceptance of the inscrutable succession of events is also reflected in the sentence structure, for example: "Eine kam an die Reihe, jünger als alle vorher, keine Tante eigentlich, wiewohl auch kein Mädchen mehr, eine ganz entfernte Verwandte, nur aus Briefen halb bekannt." (371) The succession of clauses imitates the way Raymund might think or record events—a series of modifiers, apparently without particular design, without main or subordinate clauses in their expected order, giving the impression of an arbitrary list of qualities as they might have occurred to Raymund. Later, when the war is over and parents have returned, Raymund lies in bed one night thinking in his usual manner: "Ungeordnet fiel ihm ein: . . ." (374) There is neither order, nor security, nor anything to hold on to in the world into which Raymund is cast.

These paragraphs mark the two levels maintained throughout the story: the individual and the general. As described above, the language projects certain qualities of the "hero" and his relation to the environment. Read for a more general impression, it projects the characteristics of a dream, can in fact be described in terms used to describe "the dream state of humans": ". . . where we encounter . . . very little rational analysis; . . . and, most of all, a very feeble sense of individuality or self, which gives way to a pervading fatalism, a sense of unpredictable buffeting by uncontrollable events."[5] Perhaps this resemblance to a dream state is also a quality of the times, product of the predicament of the individual in a

---

[5] Carl Sagen, *The Dragons of Eden* (New York: Random House, 1977), p. 160.

world which is too unstable to provide him with a firm footing for life. Raymund *and* his times are the subjects. The last quoted paragraph above uses modifiers which describe not only the times but also Raymund's very personal experience. The next episode, for example, is his seduction by the unsavory youngest of the "aunts" who takes charge briefly of the household. Raymund's generation ("man") is "released"—"impudent" and "curious"—into the "zweifelhafte und zuchtlose" war time just as Raymund is released into the "zweifelhafte und zuchtlose" "aunt time."

Raymund's reaction to the seduction episode initiates a pattern which will repeat itself in his later relationships with women: "Er hatte aber mit ihrem ersten Worte plötzlich wieder dies Gefühl von früher: So gehört es sich, so ist es recht, so muss es wohl sein, . . ." (373) They answer his need to break out of the chaos and into an order, a dependability in human relationships. In women he will seek to overcome his uninvolvement, his outsider position, and look for the warmth and security, the "du" relationship which he lacks. The women in the Süskind stories are stronger than his "heroes." They are of an emotionally emancipated type which one might expect to encounter as typical products of the 1920's. They are more self-sufficient and self-assured, less vulnerable, more calculating, more in control than are the men.

Raymund had no father during the war years—an experience which he shares with his generation (cf. Mauriac, 355). His father would appear in officer's uniform for a few days once or twice a year and disappear again without appreciable effect on the son. Raymund was on his own, without guidance, without authority, without particular ties to home. After the war it is too late to reestablish a meaningful family life. The place of meaning is taken by empty routine, and of the traditional phrases and ceremonies only the shell was left:

> Man lief die Strasse zu Ende, wie in einen Graben fiel man in eine Prüfung und ging unberührt daraus hervor; nun sei man ein freier

> Mann, sagten die Lehrer und tranken viel beim Schlussbankett. Anzufangen wusste man nichts mit dieser Freiheit, doch begann man ein Studium, unter welchen Gesichtspunkten, das wusste der liebe Gott. Weiter sass man den Eltern im Haus; die stritten viel in diesen Tagen. Der alte Haushalt aber spülte sie wieder träge zusammen, ehe viel Zeit verging. (373)

Though Raymund thinks he ought to leave home he remains: "Doch war er sonderbar festgehalten, nicht nur, weil die Zeiten arm waren, sondern eben dieses Hauses wegen, in dem er zwei Jahrzehnte gehockt hatte, gegessen, geschlafen und nicht viel sonst." Where else ought he to go in impoverished times to seek the attachment and security which eludes him? He seeks them in familiar objects (house and furniture) but also in his own past time, i.e., in that portion of his years which is invested—merely because it passed there—in particular surroundings. Later he experiences the same reluctance to break with the surroundings of his office, though the corporation which employs him is near collapse.

Raymund belongs to an emotionally scarred generation. It is the generation which is entering the working world during the economic chaos of the early 1920's. The fast-moving world is dominated by the young, riding high on risk and sudden profits: "Nun war überall Verdienst, er [personification of "Verdienst"] lief einem über den Weg, er spottete der Schulen und der reifen Jahre." (374) Raymund enters this world by means of a chance encounter in the street. He runs into an old school chum who has turned into the epitome of a wheeler and dealer, a stylish, prosperous young man on the make and apparently rising rapidly in business. Raymund is swept along but nevertheless remains an outsider. He observes with sensitivity, but without probing or judging or deriving conclusions. He notices, for example, as his newfound associate put his foot on the running board of his automobile and ". . . winkte zerstreut dem Chauffeur, der viel älter war, schnauzbärtig, Familienvater, aber einverstanden mit allem und zufrieden, wie es *schien*." (374) (Italics mine.) One could hardly make a more telling observation about relations between the generations and who is in charge.

By means of irony Raymund's distance from this new world is established. For example, Raymund takes note of his friend: ". . . ja, er trug wahrhaftig hellgraue Gamaschen." ". . . der Freund tat in aller Eile vertraut mit der Bardame. 'Eine kleine Rekreation,' sagte er heiter und sprach das Wort englisch aus-'ja, so ein Likörchen,' sagte er." (374) Small touches such as "wahrhaftig," "in aller Eile," and the use (and English pronunciation) of a fashionable word reveal that the friend himself is a cliché of the times—modish, superficial, hectic, and not quite convincing. Raymund, as usual, seems to have no will and to exercise no control over his life. Rather he is carried by chance circumstance along pre-existing pathways: "Das sei ein glückliches Zusammentreffen, liess sich Raymund mitteilen und nickte, . . . Also war Raymund angestellt, er wusste kaum wie, in der Propagandaabteilung . . ." (375) He experiences the pace of the business day in his office building as if it were an express train. It begins slowly with a self-generating rhythm and reaches its peak speed evenings. The modern office building seems to be invested with a life of its own, disconnected from life outside—" . . . —man sah ja fast nie durchs Fenster." (375)

Though he tries to become involved, Raymund remains a stranger in the sleek environment. As a consequence he turns to the objects which surround him to fill his need for comfort and security. "Es war besser, zurückzukehren in jene Schnellzugstimmung des Hauses, der breiten Fenster, der wichtigtuerischen Klubsessel. Das alles *schien* unerschütterlich; wer da inmitten sass, war geborgen und aufgehoben. Allein schon die Briefbogen, ...—all das war höchst beruhigend." (376) (Italics mine) But his security depends upon appearances ("schien") and is actually as fragile as the overnight success of the corporation which employs him. A historian writing over half a century later describes the economic circumstances of the collapse of Raymund's employer and his ilk:

> In Deutschland folgte auf die Stabilisierung der Mark noch eine Stabilisierungskrise bis Ende 1925. Das harte, aber teuer gewordene Geld führte zur Illiquidität in der Landwirtschaft, zu einer Reihe neuer Zusammenbrüche grösserer oder kleinerer Unternehmungen und zur Schrumpfung oder Gefährdung von Konzernen, die sich in den Kriegs-, Nachkriegs- und Inflationsjahre über alle Massen gebläht hatten.[6]

The luxury, the pretense, the self-important hustle and bustle in the offices rested on a foundation of sand.

The prosperity of the corporation had been based upon the inflation economy. What the galloping inflation meant is not revealed in the story by statistics—for example, that in mid-November 1923 ". . . the official value of one dollar was no less than 4,200,000,000,000 M"[7] but by what it meant to the young, bewildered Raymund who shares the helplessness of the individual in the face of the mysterious, uncontrollable workings of the economy: "Das Geld übrigens war ein rechtes Märchending geworden. Wer dahinter stand, blieb zweifelhaft: denn diese Scheine, bunt, leichtsinnig-neu, gar nicht erst schmutziggebraucht—sie sahen aus, als kämen sie frisch aus Zauberers Hand." (376) The inflation had "made a few clever manipulators very rich overnight, . . . But for every one who made a profit there were hundreds who were ruined; . . ."[8] The corporation belonged to the former group. In its heyday a succession of visitors would appear whose motley composition tells a story about the social contradictions of the 1920's, and the air of ruthlessness, the taint of corruption in this "get-rich-quick" atmosphere: "Vertreter waren da, dicke Geschäftsfreunde mit Zigarren und neuen Witzen, stellensuchende alte Herren mit verzweifelten Gesichtern, Steno-

---

[6] Gerhard Schulz, *Deutschland seit dem Ersten Weltkrieg 1918–1945* (Göttingen: Vandenhoeck & Ruprecht, 1976), pp. 79–80.

[7] Walter Laqueur, *Weimar: A Cultural History 1918–1933* (New York: G. P. Putnam's Sons, 1974), p. 21.

[8] *Ibid.*

typistinnen mit frechen Beinen, undurchsichtige Herren von gemeinnützigen Vereinen, Beamte, die Ausfuhrerlaubnisse zu vergeben hatten." (376)[9] All were treated with arrogance by supercilious youth riding high on the coattails of false prosperity:

> Die wenigsten fanden Gnade vor den Augen des Freundes; er stand hinter seinem Schreibtisch wie ein Offizier und sah häufig auf die Armbanduhr. "Wie jung er ist," dachte Raymund, indes jener ein paar ältere Herren salopp hinausgeleitete. "Ach, das sind Oberregierungsräte," erklärte der Freund flüchtig, "sie wissen nicht recht, ob sie Geld nehmen sollen." (376–77)

The old titles count for nothing; traditional standards of virtue are out of place; corruption is ubiquitous; and a new breed is in control, represented by the director of the corporation. He is young, slender, distant, inscrutable, and unhappy despite his riches. Underneath the glitter is decay—an impoverished emotional life, an unhappy marriage, and a business with a doubtful financial base. These contradictions are characteristic of the world in which Raymund finds himself. He is invited to the director's villa for a summer party: "Man erzählte Wunderdinge von dem Luxus und der Verworfenheit, die man sich versprechen dürfe; übrigens sei die geschäftliche Position der Firma nicht sehr glänzend." (379) The ironic juxtaposition of two such disparate situations underscores the contradiction.

Raymund arrives late at the party, remains characteristically sober, and therefore finds the elegant decadence more distasteful than attractive. In the semi-darkness he glimpses bodies draped over each other in confusion on the floor. His

---

[9] Laqueur, *ibid.*, p. 22, describes these types: "The government was also blamed for its inactivity vis-à-vis the manipulators and the black-marketeers who suddenly dominated the social scene and whose speculations aroused tremendous resentment. Fat, ostentatious, vulgar, smoking enormous cigars, driving around in a luxurious car, he was depicted in a thousand cartoons."

reaction is to feel like escaping to pristine nature: "Er verspürte Lust, umzukehren, da die Nacht draussen kühl und rein gewesen war. Und über solchen Unflat spannt sie sich nun, dachte er, die Menschen sind doch Schweine." (380) But the sight of lesbian lovers, shocking at first, has the effect of transforming Raymund's attitude into tolerance and he enters the party, sober but accepting the human predicament he finds there.

While the privileged classes are trying to drug themselves with sex and drink at dissolute parties, the inflation continues to rage:

> Aber auch in den Gärten und Tanzhäusern vor der Stadt war man nicht sicher: unversehens kam vielleicht der neue Devisenkurs durchs Telephon und stahl einem das Geld aud der Tasche. Doch halfen die ausländischen Noten, die man bei sich trug und weitergab, wie verbotenes Gift. Dann entrann man der Aufregung und ergab sich den alten Wäldern und der unberührten Kühle der Nacht. (379)

Nature is always there for Süskind's characters as a counterpoint to the anarchy of the times and as solace for the speed and unpredictability of events.

The currency reform of 1923 and resulting collapse of the corporation are signaled in the story by the sudden departure *en masse* from Germany of the once prosperous foreigners, whose more stable currencies had bought them so much in the inflated German economy. By means of an ironic perspective the author exposes the implications of these events:

> Plötzlich nämlich hatte man ein Geld, das fest stand wie Eisen, und die Scheine der Ausländer blieben klein und wirkungslos in ihren Händen und wollten sich nicht verwandeln. Wie Zauberer standen sie da, denen die Gabe über Nacht entronnen ist. Ihre Eleganz sah fadenscheinig aus bei genauerem Zusehen, sie waren wohl gar nichts Besonderes bei sich zu Hause. Hierzulande aber herrschte bekanntlich Ordnung, und es war wieder ein Staat da, der für gut befunden hatte, dem Jahrmarkt ein Ende zu machen. Arme Ausländer hatten da nichts zu suchen. (383)

This paragraph is an example of the use of irony as social

criticism. At first glance, it appears to be primarily a critique of the foreigners who had so long reaped the benefits of the inflated mark and now were receiving their just due. However, more is hinted at in the first clause, namely a biting critique of Germany and the Germans. There is an ironic contradiction between the stereotyped and exaggerated metaphor of the currency as stable as iron and the suddenness ("plötzlich"), almost backhandedness ("nämlich hatte man") by which this iron-like stability seems to have come about. At the latest when we read about the "well-known order" which reigns in Germany (as opposed to the total disorder which had prevailed up to this moment), we realize that the scrutiny to which the departing foreigners were subjected is meant to be a criticism of fickle German attitudes towards them. They were lionized as long as their currency was valuable. Suddenly, with the stabilization of the mark, their weak points—threadbare elegance and probable lack of status at home—were noticed for the first time. The last two sentences use the stereotyped phrasing which reveals attitudes frozen in self-righteousness and chauvinism. The ironic contrast between this style and the rest of the story sheds a critical light on attitudes and behavior in German society.

Raymund's next relationship—he is twenty—is with his eighteen-year-old secretary, Fräulein Marion. It begins when Raymund, in the midst of dictating a letter to her, suddenly notices her hair and breaches the formal distance between them by asking her age. The beginning of their relationship is typical for the events in Raymund's life—in its unintentional, almost accidental nature (at least as he experiences it). Fräulein Marion presumes that Raymund's question implies a criticism: " 'Sie meinen, weil ich es gar nicht nötig hätte, hier zu sein? Das ist ganz richtig, ich könnte zu Hause auch leben,' sagte sie trotzig. 'Aber hier geht es schneller, sehen Sie, und man kann auch mit dabei sein.' " (377) "Dabei sein"—to be where the action is—is everything for Fräulein Marion. She is a child of the times—shallow, fast-moving, seeking excitement, available for sex without emotional involvement. Raymund is different. Drawn by a sensual quality of her hair, he caresses it. "Er merkte nicht, dass ihr Kopf seiner Bewegung nachgab, bis er mit einem letzten Ruck hintübersank und die Stirn sich ihm weiss entgegendrängte. Ihn erschreckte etwas diese Bewegung, die er nicht gewollt und doch halb verschuldet hatte; ein schuldbewusstes Gefühl kam leise und verlockend über ihn . . ." (378) *Any* feeling is tempting to Raymund, even guilt, because at least it is an emotion and indicates involvement with another human being. What kind of "guilt" could he feel as a result of such an insignificant reaction as a tilt of the head? It is guilt in the context of this world, for having related on other than a superficial level, for having shown tenderness, having bridged the accepted cool distance, brought emotions into a relationship and (apparently) aroused them. But with a knock on the door, Fräulein Marion, to Raymund's astonishment, recovers immediately (from their kiss) and resumes without transition her typing posture and businesslike attitude.

Raymund, however, seeks involvement with her. In him there still exists an interior life, deprived as it may be, which wants to be nourished, to communicate itself to others. Raymund retains the romantic sense of nature as a set of phenomena which involve and convey meaning for human beings. Fräulein Marion, a character meant to be more typical of the times, is exclusively involved in externals and the palpable present:

> Nun war Raymund viel mit Fräulein Marion zusammen an den Abenden. Wenn er dann mit ihr durch den Wald ging oder auf einer Anhöhe über dem Fluss, die Tanzmusik der Lokale noch im Ohr, fühlte er plötzlich die Wärme ihrer Hand auf seiner Schulter wie eine Mahnung, und er empfand ein Begehren nach ihr, weit über ihren Körper hinaus, ein sonderbares Gelüsten, sie auszufragen, unsäglich auszuhorchen, des langen und breiten, ins Höchste und ins Unanständigste hinein. Sternschuppen fielen durch den Himmel, ihm kam der alte Aberglaube in den Sinn und er fragte: "Hast du dir auch etwas gewünscht?" und erwartete sich

> mehr als Lachen und Nicken. Er hätte gern mehr von ihr gehört, wie das gewesen sei mit dem Krieg und den Eltern und den gefallenen Brüdern. Aber sie sprach von heute und morgen, sah ihn oft erstaunt an und ging lieber zurück zum Tanz. Da war sie einhellig mit ihm wie tagsüber im Geschäft, und sie schien nichts anderes zu wollen. (379)

Inevitably, when the corporation collapses suddenly and unceremoniously, their relationship does the same, as does the high position of the young friend who got Raymund his job: "Er stand hilflos wie ein Schuljunge und an einem Ersten ging er glanzlos ab." (384)—a departure so insignificant that it makes no difference on which first of the month it occurs. One morning Fräulein Marion simply does not appear. Raymund, uncomprehending, holds in his hand her letter of resignation "der ganz anhänglich klang, seltsam verwöhnt aber und verloren: nun habe sie das ja mitgemacht, aber für die nächste Zeit müsse sie anderswo Posten fassen, Entwicklung sei ihr erstes Ziel." (384) It is a portrait in a nutshell of (middle to upper class urban) youth in the 1920's—spoiled, lost, yet not without vestigial feelings of attachment. In connection with the incipient dissolution of his place of work, Raymund felt ". . . Anhänglichkeit, . . ." ". . . eine blinde, richtungslose Anhänglichkeit, . . ." (384) Fräulein Marion's goal, devoid of content and values, is mere process. In that fundamental respect also she is a representative figure.

Of course it turns out that she felt no deeper ties to Raymund. Their lack of emotional contact—despite physical intimacy—is indicated by the fact that in the narrative she is never called anything other than "Fräulein Marion." Her decisions are based upon cool calculation of self-interest. She is literally leaving for greener pastures—marriage to a Thuringian landowner, ". . . aber man durfte sie ja nicht abhalten, da sie klug und umsichtig handelte. Wahrscheinlich blühte das Agrarwesen in Thüringen." (385) Although he feels indifferent toward her and would never think of trying to follow her to Thuringia, Raymund tries almost desperately to hold on to Fräulein Marion: ". . . er wusste nicht wie und wem zuliebe. Ganz und gar nicht war es ihm zu tun um ihren Körper, den er kannte von Aufgang bis Untergang. Er wünschte aber brennend, nach ihr zu greifen in diesem allgemeinen Zerbröseln des Festen, da sie das einzige war, zu dem er 'du' sagen konnte, . . ."(384) She was "*das* einzige" for Raymund—not so much woman as another creature, an outlet for his emotions, a means of connecting to life.

After losing everything into which he had invested his needs, Raymund is totally bewildered: ". . . verirrt kam er sich vor, wie ein Kind in einem schwierigen Museum, . . ." (386) He returns home for lack of any other goal, falls into bed and into a sleep which lasts an entire day and is as deep and intense as the sleep of children or animals. This sleep is a retreat from the world, a form of regression to a more primitive state: "Er verlangte brennend zurückzukehren und dass alles (er wusste nicht recht, was eigentlich), dass alles nicht wahr sei." (386) It is a healing sleep which permits Raymund to recover from deep trauma. "Alle Glieder fühlten sich zerbrochen an, in einer wollüstigen Weise zerschlagen." (386) It is the deep sleep (or serious illness) which is a convention of many *Bildungsromane*. After the hero's usually tortuous development to maturity, in order that he may recuperate emotionally from his trials, he must be briefly incapacitated in a sort of hibernation to shield him from the stresses of the world. He issues forth from this state—is born again, so to speak—in a condition of receptivity for his "epiphany"—the moment when he will have achieved a universal insight, having found himself and understood his place in the community of humanity.

First, after awakening, Raymund makes one last small attempt to rescue himself by means of a woman. He visits the estranged wife of his former boss, an older woman who has attracted him. He is driven by his fear of being alone and his need to bridge the emotional distance to another human being. "Abermals überfiel ihn die Bangigkeit des Alleinseins, zugleich ein blinder Drang zu helfen und beistehend zuzugreifen." (387) It had been a woman—the distant relative who had seduced Raymund—who had first broken through the emotional vacuum which surrounded him. Since then he has continued to seek this "du" relationship with a woman. His thoughts at this moment help to explain why: "Was sind das eigentlich für Tiere, dachte er zuchtlos, die Frauen? Wie ist das denn, besann er sich, wenn eine Frau sich freut, ist das nicht ganz anders—wenn eine Frau wartet—wenn eine Frau etwas haben möchte—weiss man denn davon etwas?" (387) Women are to him mysterious creatures—"Tiere"—who probably exist in a more intimate relationship with nature, an intimacy toward which Raymund is also drawn. He asks this woman whether he might visit her often. Again he is rebuffed. Since she is on the verge of leaving town, he will never be able to see her again.

The door slams closed and Raymund stands alone on the street. With a switch to a lyrical mood, his epiphany is described:

> Irgendwo auf seinem Heimweg fand Raymund sich wieder. Er fand sich in einer öffentlichen Anlage, etwas vom Wege abgekommen, gegen einen Baum gelaufen. Seine Hand befühlte die feuchte, quellige Rinde, die ein wenig klebte und leckte—er hatte vielleicht lange schon darüber hingestrichen. Ein flaches Stück Wiese lag weit und dunstig vor ihm, dahinter waren unregelmässige Lichter im Kreise gelagert, starräugig, aber warm doch immerhin, beinahe tierisch.
>
> Der Anblick beruhigte ihn und auch die Feuchtigkeit der Luft, kalt bewegt um Stirn, Augen und Mund. Plötzlich horchte er auf: Hinter dem Lichterkranz hervor drang ein gleichmässiges, ruhiges Geräusch. Das war die Stadt; sie summte. Schlaf oder Arbeit oder Vergnügen oder Licht—nun, die nächtliche Stadt summte. Es war ein glückliches Geräusch, einladend und beruhigend: alles ging weiter, nichts war zu besorgen, es wurde gut gewacht—ach so, morgen würde es früh schon Brot geben.
>
> Merkwürdig erleichtert und doch erfüllt, wandte Raymund sich zum Gehen. Er fand zurück zu seinem verlorenen Fussweg, dem Weg, wo viele gingen, tagsüber. Jetzt war er allein, aber er

spürte mit Rührung die von vielen Füssen weiche, zerstampfte Erde. (388)

Via a brief loss of selfhood (amnesia) in communion with nature, Raymund has penetrated the barrier of alienation which surrounded him and has broken through to life. His hand which caresses (the verb "befühlen" has a considerably stronger and more sensual meaning than mere "fühlen") the bark of a tree experiences physical contact with life in its original form—moist, swelling, sticky—like the organic "soup" in which life on earth first arose. Finding life at last, he has also literally "found himself" (repeated twice in the first two sentences) in an unconscious, intuitive process. Now everything seems to Raymund to be alive; the city lights are "warm, almost animal-like." In this "public" park, after having "strayed somewhat from the path," he has found peace. Moisture and cold touch his forehead (thought), eyes, and mouth (as in Brod's "Beschneite Spinnweben," above pp. 74–75) stimulating these organs to new life. And his old dominant sense of hearing receives a new impetus—this time a happy message, inviting and soothing—that the world is predictable. It will go on dependably on its own, providing the essentials—sleep or work or pleasure or light, and bread in the early morning.[10]

Raymund's new-found certainty (no more qualifiers such as "es schien"), his sense of confidence in the order of things, had been presaged in a dream which he had as a teenager:

Hierauf, plötzlich und als langgedehntes Bild, schon halb im Schlaf, als Treppe ohne Ende, sah er kommende Tage, einen nach dem andern, eine unendliche Reihe. Es war der einzige Weg, der

---

[10] The view of the city, by contrast with Stefan Zweig's "Phantastische Nacht" (see above, p. 33) and the attitudes it represents, is positive and supportive of "life."

ihm gelassen war, merkte er träumend; er fühlte sich tief beruhigt, tat den ersten Schritt, stieg dann und stieg. (374)

In the past only in a dream, but now in reality, a sense of continuity has led to a resolution of tensions between the individual and the community. This resolution is the prerequisite which allows Raymund to return to *his* lost way and to join, not a particular individual (woman), but the "many feet" which trod the path before him. He was not destroyed by disappointments, but has found a new level of existence in contact with organic nature ("the soft earth") and in a sense of community with the mass of humanity.[11]

There is an acute contradiction between this resolution and the conflict which preceded it. Raymund found himself in a very modern existential predicament. A lonely outsider—in a sense a lost soul—he suffered from alienation and a feeling of powerlessness. Yet in a resolution which harks back to the mentality represented in the earlier works by Kayser and Zweig, the conflict is extinguished in a rhapsodic union with the forces of "life." The resolution is foreign to the rest of the story and gives the impression of having been imposed in order to force a solution upon an insoluble problem. The conclusion, in other words, skirts the problems which were presented. The switch in mood and tone signifies a kind of escapism. An implausible happy end provides a private solution to the hero's difficulties. These difficulties had been presented, however, as representative of an era and a generation.

---

[11] The resolution of "Raymund" illustrates the "invidious contrast" to which Peter Gay, in *Weimar Culture: The Outsider as Insider* (New York: Harper & Row, 1968), p. 80, refers: ". . . Ferdinand Tönnies' classic in sociology, *Gemeinschaft und Gesellschaft*, first published as far back as 1887, made its fortune in the Weimar Republic, with its invidious contrast between the authentic, organic harmony of community and the materialistic fragmentation of business society."

The resolution brings "Raymund"—despite its stylistic departure—into line with the previous affirmative stories and with Kayser's predilections of the early twenties. While the style is modern, the ultimate message is ideologically regressive.

Mechtilde Lichnowsky's "Das Rendezvous im Zoo" (June 1927, I, 599–621) is a distinctive member of the affirmative category by virtue of the consistently light touch, playful irony and humor with which it presents a problematic relationship. Like Süskind's, Lichnowsky's characters are urbane citizens of the twenties. The subject once again is an obsessive love which is not fully returned by one partner in the affair. In this case, however, we enter the mind of a woman. "Teini" is sensitive, intelligent, charming, married, and helplessly in love with a rather obtuse entomologist who has the equally unlikely name of "Boy"—as in "Raymund" the modish English jargon is a sign of the times. As loving as she is, Teini is never able to communicate her feelings and her needs to the imperturbable Boy because he always thinks and speaks in terms of the category "women" and this block prevents him from acknowledging Teini as an individual. Teini, who is emancipated in outlook, has perspective on the situation, is fully aware of her lover's "male chauvinism," but loves him just the same. She suppresses her frustration and all the thoughts which she cannot express because Boy "hates discussion," "hates arguments," and calls any expression of an independent outlook on her part an "argument."

The title refers to Teini and Boy's meeting at the zoo where they are placed in the midst of a cast of creatures—lions, elephants and so on—which the author playfully uses to symbolize aspects of their relationship. After a particularly frustrating conversation during which Boy shows himself once again to be impervious to the emotional reality of the relationship, Teini, who usually prides herself on her self-control, is driven to tears. Finally, in a great effort of will she is able to achieve the "philosophical distance" for which she strives—i.e., to accept Boy for what he is and not to expect more since she loves him and he is unable to rise above his prejudices. She achieves it by means of communicating with the "wisdom" of one of the gentle creatures at the zoo. Unlike Boy, the animal is able to accept and give love and tenderness without social inhibitions or embarrassment. Its naturalness and serenity impart to Teini a new composure and altered perspective:

> Sie sehnte sich nach der rotbraunen Antilope, die zwischen Auge und Mund auf jeder Seite Platz für sieben Küsse bot und sich so gern ihren Liebkosungen hinzugeben schien, den Kopf weit aus dem Gitter streckend.
>
> Nun waren sie also bei der rotbraunen Antilope. Teini umklammerte den Nasenrücken, der hart und lang wie ein menschliches Schienbein zwischen zwei deutlich sichtbaren Adern lief. Ein überlebensgrosser, zart durchlochter Trüffel schnupperte über dem melancholisch lächelnden Mund, und hoch oben glänzte das feuchteste, schwärzeste Auge, ein Meer von Sanftmut. Teinis streichelnde Finger waren am Ansatz der Lauscher angelangt, und ihre leichte schwedische Massage schien die Antilope besonders zu lieben. Sie legte den Kopf auf Teinis Schulter und atmete befriedigt aus und ein. Man hätte denken können, dass sie lächelte. Teini sprach sie leise an, und im Spiegel das nahen Auges sah sie sich selbst, in kleinem Format, aber unheimlich deutlich. Sie schämte sich ihrer grässlichen menschlichen Klugheit, die zu nichts langte.
>
> Dann wandte sie sich um, blickte den kleinen Boy an und liebte ihn mit Antilopenweisheit, überlegen und bescheiden. Sie lächelte ohne Melancholie, Pantherkatze plus Antilope, minus Adam und Eva, und Paneuropa, hol's der Kuckuck!
>
> Dann standen sie zum Abschied in der Sonne, der Boy lächelte, als wollte er einen sehr guten Witz machen, und sagte das beste, was er wusste:
>
> "Teini, Darling, also morgen um?"
>
> "Um 4,30, du Zebra," sagte sie. (620–21)

It is an epiphany as we have been accustomed to finding in the affirmative category—stimulated by the soul's communication with nature, but this time in more modern dress than the earlier stories, with ironic distance and a touch of whimsical humor. The resolution is not forced and incongruous, as in the Süskind story, but is appropriately modest and lighthearted, in consonance with the atmosphere of the work as a whole.

The next story in the affirmative group is Hans Reisiger's tale of the woes and joys surrounding a group of adolescent boys' final exam and prospective graduation from *Gymnasium*. "Not und Verklärung" appeared in March 1928 (I, 280–93). It was Reisiger's second *NR* story during our time period.[12] This March 1928 issue also brings some significant remarks by Rudolf Kayser which are pertinent to our quest for the shape of *NR* literature under his guidance. In his "Europäische Rundschau" section (330–36) Kayser included a brief refutation of some main points touched upon by Otto Flake in his lead essay in the February issue: "Rassefragen" (I, 113–22), which attempts to justify anti-semitism as a legitimate philosophical alternative and in the course of doing so relies on most of the standard anti-semitic shibboleths.[13] That this essay should have been published in the *NR* is startling. Kayser's response is a model of tolerance and restraint. Most interesting for our purposes are his general introductory remarks (addressed directly to his "dear friend Otto Flake"):

> Wir sehen beides manches jetzt anders, d.h. knapper, zweckhafter, kritischer, eingeordneter in die Systematik des Lebens an

[12] Reisiger's "Stehe auf und wandle," which belongs to the negative category, appeared in August 1926, II, 127–55.

[13] Flake's essay represents a low point in the *NR*. It includes such statements as the following: "Er [Antisemitismus] ist, philosophisch betrachtet, der Kampf der Monade gegen die Universalität, des Konkreten gegen die Idee, des Gewordenen gegen das Fliessende." (116) "Was ich sagen will? Dass der Antisemitismus eine der Formen ist, in denen sich die Suche des richtigen Verhaltens zum Leben vollzieht." (116) Surely the kind of trash which his muddled thinking produced here marks Flake as the most overrated of *NR* authors. (See above, n. 26, p. 53 and de Mendelssohn, *S. Fischer und sein Verlag* throughout for Flake's prominent role.)

> als in jüngeren Tagen, suchen die Fragen der Zeit aus keiner platonischen Kuppel und keinem psychologischen Rampenlicht zu beleuchten, sondern nur aus ihrer und unserer Existenz, dem realen Dasein, das Geist und Ding gleichmässig erfüllt. (330)

The terminology alone contrasts sharply with Kayser's 1922 essay—apparently part of his "younger days"—which served as signpost for subsequent stories. Particularly conspicuous are the sober tone, modest goals, and mistrust of lofty and global perspectives. It marks a new skepticism of sweeping truths—whether they be embedded in psychological theory or pholosophical idealism. It is a rejection, in other words, of the mentality of the early stories[14]—Kayser's own, Zweig's, Schaeffer's and Hirschfeld's. Kayser's new convictions began to be reflected in the selection of affirmative stories around 1927 with "Raymund"—or 1926 with the Brod story—although no definitive line can be drawn between one mentality and the other, as the conclusions of both stories show.

The Reisiger story as well as the next entry in the affirmative category, Wilhelm Schmidtbonn's "Die verwegenen Girlanden" (June 1928, I, 608–29), must be reckoned to the earlier type. (Schmidtbonn's two other contributions are in the negative group.) Both fall under the heading of nostalgia. Both celebrate a bygone era—in the case of Reisiger it is a bygone time of life, in the case of Schmidtbonn a golden age when tradition and honor determined the affairs of men. Reisiger portrays the peculiar rite of passage which the final exam in the *Gymnasium* signifies. He captures the high spirits of the boys, their camaraderie, their anxiety, hopes, disappointments and triumphs. In their self-contained universe of school and its concerns, isolated from the world and the problems of adulthood, the boys are idealistic in the extreme. They are devoted to one another in loyal friendships which manifest pro-

[14] And implicitly, of over-reliance on Freud and Nietzsche.

nounced homoerotic elements (cf. "Turnlehrer Pravda" above, p. 51), inevitable in view of the circumstances of shared intimacy and isolation from girls. (The school system for the upper middle and upper classes certainly lent itself to forming the unrealistic views of women which we have found so prevalent in the previous affirmative stories.)

The epiphany occurs in the form of a triumph on stage for the main character, Anselm. His starring role in a graduation play proves to be such a success that it has the effect on Anselm of opening his eyes to previously unrecognized possibilities of adulthood: achievement, recognition, self-confidence, the capacity to be a productive human being:

> . . . den angestauten Beifallsjubel gleichsam an sich heraufriss, das er einem hinter die Kulisse in die Ohren nachrauschte—Erstlingsgruss der Zukunft! Liebesgruss, an ein Etwas gerichtet, das kein blosses Knabenspiel mehr war, sondern Lebensmächtiges, das man hier atmend in sich trug—mochte es nun tönendes Lautwerden fremder Worte sein, oder Ahnung eigener, die man erschaffen würde, oder beides vereint! O Spenden, Hingeben aus eigenem Quell, zum erstenmal nach Jahren des Hinnehmens und Widergebens von Fremden, Unerlebtem!—Mathematik: genügend. Deutsch: genügend. Latein: genügend. Aber hier war: nicht Genügen! Hier war: immer noch mehr!— (292)

The style is typical for the story and serves to convey the boys' generally rapturous, always intense feelings.

Schmidtbonn's "Die verwegenen Girlanden" is a banal tale of a clash between old and new ways in a small provincial town. It is told in a conventional manner by the narrator—a boy who spends a summer with his uncle. It develops that the livelihood—and consequently the existence—of the uncle, who is a furrier, is threatened when a competitor establishes himself in the building across the street. Modern business methods such as advertising and price-cutting are seen for the first time in the town when the competitor sets up his business. Soon the new shop attracts even the uncle's steady customers. In the eyes of the boy the ruthless businessman is a villain. Much attention is given to his hideous appearance: slant-eyes, yellow-skinned, with yellow wolf-like fangs, spewing forth saliva when he speaks. There is obvious racism in the comparison of the repulsive features to a "Chinesengesicht."

Soon the uncle is on the verge of financial and personal ruin. His life's investment was his business and the newly-expanded building which housed it. (In the hidebound social structure of that old provincial town choosing an alternative direction in life would not occur to anyone. Nor would it, under those circumstances, be possible.) However, the family is saved when the enemy turns out to be a fraud and is carted away by the authorities.

There is no doubt that the reader's sympathies are to be cast on the side of the kindly, defenseless uncle, whose near-downfall is caused by his unswerving adherence to the conservative standards of his trade. He refuses to react with competitive measures:

> Aber der Gegner schrieb nicht nur die Namen von zweiundzwanzig Hauptstädten der Erde [locations of the competitor's fictitious branch offices] an seine Fenster, sondern auch die Preise an seine Waren.
>
> Über jenes spottete mein Onkel nur, aber dies erbitterte ihn. Das ging gegen die Würde eines Geschäftsmannes von damals. Das hiess aus einem Laden eine Jahrmarktbude zu machen. (624)

The uncle's reaction is disillusionment with human nature followed by proud withdrawal from the fray. The morality of the story is simple: a division into the good old and the bad new. The author is condemning the postwar breakdown of traditional moral standards (by implication also "Americanization" which was seen as the source of modern competitive business practices). The new is fraudulent, hollow, morally and physically reprehensible (evil is revealed in outward appearance). Consequently it is destroyed. The story closes with uncle and nephew engaged in a joyous affirmation of the good old ways:

> Er hört nicht auf zu singen, ich höre nicht auf. Wir singen die ganze Stadt an, wir singen die zweiundzwanzig Hauptstädte der Welt an, die fünf Erdteile, wir singen Gott an. Der Onkel sieht zu mir herunter, ich zu ihm hinauf.
>
> Jetzt greift er in die Tasche und schenkt mir ein Dreimarkstück.—(629)

The September 1928 issue brings the next affirmative story "Sterben auf einer Pflanzung" by Kurt Heuser (II, 249–62). It is a complex and in some ways profound tale whose affirmative resolution and epiphany is qualified by an ambivalence which is new to the affirmative category. Further evidence in this issue of increased sophistication of judgment is the revised thinking about the United States represented by the lead essay "Amerikanisierung Europas?" (225–35) by Max Rychner.[15] It is an insightful, balanced analysis of European conceptions and misconceptions of "Americanization," with suggestions for productive reactions to it and assessments of its potential as a positive stimulus for European ideas. Rudolf Kayser concludes his review of a French author's novel about life in California (*Hollywood Dépassé* by Luc Durtain) by placing his imprimatur upon a thought which would have seemed out of place in his remarks on the U.S.A. a few years before (see above n. 15, p. 35): "Vielleicht die tiefste Weisheit dieses Romans Kaliforniens aber lautet: 'Die Kontinente wie die Menschen verkennen sich immer gegenseitig.' " (328) The tenor of this issue is a serious concern with other cultures and their relationship to Europe. In addition to the Rychner essay this issue includes one by Georges Duhamel, "Vom europäischen Geist" (235–48), which is a plea for internationalism and receptivity to other cultures and peoples; the Heuser story whose protagonist is Africa itself; the memoirs of Joseph

---

[15] Hermand and Trommler, *Die Kultur der Weimarer Republik*, p. 56, use the Rychner essay as an example of strong pro-American attitudes which began to become prevalent in intellectual circles around 1924.

Conrad; a philosophical dialogue in honor of Tolstoy's 100th birthday—"Tolstoi-Legende" (281–90) by Efraim Frisch—which touches upon, among other things, value systems in foreign cultures; and a lengthy travel essay "Südafrikanische Städte" (291–310) by Richard Hülsenbeck.

The Heuser story of Africa shows great sensitivity and respect for the beauty and integrity of an environment which is not only alien but often deadly for the European. Heuser was a major contributor to the *NR* during out time period. Only he, Ponten and Schaeffer are represented by four stories each. One of Heuser's stories belongs to the affirmative category, three to the negative.[16]

Three of them are set in Africa and deal with the displaced European's fascination with the mysterious continent and his struggle to survive and establish himself there. The most impressive of the four stories is "Sterben auf einer Pflanzung." At issue is the power of the "dark" continent and

---

[16] Heuser's other stories are "Elfenbein für Felicitas" (August 1927, II, 125–38), "Wiederkehr der Amazonen" (April 1928, I, 347–65) and "Ein Feldzug gegen England" (August 1930, II, 226–44). In 1929 Fischer published Heuser's collected stories under the title of his first published work "Elfenbein für Felicitas." The collection is reviewed by Hans B. Wagenseil in the February 1929 issue, I, p. 288. Heuser's fate is representative of the generation of S. Fischer Verlag's promising young writers who came of age in the 1920's. Ernst Alker (*Profile und Gestalten der deutschen Literatur nach 1914*, ed. by Eugen Thurnher [Stuttgart: Alfred Kröner, 1977], p. 31) writes of Heuser's work: ". . . Bücher. . . , die (vielleicht infolge Ungunst der Zeit) nur vorübergehend Echo fanden, obwohl ihre Qualität beträchtliche Beachtung gerechtfertigt hätte. KURT HEUSER (1903–1975) war diplomierter Landwirt in Afrika gewesen. Dort Schrieb er unter dem Titel *Elfenbein für Felicitas* (1928) zusammengefasste Ersählungen, die ihn als Prosaepiker auswiesen, als Prosaepiker alten Stils; . . . Nach Herausgabe von drei weiteren Kolonialromanen schwieg Heuser und wurde ein Mann des Films." After publication of his novels *Die Reise ins Innere* (1931) and *Abenteuer in Vineta* (1933)—both of which appeared serialized in the *NR*—Heuser published only a collection of novellas, *Buschkrieg*, in 1933, and from then on wrote no more fiction. (Peter de Mendelssohn, *S. Fischer und sein Verlag* [Frankfurt am Main: S. Fischer, 1970], p. 1102.)

the predicament of white intruders in the face of that power.

The main character, a European adventurer named Staller, feels the overwhelming force of the African landscape for the first time after several years there when he ventures out one night, driven by the unbearable tension of an apparently unending drought, to try to find and confront the medicine man/rainmaker who is also a field hand whom Staller had severely beaten that day over a trifling offense. Staller senses a mysterious, indescribable force in the African night, ". . . etwas, was seine Kniee schwach machte, eine fremde unsagbare Gewalt." (256) Up to this time Staller had prided himself on being tough, invincible. Now for the first time he must admit to helplessness and vulnerability. His situation, which is representative of the rootless adventurer who has fled Europe to make his fortune and test his strength where, he believes, it is still possible to do both, is summarized in a key paragraph (which also illustrates the realistic, down-to-earth quality of Heuser's style):

> Er hatte immer damit geprotzt, dass er ein heimatloser Kerl sei, der nach Afrika passe, nicht gefährdet von geheimen Sehnsüchten. Das wäre ein Land, da könne man leben, zum Donnerwetter. Hatte er nicht diese vielen Zusammengebrochenen verspottet, die nach dem Vaterlande jammerten, heim, nur heim aus dem brennenden Busch, die in der letzten Klasse sich eingeschifft hatten, besiegt von dem Lande—und ohne Mitleid Schwächlinge diejenigen gennant, die man hatte verscharren müssen in der Einöde; zwei davon waren Kamaraden gewesen. Warum musste ihm das geschehen, dass er in diesem Augenblick, wo es ungebrochenen Mut galt, zum erstenmal diese volle Verlassenheit erkannte, und dass dies eine Niemandslandschaft war, ein Mondkrater, unfruchtbar, soviel er schuften mochte, unfruchtbar für ihn, den Fremden? Den Negern wuchs ihr hellgruner Mais ins Maul, fur ihn regnete es nicht einmal, verfluchter Spuk. (256)

Africa, inevitably, responds to the stranger's hybris by destroying or transforming him. During that same night, in a painful, humbling process at the mercy of initiation mysteries and hallucinations, Staller changes. His epiphany coincides with the reawakening of the parched earth in a downpour. It is as if Staller were rewarded for his metamorphosis by the longed-for metamorphosis of the land. Heuser's account of the miraculously awakened prodigal fecundity of the earth celebrates Africa and the reduction in that elemental environment of life questions and relationships to the essentials—no room for European existential doubts, questioning of the meaning and purpose of life, or for the castles in the air which civilization tolerates (and in that sense Staller, once his arrogance has been tamed, is well suited to the land). It is a remarkable example of descriptive prowess—vivid, dramatic, illustrative of extraordinary powers of observation and keen sensitivity to nature in microcosm:

> Wie Seen entstanden waren in den Senken, rudernde, rufende Frösche darin, und die wimmelnde Kreatur der Larven und Käfer. Wie es geflügelt aus allen Ritzen und Spalten des Bodens aufschwirrte und gleich sich suchte und fand, der Hochzeitsschwarm der Termiten und die Libellen über den Teichen, verhackt zum Doppelflug, andere Beute suchend und selbst wieder Beute. Wie die brodelnde Luft erfüllt war von Gesängen der Vögel, der Zikaden, der Kröten; wie die Stummen ihre Leiber badeten und wollüstig atmeten. Ja, wie mit einem einzigen Schlag das Land sich begrünte, das geheimnisvolle Pflanzenreich emporstieg aus dem dunkeln Kelch eines Jahresschlummers, mit einer zarten und dennoch Steine zersprengenden Kraft, ja, wie toter und seelenloser Stoff sich wandelte zu lebendigem in der geheimnisvollen Chemie Gottes und jedes Ding wieder so wurde wie es geplant war und wie es sich stets wiederholt. Selbst in den toten Hölzern regte es sich noch, Zaunpfähle schlugen aus und Schemel, es war eine ungeheuere Verschwendung von Farbe, Licht und Formen, und im geringsten Keim drängte es und wollte geboren sein, um selbst wieder fruchtbar sein zu können. Es war alles notwendig so und kein Zweifel am sein, und die Träume zerflossen vor dieser grösseren Zauberei. (262)

We are encountering here again that profound connection between human beings and nature which Kayser had called for and which has often been the context for the hero's epiphany. However, at this point the Heuser story takes a different turn—a turn away from the flight into an ideal realm which former epiphanies signaled. The idea of Staller's transformation into a feeling human being is retracted again by a cynical comment. When Staller awakens from his trauma and tries to tell his last remaining comrade, a kind and gentle man named Go, that the rains have come, he discovers that Go has succumbed to fever during the night: "Er fühlte einen Schmerz in sich emporsteigen, aber schon war er wieder so, dass er ihn sich nicht eingestehen wollte, Denn er war doch nicht anders geworden, so plötzlich ändert sich doch kein Mensch." (262) With this remark the idealistic type of resolution of earlier stories is explicitly rejected. However, it is the invariably skeptical voice of Staller, a character who finds it difficult to admit the idea of metamorphosis. And in the concluding lines doubt is cast on Staller's cynical thought:

> "Armer Go," sagte er. "Es wird nun doch sicher eine reiche Ernte geben in diesem Jahr!" Er rief den Hund zu sich her, um das Gefühl der Einsamkeit besser überwinden zu können.
>
> Dann ging er über das Feld und sah, dass alles gut begann. (262)

Staller has indeed become more feeling; he has become sensible too for the first time to the land as good. The conclusion is undeniably affirmative, but with qualifications (such as loneliness and implied future struggle) which give rise to ambiguity and thereby to a level of realism which is new to the affirmative category.

Albrecht Schaeffer's second affirmative story is "Meleagros und Atalante" (November 1928, II, 562–78). It is one of two stories during our time period which are adaptations of ancient Greek myths. A female child abandoned in the wilderness by her misogynist father is raised as its own child by a mother bear and grows up to become a protegée of the goddess Artemis who names her Atalante and makes her one of her huntresses, while at the same time also making Atalante blind to human emotions in order that the mortal may bear the sight of the goddess. Eventually the goddess permits Atalante to return to her family and requires of her an oath that she will not submit in marriage to any man who cannot run faster than she. Atalante—more powerful than a man and manlike in appearance—returns to her home to become the pride of her father. After she has slain with her spear three suitors whom she had overtaken in a match race, Atalante is finally won, after many more trials, by the clever and honorable Meilanion who succeeds by means of intelligent strategems where others who depended upon force had failed.

Meilanion is able to win Atalante because he has learned what prevents her from being a real woman, and is able to find ways to release her emotions and her womanly nature. He wins their match race by tossing down three golden apples which Atalante stoops to pick up, showing life in her eyes for the first time. Meilanion only takes her for his wife, however, when she has also experienced pain—the death of the giant Meleagros, who had loved Atalante. "Was Lust ist—jene Äpfel—, und was Schmerz ist—jener Tote—, du weisst nun wohl alles, was deines Geschlechtes ist. Mein Haus in der Heimat ist dir lang offen. Tritt ein." (578) The moral—a woman whose heart is closed to desire and pain is not a complete or worthy human being—is an extension in the garb of ancient Greece of ideas we have already seen in the stories by Kayser, Zweig, and Schaeffer.

Part of Rudolf Kayser's (rare) editorial footnote to a literary essay in the same issue of *NR* is relevant to the ancient Greek setting of Schaeffer's message: "Vor allem scheint uns die innere Aktualität doch weit wichtiger als die äussere zu sein. Zu allen Zeiten schafft nur sie das literarische Abbild der Gegenwarten, wobei es recht gleichgültig ist, ob der Stoff der Vergangenheit oder der Gegenwart entstammt." (550)[17] In

---

[17] Jenö Kurucz, *Struktur und Funktion der Intelligenz während der Weimarer Republik* (Spich Bez. Köln: Grote, 1967), p. 55, remarks *(continued on page 106)*

accord with these remarks, we are led to examine other stories in an historical setting for their contemporary relevance.

Bruno Frank's "Der Magier," which appeared in October 1929 (II, 505–36) is a trite and uninspired tale, poor in execution. A conglomeration of stereotypes about art, society, the theatre, and success, it pretends to profound commentary on these themes. It is handicapped by lack of artistic control—over-long, packed with superfluous incident and details and one-sided, unbelievable characters, lacking balance and a structural concept. The story catalogues the meteoric rise to the heights of his profession and fame of a brilliant theatre director. The portrait appears to be of Max Reinhardt.[18] The methods of Frank's "magician"-director Meskart nearly duplicate those of Reinhardt as described by Carl Zuckmayer in his autobiography.[19] Zuckmayer also calls Reinhardt's work "magic."

After achieving the pinnacle of success, however, Meskart begins to find its satisfactions hollow, his work lifeless. At the close of the performance by his troupe of a particularly artificial play before a particularly stiff group of the European social elite, followed by a reception of baroque luxury, the director is alone at night and happens to observe from the interior balcony of his palace a young servant couple engaging in an orgy of eating and sex in the uncleared dining room below. This sight precipitates his epiphany, for the next day Meskart has departed, leaving behind wealth and fame.

(continued from page 105) on post-World War I culture: "Mag die intellektuelle Aussage nach wie vor in der Form abstrackter metaphysischer Leitsätze oder in der eines wirklichkeitstranszendenten künstlerischen Werkes gemacht worden sein, sie wurde auf die konkrete Gegenwartskrise bezogen."

[18] Details such as his Jewishness, his Viennese acting background, his productions of the classics, his international fame, and his extravagant castle home duplicate Reinhardt's biography.

[19] Carl Zuckmayer, *Als wär's ein Stück von mir: Erinnerungen* (Frankfurt am Main: Fischer Bücherei, 1969), p. 331.

He reappears, unnamed (a completely unmotivated device by the author), directing and acting in a traveling troupe of black players which performs tempestuous melodramas in the style of *Uncle Tom's Cabin*. The performances are described at length and we learn that the troupe enjoys astounding success and that the director has ambitious plans for its future. The idealized, unconvincing conclusion represents a relapse into the mentality of the early twenties' stories such as Zweig's "Phantastische Nacht" and Kayser's "Die Begegnung in Padua" where the hero who has achieved success in his métier rejects what seems to him to be dry intellectuality and sterile routine in favor of a commitment to a romantic ideal called life.

Georg von der Vring's "Aube" (January 1930, I, 106–26) is a highlight of the affirmative category. Stylistically one of the most successful, it is also the most beautiful story. It is an intricate composition, carefully developed, profound in its themes, uncompromising in its realism. Yet it rests upon a delicate, lyrical portrait of the hero, Lieutenant Aube, of the emotions with which he must deal, and the landscape against which they unfold.

The scene is France during the German army's winter campaign of 1918. The story begins:

> Der Leutnant Aube gehörte zu einem Bataillon, das um die Mitte des Januar 1918 von der Verdunfront verlegt wurde. Nach Mitternacht und bei strenger Kälte war man auf einem finsteren Bahnhofe verladen worden und dann, ohne das Ziel der Fahrt zu wissen, über dem Stossen der Achsen eingeschlafen. (106)

War is a theme; it is always there with its discomforts and demands, determining the course of lives and events. War is also a metaphor for the world. It provides the backdrop and stimulus for the hero's journey of self-discovery. "Aube" is a *Bildungsroman* in miniature. The circumstances of Aube's inner life are indicated, symbolically, in the above initial sentences: cast out into a cold, dark world, carried along on a journey with unknown goal, lulled by the momentum of circumstances, not fully conscious—at this point—of the private significance of what happens to him, and tending to try to escape by sleep (or other means—at one point later in the story Aube thinks: ". . . ich wollte doch in St. Faubourg meinen endlosen Schlaf beginnen; ich wollte doch in Loison des lieben Majors Schüler werden im Vergessen; . . ." [121]) the harshness of experience which the world, and in particular a war, thrusts upon a young and sensitive, still innocent person. On the way to the village St. Faubourg which will be his overnight quarters Aube, lulled by the rainy landscape and rhythmic trot of his horse, thinks: "Zum Katzenkraueln! Man schläft so schön, man döst so halb, träumt zu dreiviertel—irgendwo ist auch Krieg." (107) Not only does his mood capture the inactivity, boredom and purposelessness of the soldier between battles and away from the front, but it is also indicative of the state of Aube's psyche—it is as if in a cocoon, as yet innocent of the metamorphosis to which this episode in his life will lead.

The author is dealing with archetypal patterns. They are indicated early on:

> Eine halbe Stunde später erblickte Aube auf der nach links zum Dorfe abgehenden Pappelstrasse zwei einzelne Reiter, sie schwammen durch die Zeile dahin. Auch der Futtermeister schwieg, er war verkatert, von der vorigen verwachten und verzechten Nacht her, übel und kalt war ihm. Aube dagegen, in dieser schwimmenden Weite, gewann von Minute zu Minute seine Fröhlichkeit zurück, ziemlich durchnässt und heiter stierte er gegen den Rücken des trabenden Pferdes. So verloren wie oft, dachte er und sah diesen nassen Rücken genau an—seit man von der Mutter kam, und so weit von allem, ausgestossen vom Rittmeister in ein anderes Dorf, aus dem Truppenteil nach dessen Meinung zurückgesetzt, jedoch in Wahrheit wieder einmal vorangestellt. (107)

One archetype is birth—the traumatic departure from the womb.[20] The second is the journey; the story receives its

[20] It seems hardly necessary to mention Freud again here.

rhythm and momentum from Aube's travel by train, horseback, foot, bicycle, and horseback again through the French countryside and internally toward his epiphany, when finally he will have accepted the loss of mother and risen above the trauma of having been abandoned to the world.

Aube goes so far as to have himself transferred twelve times in three years—another aspect of the journey archetype. In so many words: "Leutnant Aube 'wanderte' gern, . . ." (107) In order to preserve a certain distance to his fellows Aube would, as soon as he got to know them well, request a transfer. Apparently these frequent transfers incidentally also saved his life. A friend wrote: "Du wanderst am Tode vorbei." (107) But on another level it becomes clear that this is a device on Aube's part to shield his soul; his transfers are precipitated by his comrades getting to know *him* better.

As in the beginning of the above-quoted paragraph, the setting, the landscape, his fellow soldiers are seen through Aube's eyes as if in an impressionist painting, except for the few times when he chooses to focus close up, as if through a magnifying glass, on a particular feature. This stylistic device also conveys the self-defensive, fetal posture of Aube's psyche, folded in, wrapped cocoon-like, except for the intrusion of an occasional strong visual impression in bold relief. For example, continuing his ride to St. Faubourg:

> Daran dachte dieser [Aube] soeben, als ein Reiter neben dem Wagen auftauchte, der sein Pferd zügelte, wendete, tanzen liess und sein wütendes Gesicht so nahe als möglich zum Leutnant heranbrachte.
>
> "Stollen bei Tauwetter!" schrie dieser Offizier—nur Gesicht, wie es Aube schien, nur hüpfendes, höchst unzufriedenes Gesicht, Pfütze von Antlitz über dem breiten Zimt mit Zuckerfarbenem Pelzkragen. "Ja, Stollen!" schrie er, tanzte und deutete. (107)

The sudden close-up of a face is an important symbol in the story. Twice at crucial moments Aube inadvertently glimpses his own face in a mirror and is shocked by the difference between the reflection and his sense of self. The first time he turns away in annoyance. The second time the reflection remains but Aube is made ill at ease by it and abruptly stops his conversation. Finally, when self-insight, his epiphany, is near Aube thinks: "Ich wurde geboren in St. Faubourg. Ich bin ein Kind, klein und zart. Nirgends ist hier ein Spiegel, der mir's bestreitet." (124–25) The mirror is used to symbolize progress toward consciousness of self.

The rebirth in St. Faubourg to which he refers is the consequence of a middle-of-the-night visit to Aube's room by the attractive daughter of the French family whose home he is occupying for one night. In the few words of his reaction to the unexpected visitor Aube's self is revealed with a subtle realism, economy of style, delicate humor and restraint which are unique in the stories up to now. We learn that Aube is very young in spirit, childlike, gentle, inexperienced:

> Mitten in der Nacht erwachte er, hob den Kopf und fragte: "Hatte ich denn nicht abgeschlossen?"
>
> "Bestimmt nicht," flüsterte jemand, der im verdeckten Mondlicht mitten in der dreieckigen Kammer stand. Es war nicht die alte Dame, wie er gedacht. Ihr Haar hier war schwarz und lang, ihr Kleid weiss. So war's die Junge.
>
> "Gehen Sie im Monde?" fragte erschrocken Aube, wollte aufstehen, war doch nicht angezogen. "Nein." Es lachte nun aus ihrer Kehle, schnurrte, platzte los: "Ich friere hier!" "So liegt dort mein Mantel. Warten Sie, ich stehe auf . . ." Er stockte: "Ist's ein Traum?"
>
> "Wir tun's einfacher," sagte schlicht das junge Weib und kam in sein Bett, nicht ganz nahe. Ihr Mund flüsterte: "Sie reisen ja morgen fort, so blieb ich wach."
>
> Noch war es wohl Aube ein halber Traum, doch drang Wärme zu ihm her, ganz nahe Wärme. Er begann plötzlich zu weinen, griff zu; da griffen sie sich beide. (111)

Slowly, once he has returned to the normal deprivation of the soldier's life, Aube begins to realize that this experience has changed him for the better, provided him with comfort and support which he had not known before—even though when he returns a short time later to propose marriage to the girl (whose name he does not know), she and her family have fled and Aube is not likely to see her again. In his mind he compares her flight to a second abandonment by his mother. The first occurred when his real mother died during Aube's childhood.

The tender scenes stand in drastic contrast to the scenes of bleak conditions in the military encampments, with physical hardships such as cold, dampness, filth and fleas:

> Im Februar dann lag wieder Schnee, kehrte der Frost zurück. Leutnant Aube hatte keinen Strohsack mehr und lag auf Draht. Draussen und drinnen wehte Ostwind. Heck verschlief den Ofendienst. Auf dem Gesicht lag die Kälte wie eine Scheibe Eis. Man erwachte, warf Wäschestücke sich übers Gesicht, stülpte die Feldmütze auf. Unterm Bette im Gurkentopf fror Urin. Gegen Morgen wurde die Kälte unerträglich. (113)

This kind of physical realism has never before appeared in the affirmative category. With the exception of Hirschfeld's maudlin leprosy story which depends not upon realism for its effects, but upon sentimentalized gore, manifestations of the unpretty physical side of life have been completely missing. Even in Heuser's earthy jungle story, while it is said that life in the jungle is full of physical hardships, the reader is never given a sense of these. If the characters are sweaty, fly-ridden, itchy and uncomfortable as they really would be in such an environment, the reader is spared this unpleasant knowledge. Yet in the most delicate, lyrical story these matters are not ignored. One aspect of the brilliance of the composition and its profound realism is von der Vring's successful conception of the interaction between a hero of flowerlike sensitivity and poetic sensibilities, and the harsh environment of war.

The presentation of nature is always appropriate, sometimes arresting, never trite. The landscape, the weather, animals, trees and flowers are integral to Aube's sensibility. They can be reflections of his moods, extensions of his feelings, or symbols of the emotions with which he is grappling. Once spring finally arrives, Aube and his orderly Heck, seeking a supplement to their meager diet, shoot a rabbit. Heck discovers that it was pregnant. Aube, saddened and disgusted, tells him to bury it. Immediately Aube's thoughts turn once again to the womb and his need to return: "Er ass Brot, dachte: Ich will sie heiraten! Dann: Wer hat uns lieb, wenn nicht diese Frauen, die einfach da sind und liebhaben. Ich will in ihrem Bauche verschwinden und wiederkommen am Jüngsten Tag." (116) These thoughts precipitate his sudden return to St. Faubourg to propose. Finding the young woman gone, Aube's spirits ebb to their lowest, darkest point. He despairs of life in a tone and symbolism reminiscent of Büchner's Woyzeck:

> Er aber war nun arm; er legte eine Handfläche gegen die Flurwand dieses Hauses—war nun arm. Plötzlich blies der Wind die Tür weit auf, so dass er drüben sein Fahrrad stehen sah. Ihm war zum Umsinken traurig. Wozu dies gut ist? dachte er—wozu wohl?
>
> Dann trat die Magd aus der Küche, ein Messer in der Hand, wollte sich wohl Löwenzahnsalat sammeln. Aube rief: "Schneiden Sie niemand damit!"
>
> Sie schrak zusammen, verbarg das Messer, wählte die Hintertür. Nun blies der Wind strömend durchs Haus—Aube liess sich ergreifen, kam durch den Vorgarten und hob sein Fahrrad, durch dessen Speichen fauliges Laub wehte. (117)

The death of Aube's hope of returning to the mother figure had been presaged by the killing of the baby rabbits in their mother's womb. (Later, Aube admonishes a rabbit-hunting colleague: "Für Hasen ist Schonzeit." "Schonzeit gibt es nicht," (118) responds the other officer, illustrating again the vast emotional distance between Aube and his fellows.) The nature symbolism is continued in the resistance of the weather to Aube's return to his encampment.

> Er fuhr zurück, kämpfte gegen den Wind, seine Mütze raschelte ihm am Ohr. Er weinte nicht, kam zurück wie von einem Todesfall und Begräbnis, sparte sich dies und jenes an bohrenden Gedanken für später auf. Manchmal wollte sein Rad stehenbleiben, dann wieder überwand er den Sturm. (117)

At this point Aube decides that he must again apply for a

transfer because he is on the verge of inadvertently revealing himself, his thoughts, his interior world to his fellow officers. Here the last of the major themes is introduced: memory. The capacity to remember gives meaning to life and a reason for living. (It is the same conclusion and means of reconciliation with himself and life which is arrived at by Schickele's hero in "Tulpen.") By accepting memory—against the advice of a much-admired older officer who tells Aube that the most important, in fact the only important thing in life is the capacity to forget—Aube affirms life. He replies to the major who so successfully forgets: "So sind Sie schon beinahe tot!" (118) For himself Aube rejects that means of coping:

> Das wäre eine Kur, dachte er, das wäre in der Tat eine gewagte Kur, "sie" vergessen zu wollen. Es wird nicht gehen, denn ich habe ja auch meine Mutter nicht vergessen, bin zwar allein, habe aber den Kopf so voll wie nur möglich. Lebt wohl, Bilder! ihr entzückenden Schmerzensbilder—da seid ihr! da seid ihr! . . . Lebt wohl—wieder da! (118)

All memories are precious to Aube, even the memories of pain. Accepting them, he knows, means accepting life. It will lead, in a growth process which integrates the up-to-now separate levels of his existence and his sensibility, to Aube's epiphany (or "dawn," which is the meaning of "Aube" in French).

During a last night celebration at the makeshift officers' casino, Aube becomes involved in a rambling, tipsy conversation. It is a realistic scene which reveals the anxiety and tensions of men in wartime who are temporarily removed from the immediate dangers of the front which, however, are ever-present in their minds. Inevitably the conversation turns to the topic of death. It stimulates Aube to think of his own death and of an enemy soldier he killed when he was a new recruit. The occurrence has remained in his mind as the image of a tam-o'-shanter with colored ribbons which flew into the air when Aube shot its British owner in the head. The image is an example of the author's mastery of the technique of understatement. He does not have Aube's thoughts express the obvious—that he is haunted by his deed. Instead Aube remembers that at the time he had been proud of the shot and praised for it, but now all pride and praise are gone and only the image of the floating tam-o'-shanter remains. The extraordinary image of death—colorful, lighthearted, almost whimsical—conveys with terrible poignancy the tragedy of war. His review of it marks the beginning of a catharsis for Aube. It concludes that night with a dream of the young French woman which reaches a new level of reality and intensity: "Als leichter Schatten war sie da und ihm nahe, solch eine Liebe hatte er nie geahnt noch gefühlt. Sie wurde erst jetzt seine erste Liebe." (124)

Aube's battalion is ordered to move on. In conjunction with the movement of the troops, Aube progresses to the next stage in his personal development. It is marked by resignation—stoic acceptance of himself and his fate whatever the war will bring:

> Das ist nun alles zu Ende, dachte Aube; als ich Junge war, als ich gross wurde—alles dies ist zu Ende. Es ist irgendwo zurückgeblieben, drüben, wohin die feindlichen Bombenstaffeln fliegen. Ich wurde geboren in St. Faubourg. Ich bin ein Kind, klein und zart. Nirgends ist hier ein Spiegel, der mir's bestreitet. Ich werde jung bleiben und in der Jugend sterben. Man lässt Kinder nicht in einen Krieg ziehen! Ich darf auf alles, was ich mir einst ausdachte, ein munteres Leben auf dieser Erde, verzichten.
>
> Jene Mutter, die kraushaarige, früh alt gewordene—nur dass sie kraushaarig und alt gewesen, war ihm noch im Gedächtnis geblieben. Jener Vater aber—er hatte ja sein Stuck Leben, das er, Aube, doch war, seinen hilflosen Sohn verlassen. Damals hilflos, heute—bewehrt! Heute ein guter Sohn, ein ganz ergebener Sohn einer anderen Mutter, welche ihm die erste nicht verdrangte noch aufhob, sondern sich mit ihr verschmolz—und so der ersten das gleiche nachtat, nämlich, sich wieder aufzumachen und fortzureisen. So war er zum zweiten Male allein, doch das war ja ganz und gar kein Grund zur Trauer. Zeitlichkeit und Gegenwart in der Liebe, ihm war es nicht überaus wichtig. Er sass im Sattel, er war ein ganz getroster, ein beinahe schneidiger Leutnant. Er ritt durch

den Wald, es wehte eine Luft, wie die Luft des jugendlichen Lebens weht. Diese Hand, welche die Zügel hielt, war noch heute angefafst in einem verborgenen Sinn. (125)

This interior monologue is comparable to a psychoanalysis which Aube is carrying out on himself. After the stages of his life—with all their unhappy implications—have been called forth for review, Aube is able to reconcile himself to his orphaned status, his loneliness, and deprivation—or at least is able to put on a brave front.

Riding along with the troops Aube sees a young soldier climb over a fence with a bouquet of primroses in his hand, and stares at him in shock because the soldier looks just like Aube's young "mother" in St. Faubourg. When the soldier senses that he is being observed by his commanding officer he drops his bouquet to salute. Aube instructs him to pick it up and join the ranks. When the soldier has gone Aube notices one primrose lying on the road. As soon as the troops are out of sight Aube picks it up. This is the moment of his epiphany, when to insight and acceptance of life is added joy, when everything he has felt flows together into one great affirmation—his love, his search for the mother, the springtime landscape and flowers, past and present, joy and pain. It is the triumph of remembrance over death. The past is alive and present in the imagination. With this joyous feeling Aube rides to face whatever will come:

> Eine der Primeln aber war hier noch liegengeblieben. Als die Kompanie um die Dorfecke bog, stieg Aube ab und griff sie sich. Das also ist sie! dachte er und empfand in diesem Augenblick, dass sein Leben im Begriff sei, sich zu vervielfältigen, sich zu dehnen. Er küsste die liebe Blume, sie war ein wenig schmutzig, sie roch nach dem alten Frühling der Welt.—"O Gott," flüsterte er, "lass mich beten!"—Dann, den Fuss bereits im Steigbügel: "Du bist ganz nahe in Zeit und Gegenwart!"—Mit einem heissen Schaudern, in dem Glück und Schmerz sich mischten, stieg er in den Sattel und ritt langsam, die Blume, die Blume in der Hand, dem jungen Soldaten nach. . . (126)

Süskind's second contribution—"Beginn einer Liebe"

(March 1930, I, 370–89)—shows development in a number of ways from "Raymund." The hero—at least in a love relationship—is a decisive person. Süskind's choice of verbs in the introductory paragraph formulates this difference:

> Als er sie zum erstenmal *sah*, *war* alles schon *entschieden*. Er *erlaubte sich* später manchmal an dieses erste Zusammentreffen *zurückzudenken*, und dann *musste* er *erkennen*, dass ja alles in ihrem ersten Anblick *enthalten war*, alles, wie es später *kam*, ihn *verwirrte* und *sich* dennoch *auflöste* Das *machte* ihn *froh*, denn er *merkte*, er hatte *sich nicht getäuscht*. (370) (Italics mine.)

They are verbs of understanding, of planning, control, will, calculation. The hero's thought and decisions are definitive. He is not, as Raymund was, a passive bewildered object, nor does he seem at a loss for explanations. He makes a conscious decision, for example, to fall in love and calls it "Liebe auf den ersten—nein, nicht Blick, sondern auf den ersten Entschluss." (371) The contradictions between the individual and society do not play a role, nor does life in its multiplicity of practical demands noticeably intrude. The story is entirely an interior happening. In fact, it is limited to one aspect of human relations—romantic love. The hero is referred to throughout the story only as "der Liebende." We learn almost nothing about his life beyond his preoccupation with the twenty-year-old girl who is his love object. The story is an attempt to articulate the inner lives of those two people (in particular, the man) as they relate to each other. Both are unusually observant, analytical, and self-conscious types.

This psychogram of love and the lovers does not always succeed. It is predicated on the translatability of emotions and impressions into logical terms and therefore is not always convincing. The minute examination of feelings and interpersonal relations is conducted in the third person which permits a certain ironic distance, but at the same time creates an air of artificiality, an impression of the characters as elegant mannequins. An all-knowing narrator intrudes too self-consciously and without ample justification. These along with more successful ironic devices, such as several uses of paradox, serve to prevent the pervasive romanticism of the story from deteriorating into sentimentality. The story is replete with positive value-charged terms such as "Güte," "Seele," "Geist," "Anmut," "Schönheit," "Gefühl," "Teilnahme," "Glück," "Harmonie," and above all "Liebe" (love as entity and process)—which represent the true focus of the narrative. Lines such as the following, despite the concluding gently ironic qualifier, are evidently meant to be sensitive and serious statements on love:

> Recht wirre Gedanken bedrängten ihn: dass es zweierlei Liebe gebe, eine, die sagt: ich liebe dich—aber die kann alt werden und Runzeln bekommen. Und eine andere, die sagt: ich habe eine grosse Liebe für dich, ich kann gar nicht anders als dir nachgehen, denn du bist eine Brücke, die führt von einem Punkt in mir zum anderen. Eine aufmerksame Liebe habe ich für dich, so als wärst du ein Kind in meinem Haus, nein, eine Frucht meines Leibes—Dies klang ihm zu katholisch, und er stellt das Denken ab, wie er's heimlich vermochte, wenn etwas nämlich zu schön wurde in ihm, so wie man als Kind den besten Bissen beiseite legt. (379–80)

"Der Liebende" experiences moments of "pure love," as he studies his love's hand during a palm-reading game, but the commentary after this experience contains one of the paradoxes which the author likes to use as an ironic device: "Während der Liebende dies alles erlebte (freilich nicht so romantisch, wie es in Worten aussieht, sondern mit der Sachlichkeit des Gefühls), . . ." (383) Although qualified by irony, this statement sounds like a holdover from the antirational attitudes of earlier stories (Kayser, Zweig, Schaeffer), i.e., feelings are more "objective" than the written word. Irony and paradox create a tension in the story between traditional and romantic values, and the attempt to maintain a certain skepticism.

In the traditional and romantic vein is the treatment of the young woman protagonist. She is placed by the hero on a pedestal in an almost medieval manner, although she is an emotionally sturdy modern girl whose qualities are captured by such terms as "Selbstschutz," "gesund," "Ruhe," "Wohlbefinden," "Gelassenheit." The portrait of her in the eyes of the hero, however, is reminiscent of the mysterious and bewildering qualities with which Raymund endowed women.[21] Listening to a conversation, she is observed from a distance by "der Liebende":

> Es hatte nämlich den Anschein, als lausche sie auf etwas Höheres, auf einen unhörbaren Orgelpunkt aller ringsum geäusserten Ansichten. Was im einzelnen vorgebracht wurde, sah man, verstand sie nicht alles, aber was eigentlich damit gemeint war, was noch um eine Stufe höher und klingender und richtiger war, dafür war sie bereit, dessen Blume sah sie schon und dessen Harmonie hörte sie. Was die Männer sagten, war auf dem Wege dazu und sie begleitete es mit dem leisen Spott ihres lächelnden Gesichts. (379)

The female is a special creature with higher intuitive powers. The hero thinks on two occasions of himself (and once of another man as well) as knights or knightly in their attitudes toward their respective women friends: "Er hatte etwas vom Ritter, der durch die Lande zieht, in den Farben seiner Dame, selbst in diesem Jahrhundert." (381) There is a contradiction between these old-fashioned, romantic views and the independent, self-reliant qualities of the women characters in the Süskind stories.

The young women typically lack a well-developed conscience:

> Manchmal, wenn ihr Bitte oder Vorwurf dringlich ins Gesicht schrie, machte sie sich ein Gewissen aus ihrer Ruhe. Aber selbst das dauerte nicht lang, weil Gewissen und Wohlbefinden bei ihr in einer natürlichen und unschuldigen Nachbarschaft lagen. Irgendwie muss das in ihren Zügen zu lesen gewesen sein, denn man umgab sie, selbst wo sie enttäuscht hatte, noch mit Hochachtung, mehr als sie grob gesehen verdiente. (375)

---

[21] Cf. also Süskind on Joseph Conrad, above pp. 76–77.

We see here a series of stereotypes of the woman—strange, desirable creatures who function on a more instinctive level than men and do not share men's logic or moral codes.

Like Raymund, "der Liebende" is receptive to nature. For both heroes, landscapes are fraught with meaning for human beings. It is a traditionally romantic view—that of nature and man in consonance:

> Unterm Dache der Nacht sah er Strassen sich hinschwingen, Sterne sich senken, Büsche die Häupter neigen, und indem die Natur so auf ihn zuströmte, war nur dies gemeint: es gibt Bedeutung genug in der Welt, in jedem Augenblick und allein schon in deinem Schritt und Herzschlag. Also verlass dich auf deinen Schritt und sieh zu, dass dein Herz schlägt. (379)

The comforting message is that life has meaning; life is worth living.

The feeling of oneness with the universe is finally achieved by "der Liebende," as it was by Raymund, in an epiphany which occurs as the consequence of profound disappointment. "Der Liebende" and his loved one attend a costume ball. The girl had already decided, however, that she would rather spend the evening with an old flame who has turned up unexpectedly, and she deserts "der Liebende." He remains at the ball alone, melancholy, dazed, when toward three in the morning he is overcome by an extraordinary sense of metamorphosis: ". . . ihm wuchs eine andere Haut, . . .—er hatte noch nie im Leben so unvorbereitet, so eiskalt das Gefühl gehabt: ich werde ein neuer Mensch. . . . Sein Körper übernahm das Kommando über ihn." (388) He quickly calls a cab and on the way home is overcome by a fit of uncontrollable sobbing which leaves him drained and exhausted. Never before had he experienced such a breakdown and he resists it as best he can, but without success. As the mercy of his pained and weakened body, he collapses and cries himself to sleep. He awakens a transformed person and greets the new day as a miracle. Leaving the area by train, he observes from the window an idyllic rural scene:

> Auf den Feldern, die schwarz aufgebrochen waren, lagen da und dort Gaben von Kunstdünger wie dünner Reif. Pferde waren an Pflüge gespannt, der Zug rollte melodisch, die Sonne sprühte in einem goldenen Perlglanz durch die befrosteten Fenster und weckte steigenden Rauch am Horizont. Alles stimmte zusammen, alles war gesund, alles war beschäftigt zu seinem Teil. Der Liebende, von der Fahrt sanft geschaukelt, stand am Fenster, und indem er, eingewebt in die Landschaft und ihre Zusammenhänge, das Bild der Geliebten herbeidachte, füllte ihn Zuversicht und der Stolz, der manchmal unsere Stirnen zeichnet und uns mehr verbindet als Liebschaft und Wohlgefallen, mehr als Leidenschaft, der Stolz, ein wenig der Zeit zu trotzen und immer noch dabei zu sein, heute noch und morgen und noch lang. (389)

The vision, like Raymund's, is of harmony. Each element plays its appointed role in consonance with others as part of a healthy order. The hero and his vision of his loved one are part of this stream of life. The new insight which he has achieved is expressed by confidence and pride in the mere fact of being alive, of continuing, despite setbacks, to share the communion of existence.

Both the self-imposed limitations of the subject and the nature of the concluding vision smack of escapism.[22] "Der Liebende's" obsession is a romantic and a private one, and it is resolved in a private and romantic vision. The contradiction is as striking as in "Raymund" between the style, character types, and the artificial, almost "völkisch" conclusion—a picture of the fecund earth and each element of life healthy, industrious and engaged in harmonious cooperation with the others. Beyond its ideological implications, the peaceful idyll is a most incongruous scene for the year 1930.

The mood of the rest of the March 1930 issue is in keeping

---

[22] Siegfried Kracauer, one of the most reliable critics on the Weimar cultural scene, writes in the June 1930 *NR* (I, p. 863) in a review of "Der blaue Engel" about a trend (which the film represents) toward an avoidance mentality, a denial of reality, and attempt to escape from it.

with "Beginn einer Liebe." It is surrounded by travel essays on Switzerland, Amsterdam, and the U.S.A., by an installment of Hermann Hesse's novel in a medieval setting, *Narziss und Goldmund,* by Samuel Saenger's mere three and a half page commentary on the implications of the Hague Convention, several reviews, and a lead essay on Hugo Preuss and political theory (289–303) by Carl Schmitt.[23] This essay culminates in a plea on behalf of an ever-present higher entity called the "Geist der Nation," in the service of which the author would enlist those members of the bourgeois intelligentsia who will remain independent of and above the "daily polemics" of party politics.[24] It is the old story of avoidance of ambiguous reality by pointing to a sphere of supposed uncompromised and uncompromising truth. There is a note of nostalgia in Schmitt's reference to "dem heute kaum noch fassbaren Sicherheitsgefühl der Vorkriegszeit." (290)

The distance between Schaeffer's "Das Gitter" in March 1922 and Süskind's "Beginn einer Liebe" in March 1930 marks a development in the affirmative category. Keeping in mind that it is not possible to establish a one-to-one correspondence, we are able nonetheless to determine that more or less in keeping with a modification in editor Rudolf Kayser's expressed outlook, a change took place in the tone of the stories.

---

[23] Schmitt was a prominent political theorist of the right. For his positions see Kurt Sontheimer, *Antidemokratisches Denken in der Weimarer Republik* (Munich: Nymphenburg, 1962), pp. 104 ff.

[24] "Es war den Ruf nach 'Überparteilichkeit,' der auch in der Weimarer Republik immer dann ertönte, wenn nationalistische Interessengruppen, die doch selbst durchaus nicht überparteilich waren, sich durch das natürliche demokratische Diskussions- und Kontrollbedürfnis bedroht fühlten." (Karl Dietrich Bracher, *Die Afflösung der Weimarer Republik* [5th ed.; Villingen/ Schwarzwald: Ring, 1971], p. 15.) Bracher's is a cogent and insightful comment on this phenomenon. *NR*'s own Samuel Saenger expressed the same idea in a pithy sentence in his April 1925 (I, 436–43) essay "Der Reichspräsident": "Das im politischen Leben immer verdächtige Wort der Überparteilichkeit gehört in das romantische Vokabularium unserer Dunkelmänner." (443)

Broadly speaking, and with a number of exceptions, the movement in the affirmative group has been away from anti-rationalism, away from the rhapsodic and the mystical, away from absolutes and from moralizing. The movement has been away from a dualistic and therefore reductionist world view, from the categorizing of experience and phenomena into dichotomies such as intellect/soul, science/life, reason/nature and so on that was so prominent in the early stories and in Kayser's thinking, and toward an integrated and therefore more complex perspective. The changes also have a political component which is evident early on in the embrace of a kind of anti-rationalism that is an integral part of the idealism represented here and is fundamentally anti-progressive and anti-democratic in tendency. This aspect—with several exceptions—fades in the later years in conjunction, I believe, with the changes in Kayser's thinking. With many qualifications the affirmative category can be said, in these respects, to reflect in microcosm developments in the *NR* stories overall during the years under investigation.

Certain key themes and stylistic devices serve as means to arrive at a story's basic posture. The positive transformation and epiphany is both a theme and structural device which is intrinsic to the category. Its variation catalogues changes through the years. The same is true for the portrayal of nature. Both theme-devices have an ideological component which is relatively uniform throughout the affirmative category: both provide alternatives in a world which is otherwise unacceptable or difficult to accept.[25] The individual's relationship to

---

[25] This point is made about the role of nature by Wolfgang Wendler, "Die Einschätzung der Gegenwart im deutschen Zeitroman," in *Die deutsche Literatur in der Weimarer Republik*, ed. by Wolfgang Rothe (Stuttgart: Reclam, 1974), p. 171: "Ein Halt in der widerwärtigen Zeit wird nach altem Muster in Gedanken an das Ewige der Natur gesucht. Das relativiert die bedrohliche Gegenwart und macht es zugleich möglich, dem Leben trotz allem zuzustimmen."

nature is often the vehicle for his epiphany. The portrayal of women in a story can also be an important indicator of its standpoint. The portrayal of the hero is the touchstone in every story. From Schaeffer's artist Bruno to Süskind's "der Liebende" the heroes are (with several exceptions) modern in the sense that they are non-heroic. The differences between them account for development within the affirmative category. What they share in common—the hero's capacity to undergo a positive transformation—accounts for their stories' belonging to the affirmative category. In general the heroes (and heroines) play a passive role in this process. The transformation happens to them, although they may ready themselves in certain ways, i.e., develop a receptive consciousness. The credo of the stories is individualism. Concentrating as they do on the psychology of the individual and introspection, many of the stories are indifferent to social problems. Most take an implied elitism for granted. The central concern is an individual's development—not any individual, but the exceptional individual in the positive sense. All together the affirmative represents almost a cult of the exceptional person. The significance of this individual's fate is emphasized and by implication the ultimate value is the maintenance of his uniqueness. In later categories this will no longer be true.

One variation is the paean to the collective which occurs at the conclusion of the two stories by Süskind. They illustrate—more than others in this category—the dialectic of the era because they contain within themselves a fundamental tension. In style and tone they are very much bound to the modern twenties. But the heroes stand apart. When their moment of revelation arrives it gives them insight into an entirely different world—a world of conservative traditions, of the folkish-collective, and the mystique of the soil—as antirational and committed to a rhapsodic and amorphous ideal of "life" as the earliest stories, and harboring the seeds of reaction.

What is uniform to all affirmative stories and distinguishes them from the stories in all other categories is their forward momentum. As in a *Bildungsroman* the hero progresses toward a positive resolution. Therefore a certain hopefulness and faith in the possibilities of the individual are intrinsic to the affirmative category. By its very nature, it requires of all stories an underlying idealism. Consequently the affirmative category has closer ties than do subsequent categories to tradition and to the optimism of a bygone era.

The chronological distribution of affirmative stories is noteworthy.[26] They are more heavily clustered in the earlier years. It is significant that affirmative stories appear at the very beginning of our time period but not at the end. There are none at all between March 1930 and March 1933. By contrast the negative category does not begin to appear until the end of 1923, tends to cluster later than the affirmative, and extends more than two and a half years (to December 1932) beyond the affirmative. Comparing the two distributions we can begin to ascertain a shifting of emphasis which will become marked with the fifth and final category—the nihilistic.

---

[26] See introductory chart, p. 18.

Chapter III

Stories in the Negative Category: The Early Phase 1923–29

The negative sensibility is the reverse of the affirmative. That is to say that the stories in this category presume the same values and ideals as the affirmative stories, only the negative ones find their resolution in defeat or destruction or refutation of those values and ideals. Inevitably they are tales of disappointment, disillusionment, hopelessness, bitterness or despair. Sometimes the main character experiences a reverse epiphany, i.e., his moment of insight brings a negative and unhappy insight. In order for these negative processes to take place their contraries must be presented or at least lurk in the background as silent presuppositions. For there to be disillusionment there must have been illusions, for ideals and values to be refuted they must have existed in the first place, where there is disappointment there must have been hope. The negative is the other face of the affirmative. They both rest on the same premises, but with a different outcome.

A concomitant of the negative posture is increased social criticism. In the first four stories in particular attention is directed toward social injustice, greed, hardship and exploitation. This is true also of the Heuser, Ulitz, and Regler stories, and to some extent of the Kesten and Schaeffer stories. The remaining stories confine themselves more to the private sphere.

Jakob Wassermann's "Das Gold von Caxamalca" appeared in November (II, 981–99) and December (II, 1100–18) of 1923. The narrator is a former soldier with Pizarro's army who thirteen years after the conquest of the Incan empire became a monk and wrote this chronicle of the conquest. Like a later story in the negative category—Schmidtbonn's "Zwei Indianer" (February 1926)—and unlike any story in the affirmative group, Wassermann's is a strong condemnation of European civilization. The Spanish invaders, brutal and treacherous, driven by all-corrupting, insatiable greed, savagely destroy a higher civilization. Their religion is a sham, invoked only to justify criminal behavior. Incan life is portrayed as idyllic, fostering all those virtues which the Europeans conspicuously lack. The narrator, even while a participant, senses the underlying clash of cultures and is deeply disturbed. Only years later does he realize its full import.

The style (up to the concluding section) strives for the feeling of simplicity which would be expected from a translation of the writings of an untutored monk. In keeping with the spirit of a number of stories in 1923 (see above, Ch. I) there is an aura of mysticism. The narrator, who was more humane, more thoughtful than the typical soldier in Pizarro's army, began to identify with the captured, doomed Incan emperor: "Dann drang meine Seele mit sonderbarer Gewalt in die seine, so dass ich es wie einen Fluch fühlte und alsbald wie eine höhere Stimme und wie etwas, das Gewissenslast und Trauer verursacht." (1101)

After years of contemplating inhumanity, death, and destruction of an entire land, the narrator has arrived at a posture of humility in the face of the general and inexplicable injustice on earth. The insight which he developed in a kind of slow epiphany led him to total disillusionment and black despair for the world:

Ich sah den Tod in jeglicher Gestalt, den er auf Erden annimmt; ich sah die Freunde hingehn und die Führer fallen und die Völker enden und die Unbeständigkeit jedes Glücks und den Betrug jeder Hoffnung und schmeckte den bittern Bodensatz in jedem Trunk und das heimliche Gift in jeder Speise und litt an der Zwietracht der Gemeinden und an der Torheit selbst der Erleuchteten und an dem grausam gleichmütigen Rollen der Zeit über diese schmerzbeladene Erde und erkannte die Nichtigkeit alles Habens und die Ewigkeit alles Seins, und mich erfüllte das Verlangen nach einem besseren Stern, den die herrliche Sonne reiner durchglüht und edler beseelt hat.

Dieser, auf dem ich leben, ist vielleicht von Gott verstossen. (1118)

In keeping, again, with the approach which the early affirmative stories have led us to expect (and with an approximation of the thoughts of a sixteenth-century monk), the lament is abstracted to a universal level—a diffuse and helpless *Weltschmerz*—rather than being applied to the actual social forces which were to blame.

Other contributions to the December 1923 issue also reflect a bleak mood (cf. Kayser's "An die Leser" of March 1923, above p. 22): Saenger's discouraging political analysis in the lead essay "Perspektiven" (1057–62), three poems by Oskar Loerke called "Deutsche Zeit" (1119–22), and the only contribution by Brecht during our time period, "Ballade über die Anstrengung" (1131–32), a paean to drink and the dissolute life, preaching cynicism and reeking of disillusioned romanticism.

Of the entries in the negative category, Arthur Schnitzler's "Fräulein Else" (October 1924, II, 993–1051) is the most impressive. It is a merciless exposé of contemporary society. Most remarkable is the totally convincing point of view: the consciousness of a nineteen-year-old girl. The story of Else is familiar. Despite a veneer of privilege she is trapped on all sides—between demands of family loyalty and fear of exploitation, between economic necessity and dread of humiliation. She is thrust into a situation which tests her beyond her years with a challenge to her integrity as a human being. Developments reveal that Else is completely alone—either resented, exploited or misunderstood on all sides and without anyone who cares unselfishly about her. Even as she is presumably dying by suicide, the people in her environment remain self-centered. In a setting as corrupt and scheming as the society portrayed by Schnitzler, a creature as genuine as Else must be destroyed.

Else's situation exemplifies the pseudo-liberation with which young women were deceived. They were permitted a certain superficial erotic leeway—freedom to flirt, for example, and to engage in vigorous public sports such as tennis—and thereby to have the appearance of independence. But the pseudo-emancipation is not sufficient to conceal Else's true helplessness, psychic as well as social, when the fragile supports of her social position collapse. More than any other, this story reveals woman's actual situation in the contemporary upper middle class society. She is victimized by a whole series of demands, some of which are in conflict with others. She is tied and bound in a way a man is not by the familiar lack of education and training or any foundation for being independent, and above all by the concomitant and resultant fact that as an individual she is taken seriously (and finds her economic potential) only as a prospective sex object (normally on the marriage market).

Else's psyche is that of the teenage young woman, with the inevitable emotional turmoil which that time of life implies. Schnitzler justifies her peculiar vulnerability to emotional stress at the time of the events of the story by connecting it to the symptoms of "unwohl sein" which Else feels. At ay rate, Else becomes distraught to the point of committing suicide when she cannot reconcile herself to acquiescing in the pervasive corruption.

From the exceptional individual in the positive sense who dominates the affirmative category we turn in the negative category to the pejorative meaning of the term "exceptional." The protagonists of the negative stories are misfits. The *ne plus ultra* misfit is the title character of Leonhard Frank's "Der Beamte" (May 1925, I, 492–504). "Der Magistratsbeamte" Höfer, a Spitzweg-like character, devotes his life to the minutiae of an unvarying, drab and soulless daily routine, believing that by being punctual in all things he is doing his part to uphold order and restore the *Reich* to its pre-World War I condition. Constantly trying to make ends meet on his meager salary, he blames not the inadequate salary, not inflation, but himself for his inability to do so. His is the epitome of the subaltern mentality. One day his alarm does not go off and he does not arrive at the office in time, loses his job, becomes derelict, falls into the shabby company of the destitute and hungry which he had always studiously avoided. His downfall occurs that abruptly, showing how fragile the supports of existence at the lower end of the social ladder were during the great inflation.[1] Once Höfer has sunk to the prevailing level of misery his end is the not uncommon one for the negative category—suicide.

Although the portrait of Höfer is certainly a caricature—depending upon that fine balance of exaggeration and truth which is evident in Spitzweg's paintings of eccentrics—it

---

[1] The sudden breaking out of the humdrum mold and descent into the lower depths of society was a common theme. Georg Kaiser's expressionist play *Von Morgens bis Mitternachts* was an example. Walter Laqueur, in *Weimar: A Cultural History 1918–1933* (New York: G. P. Putnam's Sons, 1974), p. 240, writes about the films of the twenties: "Perhaps most characteristic for the film of the 1920s was the 'street theme': Karl Gruene's 'Die Strasse,' produced in 1923, had paved the way and the topic was to preoccupy German filmmakers one way or another for a whole decade. In Gruene's film the street is a place full of temptation and danger. Following a sudden impulse, a lowly office-worker breaks away from conventional life. He enters a night club, follows a prostitute [as Höfer did also] and spends the night with her. The next morning he returns home, having realized that 'the street' is a cruel place, that it spells ruin and destruction, . . ." The difference is that Höfer did not choose his fate and had no home to return to.

nevertheless makes a serious comment on the isolation from reality which was characteristic of the civil servant caste. Höfer was an anachronism. The isolation in which he lived and the fiction of an orderly world could no longer be maintained in the post-World War I collapse. Frank's story is an indictment of prevailing conditions, although in the story the origins of social injustice remain as mysterious and as much a matter of inexplicable fate as they are in the mind of the protagonist. The story is also an indirect indictment of conditions prior to the collapse. To all intents and purposes Höfer fit very nicely into the pre-war world. At least he went unnoticed and smoothly integrated into a well-functioning order—a testimony to the psychic disorder of that apparent order.

"Der Beamte" is one of only a few negative stories in which nature makes a significant statement. Like "Das Gold von Caxamalca" "Der Beamte" concludes with a description of horrors—the most abject suffering, brutality and death everywhere. In the face of this suffering nature is indifferent, not involved in providing support and comfort as it does in the affirmative stories:

> Eines Tages bei frühester Morgendämmerung, unter der die Felder noch schwarzgrün lagen, taumelte er [Höfer] hungerschwach aus dem Stall und liess sich, Augen geschlossen, den Abhang hinabgleiten in den Fluss, der lautlos seinen grossen Bogen zog.
>
> Das Land stieg mit grandioser Selbstverständlichkeit in das stärker werdende Licht empor. Dicht über dem Wasser standen kleine, flockige Nebelwölkchen, von der Morgenröte durchleuchtet. Mit wunderbarer Gebärde deutete der erste Sonnenstrahl über das dampfende Land. (504)

At the end of Süskind's "Beginn einer Liebe" the hero observes the fertile fields in a harmonious landscape which corresponds with his own inner peace. Here by contrast there is no romance of the soil and no connection with the protagonist who is sliding toward his death. The river continues its silent flow without the slightest turbulence, not even a splash to indicate his end. The land is beautiful, majestic, remote from the fate of a human being.

The year 1926 was conspicuous for negative stories in the *NR*. Of five stories that year four were negative and one—the Brod story—affirmative. "Die zwei Indianer" (February 1926, I, 138–50) is another sentimental Schmidtbonn tale with strained plot and undistinguished style. It is related to the Wassermann story, being an account of man's inhumanity to man in the context of an encounter between mutually alien cultures. This time the victims are not an entire people but two hapless (American) Indian waifs who drift ashore on the North Sea coast in pre-Christian times. They become exploited and misunderstood victims of loutish ignorance and brutality. Finally after many trials they land in the hands of the Roman governor of Gaul, a representative of a higher civilization, whose care of them is kindly and tolerant. But the two innocent young men, who had survived the most terrible deprivations, succumb in the midst of plenty. The reason is that their solidarity and love for each other is pierced by the attention of the governor's beautiful wife for one Indian and not the other. Love accomplishes what torture could not. It divides them and wounds their souls. One dies of a broken heart when the governor's wife leaves on an extended journey; the second dies of a broken heart over the grave of the first. "Die zwei Indianer" is characteristic of this issue's emphasis upon understanding other cultures. In the lead essay, "Rasse und Stämme im deutschen Volkstum" (113–38), Willy Hellpach shows that the conventional use of the term "race" to draw distinctions between peoples has no basis in fact. There is also a travel essay on India by Arthur Holitscher, entitled "Madura, das dunkle" (181–202).

The March 1926 issue contains the story "Marengo oder das Leben ohne Illusionen" (I, 233–55) by Ernst Weiss. According to its title it would appear to be the negative story *par excellence*, and it does indeed present some of the central themes of the category—loneliness, isolation, the inability of people to break through barriers to communication and mutual understanding. However the resolution is an enigmatic one and atypical of the category.

An essay of considerable significance to this investigation also appears in this issue. It is Klaus Mann's "Fragment von der Jugend." (285–95) The author begins by remarking on the mood among many Europeans of impending crisis, the sense that European culture is on the verge of collapse to be replaced by radically new values. Everything is being called into queston, but above all art. Young people in general seem more interested in boxing and auto races. The young generation of writers wonders what the point is of trying to create; what they can say that is new; and who will read their books. (Mann does not call this the conflict between "Geist" and materialism as Kayser does but basically it is the same thing.)

The young generation does not know where to turn for leadership or advice. On every street corner would-be prophets offer this or that ideology, none of which is convincing. The gap between the young and the generation of their parents was made unbridgeable by the World War. Parents and children are strangers to one another. Many young people blame their parents' generation for having created the uncertain world in which the young find themselves. They want to break with the past but do not know in which direction they ought to go. Their symbol is the homeless foundling "Kaspar Hauser" who had no known family, no ties, no roots, no prescribed direction in life. But in the rootlessness of the young generation lies also the freedom to choose new directions and therefore hope for the future.

When he was younger, Klaus Mann's ideal as a writer was the work of Herman Bang[2] because of the union he found

---

[2] The rediscovery of the works of Herman Bang by the young generation of writers and his profound influence on them is discussed by Peter de Mendelssohn in *S. Fischer und sein Verlag* (Frankfurt am Main: S. Fischer, 1970), pp. 1090 f.

there between love of the human body and love of life. In this concept Mann finds guidance and hope:

> So wollen auch wir das Leben lieben, wie wir den Körper lieben müsen: mit solcher Hingabe und mit solchem Verzicht.
>
> Wir gehen, ohne zu wissen wohin, wurzellos und allen Möglichkeiten offen. Aber da wir an das Geheimnis des Leibes wieder mit solcher Inbrunst glauben, kann unser Weg nie ganz ein Irrweg sein.
>
> Wir haben beinahe nichts, beinah' kein Wissen. Aber neu ist in uns allen erwacht der Glaube an dieses Mysterium, das zwischen Tod und Leben das Bindeglied ist, dunkler Klang aus der Unschuld des Jenseits, grosses Licht in der Wirrnis des Lebens. (292)

His feelings are understandable as the reaction of a humanitarian to the waste of life during wartime. But the supports of Mann's affirmative conclusions seem poignantly fragile in the face of the grave psycho-social problems which he describes.

From this concept, or faith as he calls it, Mann extrapolates the characteristics of a literature which his (young) generation might produce. It must treat the dynamics of life, take place perhaps in foreign lands which have something to teach the European:

> Vielleicht müssten sie [die Bücher] viel auf Reisen spielen, in den fernen Ländern, nach denen unsere Sehnsucht geht und deren Weisheit, die uralte und die allerneueste, wir in uns aufnehmen wollen. In Afrika, dessen braune Wüstenunermesslichkeit uns heute mehr verlockt als Italien, dessen Schönheit uns wie ein ausgeträumter Traum erscheint, in Indien und China, in Amerika dann—(294)

Perhaps these feelings are partly a response to the nationalistic insularity of Germany during the war. Italy, which the young and adventurous reject as tame and outworn, had been the exotic goal of earlier generations and continues to be the romanticized setting of several authors represented by less progressive stories in our time period (stories by Flake, Kolb, and Kayser among the affirmatives; by Reisiger, Strauss, and Lübbe among the negatives), preoccupied as they so often were with the contrasts between north and south (above all, Ponten's "Die Frau im Süden" and Schaeffer's "Das Gitter"). Despite these differences, the reaction seems to be similar—to seek, whether it be in Italy or a more exotic place, something not provided at home.

Klaus Mann and his fellows are committed to works which do not preach to the reader: "Ohne Lehre müssten diese Bücher sein, ohne Anklage, ohne Moral, fast ohne Frage." (294) (Obviously, there is a certain naiveté to Mann's statement if taken literally, since some kind of moral or ethical standpoint is always implicit even in non-didactic, non-accusatory works.) This is, perhaps, a representative modern goal, at least for the young intellectuals of Klaus Mann's type, i.e., those not prey to ideas from the right. It is a goal which separates him from the type of the Wassermann and Schmidtbonn stories in the negative category and from the earlier affirmative stories of the Schaeffer, Zweig and Hirschfeld type. The goal is most closely realized among *NR* stories in our last category, the nihilistic.

By contrast, the qualities which Klaus Mann finds most admirable in young writers—he mentions Klabund and Brecht—and most indicative of future directions are qualities which sound reminiscent of an earlier era, sound in fact like Expressionism:

> Und was das Beste und Zukünftigste in neuer deutscher Dichtung ist—die Lieder Klabunds etwa oder die schönsten, gleichsam winddurchwehten Stellen in Bert Brechts Theaterstücken—ist eben darum gut, darum zukünftig, weil es wieder glaübig ist, ohne Gedanke, ohne den kleinen Zweifel, nahe dem Rauschen—(294)

His emotional, almost ecstatic vocabulary and nebulous concluding vision sound as if they could have been lifted from Zweig's "Phantastische Nacht":

> Aber ob es gestaltet wird oder nicht—so wollen wir vor dem Leben stehn: fromm vor seiner Buntheit, gläubig an den göttlich-geheimen Sinn seiner Bewegungen und Zufälle, weinend vor

> seiner Schwermut, täglich aufs neue erschauernd vor seinem Rätsel.
>
> So wollen wir immer im Leben stehn. (295)

The remarkable aspect of this essay is the unresolved contradiction which relates it to Ernst Weiss' story "Marengo" as well as to the Janus-faced W. E. Süskind story "Raymund." To reduce it to the contradiction rational/irrational would be an oversimplification. In "Raymund," which appeared a year later than Klaus Mann's essay, the contrast was between the sober realism, ironic almost cynical tone of a portrait of the twenties and a utopian idealism based on a sense of universally shared life. The comparable contradiction in the Mann essay is between sober analysis of the circumstances and philosophical predicament of a generation, cool proscriptions against moralizing in literature and mystical, rhapsodic language such as "göttlich-geheim" in praise of life. Klaus Mann's essay, in fact, could amost be a script for "Raymund."

The Klaus Mann essay shows us a young writer who feels acutely the existential dilemma of his generation which sets it apart from its forefathers and seems to him to be unique. Nevertheless he turns to the generation of the fathers for an answer. It is startling to find again that same vague organicism expressed in the same terms, that same amorphous idea called "life" in the thinking of one who believes himself to be grappling with contemporary existential issues. Hamsun, Klaus Mann says, is the greatest living writer:

> Wenn unsere Bücher dem Rauschen allen Lebens einmal so nahe sein dürfen, wie die seinen, so übervoll von des Lebens Schönheit, so voll des Lebens Trauer und von seiner erhabenen, unruhigen, wunderbaren Sinnlosigkeit: dann freut euch auf unsere Bücher, dann werden sie herrlich sein. (294)

There is a surprising familiarity to these remarks. They are the last one would expect to hear from a young man who wants to move forward to new means of coping with new conditions. As vague as they are, such thoughts are impossible, of course, as a prescription for literature. The essay can be taken seriously, however, as further evidence for the dialectic of an era. The antitheses in the essay are in a sense also the antitheses of the times during which it appeared—between opposing mentalities (in groups of people) as well as between contraries within the minds of individuals. For our purposes it represents a middle stage (not with chronological precision) in outlook between Kayser's 1922 essay and one by Herbert Schlüter (discussed below, p. 238) in the February 1928 *NR*.

"Marengo oder das Leben ohne Illusionen" also deals with the entity "life." The story proposes the desirability as well as the dificulty of making a wholehearted commitment to it. In this case the obstacle is the habit of single-minded devotion to success in business. Its open-endedness puts "Marengo" at the opposite pole from, say, Zweig's, in which the hero is successfully transformed (by unexplainable forces and irresistible emotions) into one committed to "life." The Weiss story also contrasts with "Raymund" where again a mystical transformation occurs. For Weiss's protagonist the matter is far more problematic. His Felix is important because, along with Raymund, he is one of the only several distinctly modern protagonists in the first two categories. This characteristic is pinpointed in the opening paragraph:

> Felix R. war ein Mensch, den man aus einer Menge gleichaltriger Leute seiner Klasse schwer herausgefunden hätte. Mittel die Gestalt, mittel der Geist, mittel das Herz. Und doch verbrachte dieser Mensch sein Dasein nicht wie in einem Zuge gleichartiger Heringsbrut, in trübem Schuppengewimmel an seines gleichen angeschmiegt, sondern er lebte ein fast ganz vereinsamtes Leben, das von dem der meisten sehr verschieden war. Man nannte ihn in der Schule Marengo, weil er nach dem frühen Tode seiner Eltern stets schwarze, grau melierte Stoffe trug, die "Marengo" hiessen. Schwarz, weil er Trauer trug. Grau, weil er selbst doch weiterlebte. Niemand rief ihn unter seinem Namen Felix, und so nannte er sich selbst, wenn er an sich dachte, Marengo. Er war weibisch von Herzen, männlich von Gehirn. Leidend mehr als tätig im Gefühl, ohne ein überragendes Ziel, ohne verzehrende Leidenschaften; abwartend, zu Wohlwollen eher geneigt als zu Hass und Neid. Er war der einzige Sohn eines Hauses, das es in Wirklichkeit nicht

> gab. Wäre ein braver Sohn gewesen, aber die Eltern starben ihm zu früh. Ein guter Gatte, denn es war ihm natürlich, treu zu sein. Aber wem? Er kam in keines Menschen Hände, und in seine Hände kam kein Mensch. Er war hungrig nach Illusionen und bereit, sich dem sehr fragwürdigen Trugschein einer Illusion zu folgen, aber sein männliches Gehirn liess keine Illusion zu. Sein Gehirn macht ihn praktisch, energisch, fleissig. Er war ein Mann der Mitte, aber nicht des Durchschnitts. Gewillt, mit sich zu rechnen, dem Notwendigen sich nicht zu versagen, Bilanz zu ziehen in jeder ruhigen Minute, gegen sich gerecht und gegen die andern billig zu sein. Er verlangte wenig von der Welt, sie verlangte nichts von ihm. (233)

The style is unfortunate—bland and unpromising—a list of qualities rather than illustration of their function, a description rather than portrayal of character. Several characteristics are familiar—passivity, aloneness, emotional deprivation, rootlessness, a certain colorlessness (indicated here in a literal sense). For such an individual, of course, the name Felix is ironic. The modern protagonist is an outsider but does not stand out (in contrast to the old-style exceptional hero in a story like Bruno Frank's "Der Magier" and other affirmative stories). The world, in which he may fit so well as to enjoy moderate professional success, pays no particular attention to him. He is marked by felt contradictions. A central one is the craving, blocked by natural skepticism, for the satisfactions which illusions can give. As in the case of "Raymund" and "Aube" the author uses the psychology of an emotionally deprived childhood to explain the adult, and as in "Raymund," to justify the adult's difficulty overcoming barriers to emotional communication with others.

The modern protagonist finds his only security in the functions of daily life which he can control (rather than in ideology, faith or dogma, idealism or global philosophizing). They are his only means of gaining purchase on an otherwise elusive existence: ". . . und da die mit der Regelmässigkeit einer astronomischen Uhr betriebene Arbeit für ihn die einzige Sicherheit in dem sonst für ihn unbegreiflichen Leben darstellte." (234)

In his thirty-second year of life, after uneventful years of business success, Felix becomes aware for the first time of discontent, a feeling of emptiness, the sense that he has not lived. The awareness comes in conjunction with looking at himself in a mirror (a symbol of awakened self-consciousness, as in "Aube") and remembering his mother's tenderness toward him during childhood (also reminiscent of "Aube"). The central experience which adds insight to awareness—the negative epiphany—occurs toward the middle rather than at the end of the story. Nature plays a crucial role. From the window of his room in an Alpine village where he is vacationing Felix has been watching a dramatic lightning storm with heavy rainfall when he goes to turn on a light in the bathroom and notices a wood louse on the wall. Felix observers it closely, examining its movements and wondering about its mysterious ways. The smallness of the insect, its limitations, its vulnerability, and lack of knowledge of a larger world, the inscrutability and apparent pointlessness of its behavior preoccupy Felix and become a symbol in his mind of the mystery of life. The insect reminds Felix of himself: "Auch sie lebte 'nach der Uhr,' freilich nach einer kleineren, noch dürftigeren als der seinigen, aber sie verfolgte ihre Bahn unbeirrbar; mutig durch Unwissenheit oder durch Gewissheit, niemand entschied es." (242)

After his return home Felix for the first time has occasion to notice the physical presence of his secretary, Margot. The inadvertent manner in which this occurs, stimulated suddenly by a previously unnoticed sensual impression, prefigures the scene in "Raymund" when Raymund first becomes aware of Fräulein Marion by way of taking notice of her hair; this couple too have never engaged in a conversation:

> Seine Sekretärin stand neben ihm, ein blühendes, hohes Geschöpf, stumm, denn sie sprach nie unaufgefordert zu ihm. War sie es, die nach Reseda und Champignons duftete, einen Duft, der ihm bekannt sein musste, da er Jahre schon Tag für Tag acht Stunden in der Nähe dieses jungen, blonden, üppigen, schnell

atmenden Geschöpfes verbracht hatte? Er sah sie überrascht an, sie erwiderte seinen Blick mit einem schwer zu deutenden Lächeln, sprach aber nichts, und auch er richtete nicht das Wort an sie. (244)

As in "Raymund" there is a physical response to one another but no further communication. In fact Margot never utters a word in Felix' presence and his remarks are seldom and perfunctory. As in "Raymund" the man and woman remain surface for one another. Margot herself remains as distant and unreal as Fräulein Marion and some of the other women characters in previous stories. She is no more than a caricature of a woman, a mannequin, at least as far as the protagonist relates to her. His attention is concentrated on physical details. Her eyebrows, for example, make a major impression; they seem "metallic" to Felix—the ultimate non-human adjective. The adjective he most frequently uses to describe her is the clichéd "üppig." But in this story, the preoccupation with surface is meant to signal a deeper problem (as opposed to the stereotypes of women in the Flake story, for example, which point no further than themselves). It is the inability of these two people to reach one another's being, to penetrate beyond the surface to the soul or even to the other's distinctive personality. Each remains isolated, enclosed in himself, incommunicado.

At first when they take a boat trip together surrounded by an evocatively beautiful landscape, Felix feels as if in the presence of Margot he has discovered life. The dreamy river and magical atmosphere of a sunny afternoon carry them both beyond a sense of time and without knowing what they are doing they make love in a grassy clearing on the river bank, showered by the rain which begins to fall. Instead of the expected consequence—the beginning of a deeper relationship between the two—exactly the opposite occurs. Margot is silent. Felix does not know what to say. To his own surprise he had been swept away, not by the other human being, but by the beauty of the river landscape and the summer day:

> Je näher die Natur ihm kam, desto fremder wurde ihm der Mensch. Mit seiner ganzen Existenz fühlte Marengo sich ausgelöscht. Konnte man sich näher kommen? Konnte man sich fremd sein? Er fand keine Worte, keine Liebkosungen. Was sollte er sprechen? Wovor warnen, was beteuern, wie sich nähern? (251)

In a rather too-obvious fashion the moral is brought home again when Felix (whom the narrative voice sometimes calls Felix, other times Marengo, according to his closeness or distance from "life" in a particular situation) finds a wood louse curled up in Margot's hat which he is holding as he searches for Margot, who has run away. The insect again brings to his mind a greater significance whose import is a comment on the human condition:

> Den Hut trug er noch in der Hand. Das Tierchen war verschwunden; man würde es ebensowenig begreifen, beglücken, verletzen, in seinem "Innern" treffen, wie das Tier in dem Baderaum des Hotels vor drei Tagen, das nichts begreifende und von niemandem begriffene Wesen auf der unfruchtbaren Wand im unbegriffenen Raum, im Gewitter unter dem unermesslichen Himmel. (252)

The universal inscrutability of existence is the most fundamental comment which the story presents. Meaning is as little apparent on the human as it is on the insect level. Its non-conclusion carries the story far away from the affirmative category and into the modern era.

Upon his return home (without Margot) Felix finds a decrepit old man on his doorstep—the same former wealthy businessman, now reprobate, who had come begging to Felix' factory some weeks before. Felix, on the spur of the moment and for no apparent reason, decides to take the man into his home and his life.

Felix looks out of the window and into the courtyard where two dogs are rolling around together playing in sexual excitement. The scene brings to his mind his encounter with Margot on the grass and he thinks that he will never see her again nor return to that peaceful spot. In the meantime a neighbor, annoyed by the noise of the dogs, pours hot water on the animals who cry, spring apart and flee to separate corners of the courtyard. The analogy to Felix and Margot in the rainstorm is too heavy-handed. The story would have been improved had it been freed of the more obvious analogies. This third association of life with the rainstorm, in conjunction with the importance of the river in Felix' attempt to embrace life, plus the dominance of his memories of his mother (which are reminiscent also of Proust), suggest Freudian symbolism—the waters as the waters of life in the womb. Perhaps Felix' quest, like Aube's, is for that which was lost when a mother died too early.

The tale closes with some equally unsubtle symbolism whereby Felix is reminded of fundamental possibilities in life by scraps of paper torn from the Bible and from Humboldt's "Cosmos." (The bits of paper were used as casters under plants by the housekeeper.) Felix, called "der sehr zärtlichkeitshungrige Sohn," (254) reminisces once again about his mother and reviews the alternatives for his future:

> Hatte er aber noch Kraft zu einer neuen Existenz? Die ewige Bewegung im Kosmos erfassen? Den Kosmos im Buche "Kosmos" sehen, erleben? Dem Evangelium aus der Fülle des Gefühls folgen in die geliebte, die schauerliche, die unbegreifliche Welt, die göttliche, die ruhende? Konnte man etwas Neues beginnen? Allein? Mit andern? Für andere? Sollte man die alte, die erste Existenz liquidieren? Verlieren, was man nie besass? (255)

The series of questions without answers is a device which the author uses frequently. They, like the insect symbol, make an existential comment—that life is open-ended, uncertain, inscrutable and possibly without meaning. There are no answers and no final resolutions. The language descriptive of life resembles closely the ecstatic language of Klaus Mann's essay—rhapsody on the one hand and unanswered questions on the other.

The protagonist does not make progress forward toward a positive resolution as in the case of the affirmative stories. In the case of Felix the outcome remains undecided. There is no doubt that affirmative values are presented. Felix seeks life through involvement with other people. He is moved by "Kosmos" and "Evangelium." But these values remain out of reach. (His attempt to get close to Margot fails; there also seems to be an unbridgeable gap between him and his aged housekeeper who is afraid of her employer and keeps out of his way.) In "Marengo" the author's devices tend to be repetitive and all too obvious, but as a consequence they provide a more easily decipherable illustration of an important and possibly representative sensibility of 1926.

Siegfried Trebitsch is author of the third of the 1926 negative stories. "Der Geheilte" appeared in the May issue (I, 489–516). It is the bizarre case history of an obsession. The story is followed in the same issue by Fritz Wittels' essay "Sigmund Freud. Zu seinem 70. Geburtstag am 6. Mai 1926." Their proximity might indicate that the Trebitsch story is meant to be related to Freud's theories. The fictional framework is a painter's first person documentation of his interior life, published by his foster son after the artist's death. The painter was victim of a life-long hysterical illness which manifested itself literally as a pain in the neck. The pain becomes the center of the sufferer's existence. he personifies it and eventually tries to kill it by shooting himself in the neck. He succeeds in ridding himself of the pain but soon it is replaced by extrasensory perception which turns out to be a curse because it reveals to him people's true thoughts and motives, including those of his foster son. The disillusionment and disappointment which this insight brings (he believes that the son has counted on his death for the sake of inheritance) are so great that the protagonist kills himself.

The story describes, in a stilted and ceremonious style, the ultimate in subjectivity and self-absorption. It is easily one of the two or three most tedious of all the stories during the Kayser years. Most relevant to our concerns are the remarks with which the foster son introduces the narrative. They constitute an explicit rejection of the dead painter and everything he stood for. The foster father was, according to the son, an "impotent dreamer." In contrast the son is a "kraftbewusster Kerl" (490) who came into the world with "Erfahrungen, mit einer illusionslosen Erkenntnis der Realität." (490) He attributes these differences to the difference between the prewar and postwar generations:

> Was uns getrennt hat, war der Aufstieg der neuen Generation, der ich angehöre und den er nicht bemerkt hat, war die ungeheure Kluft, die mein verruchtes Nachkriegsgeschlecht von der verweichlichten, spielerischen, selbsterzerstörerischen Rasse trennt, der mein Vater zugehört hat und deren Vertreter genau so tot sind wie er, ob sie nun noch unter uns wandeln oder gleich ihm unter dem tröstenden Rasen liegen. (490)

In crasser terms, it is the same comment made in "Raymund," but without the charitable tone and conciliatory conclusion. In the eyes of the young man a new consciousness, a world, separates the two generations. There is no allowance for possible points of contact or communication. The older generation was weak and decadent, unable to cope with the serious new challenges of life. The younger, by contrast, is resilient, practical and optimistic because totally disillusioned and looking nowhere for help or guidance but to its own resources for the task of rebuilding a destroyed world. Although here oversimplified and assuming an adolescent tone of aggressive intolerance, the sense of a new beginning in the midst of destruction is the familiar one from Klaus Mann's essay (although there applied primarily to literature)—hopeful confidence in the capacity of youth to deal with life without faith or dogma or ideology in a world where answers are neither provided nor sought. It strikes one as an attitude equally dependent on illusions to which the son thought only the older generation was prey—merely a new set of illusions.

Hans Reisiger's second story "Stehe auf und wandle" (August 1926, II, 127–55) includes a number of themes familiar from the affirmative category. It is set in Italy—that environment which stimulated so many German longings—flooded with warmth and light and sun. The contrast here too is provided by the northern origins of the protagonist, in this case a transplanted Scottish physician whose description of his cold, bleak, fogbound home make it sound like the epitome of all that "north" represents to the northern Europeans infected by Italy. But Reisiger presents Italian society with considerably more understanding and sophistication than do other authors. The story concerns the *unio mystica* between the Scottish physician and his patient, a fragile, ethereal young girl who lives in impoverished circumstances. His encounter with the invalid Beata (a name with portentous meaning), his care for her and the mystical bond between them have a profound effect upon the physician, who narrates the story of the relationship to an unnamed friend in a Roman tavern. It turns out that the health of the physician's soul depends upon his ability to heal Beata (who suffers from an unspecified ailment). Beata questions, however, whether it is not better for her eternal soul for her to remain as she is, confined to her room and her bed, where she is removed from the distractions of life and able to concentrate on her spiritual well-being. Dr. B. convinces her otherwise.

The epiphany which Dr. B. has experienced as a consequence of his spiritual union with the angelic invalid expresses itself as a union with nature and the phenomena of the universe:

> Als ich durch die Haustür wieder auf die Strasse trat, war das Abendgold erloschen und die Laternen blitzten in dem kalten, glasigen Nachtlicht der Dämmerung—'l'heure de la chauve souris', Fledermausstunde, wie die Franzosen es nennen—Stunde, die den Erdball in Nacht dreht—Stunde, in der die Empfindungen von uns ausstrahlen, wie eingesogenes Licht aus den Dingen, und in deren klarer Magie sich die Grenze zwischen Ich und Ihr zu lösen scheint. Die Wipfel der Bäume, die Dächer der Häuser, die Drähte in der Luft scheinen deutlicher entlang zu streifen am Weltraum in der Drehung der Erde, und es ist uns zumute, als wäre selbst das Strassengebraus einer Grosstadt nahe daran, sich in Musik zu verwandeln, gleich der eines singenden Kreisels. (139)

Finally, one day in early spring Dr. B. decides that it is time to take Beata on an extended excursion in the wheelchair he bought for her. The city is engulfed in brilliant sunlight which seems to impart a more vivid existence to everything visible. Here Reisiger's character provides an example of those misconceptions about women which we have encountered in other stories: "Ich weiss nicht, ob Südländer und ob zumal Frauen den Rausch der Sonne so empfinden können wie ein nördlich geborener Mann." (148) Dr. B. experiences the sunlight as a kind of intoxication that leads him to thoughts about the fragility of life on earth which depends upon an accidentally propitious distance from the life-giving star. He sees the threatening aspect of the sun in an Icarus image—inevitable destruction for the one who dares too much and flies too high. This is the second time the Icarus myth has appeared in the stories. The first was in Schaeffer's "Das Gitter" (above, p. 42). On both occasions it represents a cult of the exceptional individual. In both cases the Icarus myth applies to a love forbidden by social or moral taboos. The difference between the two (other than the spirituality of the love in the Reisiger story) which is responsible for their assignment to different categories is the fact that in the Reisiger story the impossible love is lost without compensation for the loss.

The sunlit world is too vivid, too stimulating for Beata. She gets up and walks a short distance, collapses into the arms of Dr. B. and is dead. She was too pure to survive in the material world. The ideal remains out of reach, an object of yearning but beyond the capacity of mortals to grasp and hold.

In the conclusion the pathos characteristic of Reisiger's style lapses into maudlinism. Dr. B. arrives at the end of his story. We know from an earlier reference that he is about to embark for Africa where he will dedicate his life to finding a cure for sleeping sickness:

> Er füllte sein Glas, goss es nochmals hinunter, stand auf, hielt es hoch, schrie: "Sierra Leone!" und schmiss es klirrend auf den Tisch.

> Dr. B. stand, sah mich unter zusammengezogenen schwarzen Brauen an und sagte scharf zwischen dünnen Lippen: "Es ist falsch, zu leiden." (155)

Dr. B. no longer values his life because it has been robbed of the ideal, personified by a human being of a transcendental nature. We will encounter the same situation in a 1931 story set in Italy—"Gertrud und Bianca" by Emil Strauss. Such stories represent the negative posture *par excellence* for they amount to the reverse face of representative affirmative tales.

Italy in the year 1001 is the setting of Axel Lübbe's dramatic tale of a transcendental and forbidden love, "Hugo von Brandenburg" (January 1927, I, 34–52). A story of Shakespearean dimensions, it too deals with the loss of an ideal love, but in this case it is an overwhelming erotic passion which robs two people of their peace of mind, their free will, and ultimately of their lives (one in the literal, the other in the figurative sense). The protagonist, Count Hugo von Brandenburg, is the imperial governor of Tuscany. His story begins with a mysterious and horrifying dream which is so vivid that it leaves the strong-minded, powerful, middle-aged ruler shaken, helpless as a child, and unable to distinguish between dream and reality. He is, in fact, a successor to the type of Kleist's Prinz von Homburg whose functioning in the real world, whose efficacy as a leader, whose very life was threatened by his inability to cast off the impression of a lifelike dream or to distinguish between it and waking reality. In the case of both protagonists the power of the subconscious surged beyond its prison of inhibitions and controls, asserted itself and took command of their conscious lives.

In both the Kleist play and the Lübbe story a dominant theme is guilt. Hugo von Brandenburg—who is faithful to his devoted wife Judith—represses, conceals, refuses to admit even to himself his passion for a beautiful, angelic young woman, Bianca dei Forti, the daughter of an archenemy. Bianca has visited the Count in order to beg him to spare her father's life. She too cannot admit to herself that she returns the passion which has assumed control over both of them.

The Count's dream turns out to have been a premonition of dire events. When he rides off to conquer rebels in another city, one of the rebel leaders he captures there is Bianca's father, who kills a young Florentine nobleman in an abortive attempt to murder the Count himself. The Count is required to judge and sentence Cesare dei Forti. At this point events begin to unfold in life exactly as they had unfolded in the Count's dream. The insoluble conflict on the deepest level of his psyche between the welfare of the creature he loves above all else, and his duty to mete out instant retribution toward a murderous rebel, drives the Count into a state which in clinical terms would be called hysteria. He is unable to think, speak or act, eventually becomes delirious and because death is the only solution, he dies when Cesare dei Forti is beheaded as a consequence of a misunderstanding by the Count's followers of the Count's ravings in delirium. For political reasons the Count's death must be concealed from the rebels, so his followers prop the body in full armor upon a horse and lead it slowly back to Florence—a scene which precisely duplicates the Count's dream.

In the meantime Bianca has entered a convent in Florence in order to escape her forbidden desire for the Count and devote herself to the service of Christ. There she experiences in a dream a union with Christ which she regards as signifying her marriage to the Savior. In Freudian terms the dream is an expression of sexual frustration released in a sexual union with the figure of the Savior which then also incorporates the figure of Bianca's father and of Hugo von Brandenburg. Aside from the obvious oedipal implications, the dream shows a transference of the forbidden worldly love to the permissible spiritual object. At the same time it offers a modern interpretation of the accounts by women saints of their ecstatic unions with Christ.

Since she regards the union as irrevocable, Bianca is horrified when the old passion wells up again as she sees the figure of her beloved in full armor riding slowly into the city again. She believes he is staring directly at her window. She feels herself torn into violation of her marriage with God and so like Oedipus she takes a sharp object (in this case a crucifix) and puts out her "sinful" eyes so that she can see only blood. Both lovers—though they have loved only in their dreams—have become martyrs to their forbidden love.

The impact of the story rests on symbols and images which recreate the climate of an era characterized by mysticism and violent emotional extremes which are undiluted by rationality or compromise. It portrays a transcendental realm which is inexplicably intertwined with forces of the subconscious so strong that they defy the most hallowed taboos and thereby create a conflict of the psyche powerful enough to destroy its victims.

With Kurt Heuser's "Elfenbein für Felicitas" (August 1927, II, 125–38), his first published work,[3] we return to a contemporary and earthbound setting. Stylistically it is not up to the level of "Sterben auf einer Pflanzung" (above, p. 100). It illustrates, however, several significant points. Again, one is the overpowering, all-encompassing nature of the African landscape. It dominates lives, thinking and behavior. Because it burns through the veneer of civilization, it exposes the true nature of the white man's character. In this story it provides an irresistible challenge to a young European who has fled, with his beautiful companion Felicitas, the weary decadence of Europe for a more elemental existence. He has chosen an exotic and dangerous world where the bourgeois values which he rejects no longer count.

---

[3] "Kurt Heuser lebt als Farmer in Portugiesisch-Ostafrika und tritt mit der Erzählung 'Elfenbein für Felicitas' zum erstenmal an die Öffentlichkeit." (*NR* August 1927, II, 224.)

Heuser's narrator-protagonist is aware that rejection of bourgeois society by the young generation has by this time become a cliché. He tries to avoid the cliché by calling his motive "sport," but it is clear that his motives are the standard ones of disaffected youth:

> Und fragt ihr, Neugierige, warum wir so reisten, so muss ich mächtig lachen, denn ich wüsste keine andere Antwort als die: aus Sport! Ich könnte sagen: weil uns diese Welt von Spiessern, Stewards und Friseuren widerlich war, aber da es so lächerlich allgemein ist, auf die menschliche Gesellschaft und die Zivilisation zu schimpfen, so sag ich lieber: aus Sport! Oder soll ich sagen: um uns Afrika zu erobern? . . . Das Leben, diese einmalige und wunderbare Tatsache, spielt sich so schnell ab, dass ich immer wieder erstaunt bin, wie alle auf Zweck und Tag bedacht sind. Wären sie nicht gottlos obendrein! Aber ein Citymann führt ein Leben, als ob er ans Jenseits glaubte; könnten ihn sonst positive oder negative Salden des Diesseits ausfüllen?—Das tägliche Brot! Das tägliche Brot! Ein Ding für Neger, nur von Hirse zu reden. Ich habe auch gehungert. Aber man kann leben, ohne Geld zu verdienen. Das Rezept für den einzelnen heisst: nicht besitzen zu wollen, verschwenden, verschwenden, was man hat, erraffen, meinetwegen, aber verschwenden! Und das Rezept für die Völker heisst: nicht besitzen zu dürfen, befristetes Geld! Business? Massenwahn einer irrsinnig gewordenen Horde. Darum lache ich, darum: aus Sport! (127)

"Stewards," "Citymann" and "Business," English (or pseudo-English) words in currency at the time, are here not used for the purpose of irony or humor, but stand for the "Americanized," "materialistic" values which the protagonist condemns. In the above paragraph as well as such lines as: "Gedichte sind unsere Sache nicht mehr" (126), the narrator has not avoided sounding sophomoric.

Before the protagonist had met Felicitas his relationships with women were the kind we are familiar with from the stories by Kayser, Zweig and Flake: "Früher, als ich allein war, riss ich Weiber zwischen mich und die Einsamkeit, aber Felicitas war kein Weib, sondern ein Mädchen." (126) The parallel to Zweig's "Phantastische Nacht" is exact here; as they had for Zweig's hero, women served as functional devices for the purpose of curing loneliness and alienation. Note the diminutive as a term of respect. As in the Flake story, to call a woman a "girl" is to give her a higher social rating.

Felicitas, it is emphasized, is the strong-willed, athletic, emancipated, modern type. Nevertheless the protagonist describes her with the clichés which have become painfully familiar from previous tales. She is akin to the antelope: "Antilopenaugen, Antilopenschritt; leiszitternde Tierflanken; . . ." (126) She is, in the protagonist's eyes, a creature of nature, like a wild animal which is able to defend itself: "Ja, aber da gibt es noch anderes, wehrhaftes Wild. Das allein soll man jagen. Das allein fordert den mann. Es ist desselbe wie mit Felicitas.—" (130) The very qualities which make a woman fascinating to the protagonist (as they had to Raymund, "der Liebende" and other previous heroes)—her enigmatic closeness to nature, her kinship with the animal—mean also that she is not trustworthy in men's terms (cf. "Beginn einer Liebe" above, p. 118). This collection of prejudices would seem to be a heritage from medieval, Church-determined views of women, the origin also of the persecution of women as "witches." Heuser's narrator-protagonist thinks how little a (any) woman can be trusted as he watches Felicitas' reaction to the treasures which a Portuguese slave trader spreads before her: "Fast schien es, als ob sie mit ihm zu spielen begönne; freilich, sie war keine Katze, sie war klug und von dieser Zeit, aber sie war weiblich." (130)

This brutal colonialist who rescues Felicitas and the protagonist from a parched, threatening landscape has amassed great wealth by vicious exploitation of the African natives. His ways are sordid and cruel; they disgust the protagonist. There is a tension between them also because of jealousy over Felicitas. The slave trader's Africa is not the Africa of the young, idealistic refugees from European corruption. The conflict between the two views of Africa reaches its climax in a hunt for a marauding bull elephant. Felicitas and the narrator come upon the animal grazing peacefully in a clearing and abandon their hunter's impulse in a mutual epiphany which coincides with obeisance before the beauty and rightness of the creature in its world:

> Die Mündung meiner Büchse sank. Und nun sah ich Felicitas; auch sie hatte die Waffe abgesetzt, sie stützte sich auf den Lauf wie auf einen Stab und stand vorgebeugt, eine Verzückung ging über ihr Gesicht, und ihr flehender Blick sagte: Nicht töten! Nicht töten!
>
> Noch einmal stand das Bild der mörderischen Städte Europas und Amerikas auf, wo man schachert und handelt, und dann versank es auf ewig. Inbrünstig riss uns die Wildnis an sich. Wir lebten. Was ist uns Elfenbein! In unendlicher Sanftheit durchweidete der Elefant die Lichtung, und wir vermeinten ihn jetzt leise untertauchen zu sehen im jenseitigen Wald und für immer. (137–38)

Meanwhile, however, an unidentified assailant shoots from the opposite direction and the wounded elephant charges Felicitas and the narrator. They are forced to kill it in self-defense. Its death marks the defeat of an idyll—of humane impulses and respect for an unspoiled Africa. The very materialism and greed which the protagonist had come to Africa to escape have proved ubiquitous. The conclusion with its sense of betrayal and wanton destruction has an up-to-date ring. With prophetic insight into the future of the continent, the narrator calls the elephant "one of the last of its kind." (137) The negativisim of this story, the triumph of blind greed and cruelty over humane ideals, raise it to a level of general validity and undiminished relevance.

Heuser's "Wiederkehr der Amazonen" (April 1928, I, 347–65) stars a group of women similar to Felicitas. A forced tale of the return to Europe of a group of amazons whose tribe has been isolated for a thousand years, it lacks the authenticity of Heuser's African stories. The strong, handsome, savage young women are seeking mates. Eventually several of them come upon and "capture" a downed pilot who takes two of them to a European city. There they create a stir which results in an uprising of all the young, "emancipated," slender and athletic women in the city. Proclaiming a "new age" and war on men, they gather on horseback for a great challenge by combat which ends in a farce when the men successfully distract the women's stallions by stationing a herd of nubile mares nearby. Despite the pretense of strength and emancipation the women's primeval instincts prevail and they are reconciled again to the normal erotic relationships with the men. Only one fanatical and jealous amazon takes the combat seriously. When she sees the pilot embrace a European girl she shoots him in the back with her arrow and he dies in the European girl's arms. The amazons disappear never to be seen again. The entire story is a denigration of women's emancipatory ambitions. Like Schaeffer's "Meleagros und Atalante" (November 1928) it strives to demonstrate that their attempt to compete with men is ridiculous and only serves to repress woman's true nature which must predominate in order for her to play her intended role. This "true" nature also happens, by the way, to accommodate men's wishes for pliable sex objects.

The March 1929 issue in which Joseph Roth's "Der stumme Prophet" (I, 344–57) appears begins with an essay by August Vetter, "Verzweiflung am Geist" (289–300), which is particularly pertinent to the Roth story and to the negative category as a whole. It is a cogent reduction of the history of ideas in the Western world since Kant to a succession of philosophical challenges to the dominance of "Geist" (in Vetter's usage roughly equivalent to reason), the latest of which are the theories of Freud. The author argues that the fate of "Geist" is connected to the fate of "the state," i.e., forms of rule. The "Verzweiflung am Geist" coincides with social upheaval. Several important stages in the onslaught upon "Geist" were: the departure from faith in sweeping truths which marked the end of the middle ages, and the feeling of isolation and separation of the individual from the masses represented in the thinking of Schopenhauer, Kierkegaard and Nietzsche. "Beseitigung der Werte zugunsten der Wirklichkeit" (291) is one phrase which the author uses to refer to the former development. The advent of modern science brought the competition of ideas with equal claim to truth: "Die Wirklichkeit hat, wenigstens für das Bewusstsein, über den Wert gesiegt, wie die Teilerkenntnisse die Gesamtwahrheit auflösten." (292) Finally, Vetter uses Kierkegaard to exemplify the predicament of the modern individual: ". . . [Kierkegaard] sieht in der eigenen Verlorenheit schon das Schicksal des neuzeitlichen Menschen vorgebildet. Überwunden wird das Einsamkeitsgefühl damit jedoch nicht, nur unendlich vertieft." (295)

The setting aside of values by the claims of reality, the victory of partial truths over faith in one truth (in other words, the loss of faith), the individual's existential aloneness, his "lostness" in the modern world—these several concepts read like a program for Roth's tale of a disillusioned, alienated former revolutionary, Friedrich Kargan. Now a drifter without ties or obligations, he had once been a legendary Communist undercover agent, inspired by idealistic motives. When the story opens, the great social upheavals and revolutions which did not fulfill their promise are past. Kargan no longer believes; he sees that his faith had rested upon a delusion. He makes a half-hearted attempt to start life over again with a woman he had loved long ago and has found again. He almost believes that he can succeed. But this promise of happiness also begins to seem hollow, as his political ideals had before. He heeds instead a call from a former comrade who is being deported to Siberia. Kargan joins him in melancholy exile with other lonely and disappointed men.

Familiar from other stories of lonely men—"Aube" and "Marengo"—is the nod toward psychoanalytical theory. The unhappy, cynical ex-revolutionary had "known neither mother nor childhood." (345) In broader terms—expressed as it has been in a number of stories (including "Raymund")—the state of motherlessness, whether symbolic or real, appears to stand for an existential sense of rootlessness, lack of nurture, lack of security. Extended to the political level, this feeling reflects the lack of a mother country to which one could pay allegiance with conviction. Expressed in the Heuser stories in the form of escape to a better world, it is apparently a representative postwar mood.[4] The consequence is exile—either in the mind or real—as indicated in the depressed view of Roth's protagonist: "Es ist möglich, dass in hundert oder zweihundert Jahren kein Mensch auf der Erde einen Ort haben wird, den er als Heimat oder Asyl betrachten kann." (345)

[4] For a simplistic version see Otto Flake's "Die zweite Jugend," above pp. 59–60.

Chapter IV

Stories in the Negative Category: The Later Phase 1929–32

The most intriguing work in the negative category is Hermann Kesten's story "Emilie" which appeared in April 1929 (I, 489 505). The destruction of ideals is so violent, the loss of illusions so complete that this tale borders on the category of nihilism. But it remains in the negative because there is a process of loss and destruction of something which had existed, although the author views that existence from an ironic perspective.

In one significant respect "Emilie" is the opposite pole to stories such as "Beginn einer Liebe," "Beschneite Spinnweben," and "Aube." In "Emilie" love is robbed of romance, exposed as a destructive, ugly obsession, entirely negative in its influence and effects. The protagonist, Georg Feist, is the victim of the same kind of consuming love as the protagonists of the above three stories, with the difference that in his case the love is for a worthless object, a scheming and sadistic forty-four-year-old whore, Emilie.

Life is presented as a downhill course. Every ideal, every romantic inclination felt by Georg is exposed as a foolish and cruel delusion. At the same time the author takes an ironic swipe at sentimentalized views of art and tender emotions.

The ironic tone is established in the third paragraph summary of Georg's personality and lonely, insignificant life:

> Er hatte mit siebzehn Jahren Gedichte geschrieben und war mit vierzig Jahren schon Agent. Gedichte schrieb er nicht mehr. Aber es war ihm die Kunst haften geblieben, Dinge zu sagen, die niemand interessierten. Er hielt sich selbst für sehr klug, und er war klug. Er hielt sich selbst für sehr gefühlvoll, und er war gefühlvoll. Er hielt sich selbst für sehr einsam, und er war einsam. Er hatte sein Leben selber geschaffen; denn er besass die Fähigkeit, seinem Leben die Farbe seines Gemüts zu geben. Seine verdriesse liche Laune schuf sein Schicksal verdriesslich. (490)

Two points are particularly pertinent. One is the new cynical tone with regard to literature: poetry as the art of saying things which interest no one. The second is the sense that Georg's personality is, inevitably, his fate. Both points contrast strongly with the world view presented in the affirmative category, where protagonists always rise above impediments of personality and fate to a better state of being, and where art (literature) whenever it plays a role, is taken seriously.

Georg, naive and inexperienced, is taken in by the appurtenances of minor elegance with which Emilie adorns herself—perfume and silk dresses. These modest decorations have an erotic effect on him. Treating this vulnerability with irony, the author also includes art which encourages romantic illusion, and Georg's sentimental attitude toward such art: "Der Arme war nicht gewohnt, den Gebrauch von duftenden Essenzen bei den Frauen zu finden. Sie trug alle Tage seidne Kleider. Auch dies Volksliedmotiv verwirrte sein Herz. Er war der Lyrik sehr zugänglich." (490)

Kesten's technique is generally to structure a paragraph so that it builds up to a cogent "punch line" which has the effect of retracting, by means of ironic surprise, the preceding sentiment. The most artful example is a paragraph which describes Georg's state of being subsequent to his unhappy marriage to Emilie. He is referred to as "Robert" because his new wife insists upon calling him that instead of his real name which she does not like:

> Robert lebte einige Zeit so in sich gezogen wie ein Marienkäferchen, das sich auf die Spitze eines Daumennagels setzte, vielleicht sich erschreckte und nun regungslos auf dem Finger sitzt, lange, als wäre eine kupferbraune Warze an einer Spitze der Hand gewachsen, mit ein wenig Grün und Schwarz vorne und zwei schwarzen Punkten in der Mitte. Bis die Warze anfängt sich zu regen, auffliegt und damit beweist, dass es keine Warze war, sonst flöge sie nicht, sondern ein zartes und phantastisches Frühlingskäferchen, ein verliebter Gedanke der Natur. Robert wollte auffliegen. Robert war Agent. Es gibt keine fliegenden Agenten. (498)

A masterly example of ironic technique—multifaceted in mood and message—it is about beauty (by implication, of the soul) despite insignificance, and about the relationship between appearance and reality. It is also self-irony by the author of his own imaginative and gently humorous metaphor, which is crushed by the hammer of indisputable fact. On the one hand an observation is made which is delicate and poignant; on the other hand an ironic world view cannot let it stand uncorrected.

Irony is the keynote and dominant technique of the story. Not only a stylistic device, it is also the bearer of the tidings about life and love which the story is to convey to the reader. The protagonist, Georg, is always the object of irony, insofar as he is the victim of illusions which the reader is not supposed to share. A prominent example is his extreme vulnerability to erotization and consequent seduction by the simplest sexual ruses. (One case, above, is Emilie's use of perfume and silk dresses.) Such situations are used by the author to very humorous effect and, by the way, to deflate the bubble of romantic sexuality. Georg's emotions are stirred by a springtime (pre-marital) stroll with Emilie: ". . . all dies und alles noch, was man Frühling heisst, und dazu noch und überdies dies treffliche, junge Mädchen, diese reizende Emilie neben ihm, . . ." (492) In Georg's poor, deluded eyes he is sharing the beauty of spring with "dies treffliche, junge Mädchen, diese reizende Emilie" who in reality is a plump, aging whore whose sole interest is Georg's modest but dependable income.

All nature seems to Georg to be in accord with his infatuation. Yet after he and Emilie have made love on the grass he feels and acts at first as alienated from her as Felix was from Margot in the story by Ernst Weiss. Like Weiss, Kesten is illustrating the impossibility of real communication between people. For this kind of loneliness there is no cure, certainly not the facile private ones illustrated by Kayser's and Zweig's heroes. The narrator, whose commentary is never ironized, conveys this message on a number of occasions: "Wenn eine Wahrheit es gibt, ist jede Beziehung zwischen Mensch und Mensch von Lüge gefärbt, von Betrug gegerbt." (495) The potential for doubt in the word "wenn" is underscored by the reversed word order which seems to indicate a questioning of whether the word "truth" is ever appropriate, whether one can assert even one "truth."

Such bitter comments would have been foreign to the stories which we have consigned to the affirmative category. Even nature is alien and deceptive, despite appearances. The more beautiful it is the more it conceals from Georg the ugly truth about Emilie. When the natural surroundings grow as dark as the true circumstances of the relationship, however, they become a vehicle for the truth: ". . . und fanden sich endlich, im Dunkeln schon, schon bei Einbruch der Nacht, in einem düstern Walde weit fort von Fürth. Da sahen sie sich zögernd beide an, so ins Gesicht, schief und aneinander vorbei, schämten sich jeder für sich und für den andern und wurden ergriffen vom Gefühl der Entfremdung. Da kehrten sie sich voneinander ab und schritten hastig durch den Wald, . . ." (495)

The falseness of human relationships which is Georg's personal misfortune can be attributed to the falseness of bourgeois morality. Georg is also a representative of his class and therefore subject to its tastes, its morality, its romantic illusions, its joy in possession and rule. These fundamental errors are at the root of his vulnerability to Emilie's exploitation. After he and Emilie had made love on the grass Georg finally overcomes his initial feeling of strangeness:

> Er fuhr mit der andern Hand schüchtern über ihr Haar, er liess seine Hand auf ihrer vollen Schulter liegen, schob sie an die Hüfte, und wie sich ihm alles bot, alles so sein war, er alles beherrschte, wie er am Morgen den Platz beherrscht, den vieleckigen, fühlte er sich so stolz und ward grossmütigen Sinns. Er war ein Bürger. Bürgerlich erst nur schien sein Glück ihm vollkommen und während. Dazu kamen noch Empfindungen der Reue, verspätet eintreffende Bedenken der Moral. Es war ihm, als hätte er ihr etwas genommen. Und sie tat ja auch, als sei ihr etwas geschehen. Also fügte es sich. Sie heirateten bald und in der Stille. (493)

The critique of bourgeois morality indicates an at least mildly leftist point of view. Weiss, in "Marengo," can be said also to have exercised a critique of the bourgeois mentality—in his case of capitalism—at least indirectly by showing his protagonist as a man robbed of his human potential by single-minded devotion to business. These quasi-Marxist explanations for private misery would be foreign to the types of stories grouped in the affirmative category.

His new wife cheats on Georg, lies to him, abuses him, squanders his money, responds to his loving nature with coldness, and subjects him to rank cruelty by having the child she is carrying aborted although Georg has pinned all his hopes and love on the unborn life. Even though Georg's life has turned into hell he is still tied to the monster he married, not only by the legal obligations but by an inexplicable obsessive attachment. Their relationship illustrates a reversal of the conventional man/woman relationship—the man is emotional, vulnerable, loving, dependent and loyal; the woman faithless and exploitative. Georg's first inkling of Emilie's true character comes to him one morning a few days after their wedding when, upon awakening, he notices to his horror through his partly raised eyelid that Emilie is staring at him with sheer hatred. It is the moment of his reverse epiphany—the insight which brings the first disillusionment, loss of hope, despair. Georg cries.

From then on his life goes rapidly downhill. Metaphors of love change drastically from the earlier romantic ones (though cast into doubt by irony) to metaphors which reveal that Georg has become aware of the sick reality of the "love" which has ensnared him. The irony now is bitter in tone: "Die Liebe war ihm wie dem Gichtkranken das Gehn, eine Aufgabe, eine Notwendigkeit, kein Vergnügen." (498) "Und doch war er noch so voll von Liebe, durchtränkt von Liebe, wie ein Lappen eines Verbandes von Blut." (499) This kind of imagery shows where the real emphasis of the story lies—not in social criticism but in a representation of the human condition, namely the inevitability of suffering and the difficulty of pinning down the cause. Of Georg the narrator says: "Kein Mensch ist leider unbedeutend genug, um nicht leiden zu können." (498)

Georg is condemned to suffer until his death. Ironically, Emilie, still his wife, even outlives him by three years. By what cause is he so condemned? As in "Marengo," instead of an answer there are a series of questions: "Er war erbärmlich, dieser Georg Feist. Aber wer hatte ihn so erbärmlich gemacht? Die sozialen Umstände, die reichen Leute, der Staat, die andern, die Menschen hatten Feist zu einem armseligen Toren gemacht? Ach warum gerade ihn, warum? Frage dein Herz, warum die Schatten in ihm aufsteigen, Sorge, Kummer, warum?" (501) Since there is absolutely no evidence that the rich, the state or others are responsible, this question is meant to be at least partly ironic. On the one hand this sounds like the chronic self-pity from which Georg suffers. On the other hand it would seem that a certain determinism is implied—personality is destiny, as mentioned at the beginning of the story. But answer is provided only indirectly if at all. Certainly it is not definitive. The negative stories all end with either a direct or an implied question: Why this injustice? By questioning, the negative stories—like Job—are rendering an implicit protest.

The Kesten story is one of the few stories in which style and world view form a successfully integrated and indivisible whole. When the very language, metaphors and internal structure conjure up the nature of a world which is merely underscored by the events of a story, there must be a fundamental congruence with the times in which it was written. An obsessive love, a marriage trap, guilelessness and exploitation in man/woman relationships could occur in the literature of any time or place. But irony which robs portrayed events, persons and their beliefs of all higher meaning, purpose or justification, which undercuts commonly held views and imparts to the portrayed life the aura of a no-win, no exit situation, is distinctive. The weak, the gentle, the sensitive appear to have no chance to come out on top. Only the amoral and unscrupulous can take advantage of such a world because, like Emilie, they have neither hopes nor dreams, nor romantic illusions, nor sentimental ideals, nor tender feelings, nor susceptibility to beauty which would make them vulnerable to the irony of existence. The world view in "Emilie" is of a piece. There is neither justice nor solace for injustice.

Axel Lübbe's second story, "Der Rettungsversuch" (June 1929, I, 779–98), deals—like "Hugo von Brandenburg" (above pp. 146–48)—with dreams, mystical experiences and extrasensory communication. But this time the context is conventional, and the execution far less successful, creating instead of drama, melodrama. The first-person narrator is a writer who is trying to rescue himself from the preoccupations of his work by taking a vacation trip across the ocean on an Italian ship. While resting on deck he sees one of the ship's musicians throw his cello overboard and then fling himself into the ocean. Without hesitating the writer jumps in to save the suicide, but instead he himself begins to drown. He is rescued by the musician who helps him back on board the ship and continues to be solicitous when he learns that the writer has caught cold. On a visit to the writer's cabin the musician tells the story of his life, his extraordinary adventures and how his cello playing always saved him in dangerous situations—either by enabling him to earn money or by profoundly influencing his listeners. But his music did not impress the one woman who means everything to him. Because she does not return his love, his music and his life mean nothing to him. The narrator, who has taken this journey in order to find relief from being absorbed with the dark side of life and the human condition, finds himself—literally and figuratively—drawn again into the depths of a tortured soul. The drowning metaphor is overused here.

The musician begs the narrator to write the story of his love so that it might one day cause the woman to love at least his memory. The narrator tries to comfort the musician and persuade him to continue to live. But during the night the musician jumps overboard again, this time undetected. Once again a character is unable to exist without the love which alone could give meaning to his life. An underlying theme is the relationship between art and life. both musician and writer can exercise power through their art, but that power becomes insignificant before the reality of a compelling emotion.

The differences between Arnold Ulitz' "Boykott" (May 1930, I, 641–63) and the 1923 version of similar themes, "Turnlehrer Pravda" (above pp. 50–52), epitomize differences between the negative and affirmative categories and illustrate development over the years to a harsher reality. "Boykott" shares with "Emilie" an equally unsparing view of human nature, the difference being that "Boykott" deals with the group as well as the individual and with moral corruption which permeates the whole of society.

Continuing the negative series of protagonists who are isolated and alone, "Boykott" is the story of *Gymnasium* student Leo Bielinski, the only Jew in his class, whose millionaire father, owner of a construction company, is convicted of bribery and corruption. The father's confessions turn out to implicate officials throughout the hierarchy of government.[1] As a consequence of the scandal, Leo's classmates decide to isolate him in their midst—a decision made readily because anti-semitism has already assured that Leo remains on the fringe of the group. The class leader who organizes the boycott against Leo later commits suicide when his own father's involvement in the Bielinski scandal is discovered. The sons are inevitably victims of their fathers' corruption. A devoted and understanding teacher helps to direct Leo's thoughts away from the suicide to which Leo at first believes a sense of honor ought to oblige him, as it did the dead Christian boy. Leo, who is loved neither by his cynical father nor by his social butterfly mother, has the integrity which they lack and cannot accept the lax morality which they regard as a necessary qualification to survive in the modern world.

"Boykott" is illustrative above all of the topsy-turvy values of the ruling classes: a sick code of "honor" means that a boy feels he must commit suicide when his father's sins are exposed; public appearance means everything; the group punishes with humiliation a member whose reputation is sullied through no fault of his own; corruption is a way of life as long as it remains beneath the surface; anti-semitism is a matter of course. Hypocrisy governs attitudes and behavior.

Since Nazism is rampant, Leo, at first unaware of his father's scandal, presumes that Nazi influence is behind the sudden coldness of his classmates: "Hat ein Hakenkreuzler eine Brandrede gehalten?" (643) The other students are a

[1] A number of similar cases actually occurred in the twenties. Two of them—the Barmat brothers (also Jews from Poland) and the Sklarek brothers scandals—are described by Otto Friedrich in *Before the Deluge: A Portrait of Berlin in the 1920's* (New York: Harper & Row, 1972), pp. 169–70 and 314–15, and have a number of features reminiscent of "Boykott."

study of the mentality on which Nazism fed. Though some are humane and many are intelligent, they are all malleable. None exercises independent judgment. None appears to have convictions of his own, nor do they have the courage to uphold ethical principles. Even the best of them are subject sheeplike to the suggestive leadership of whichever boy enjoys the highest status at the moment. According to our stories, this is the typical situation in a boys' school, making it a breeding ground for political conformity and ultimately, when combined with corrupted idealism, for mindless reaction.

The conclusion is ambivalent. Leo decides to desert the corrupt modern world which surrounds him and journey to his father's ancestral village in Poland, where he will join an uncle who is a saddler. Leo's parents had often disparagingly pointed out to him what they saw as a strong resemblance to his hopelessly old-fashioned paternal grandfather. They ridiculed this resemblance because in their eyes Leo's sensitivity and his "outmoded" scruples meant weakness, made him unqualified for survival in the world to which the parents were so well adapted. Leo's father reminds him that the uncle's hometown saddlery was dependent for financial survival upon the "corrupt" money with which he [the father] regularly subsidized it.

It is difficult to know what the author is suggesting by Leo's decision to depart. It certainly represents a kind of defeat, although Leo is looking forward to his new life. It means that Leo was defeated by the social pressures in contemporary Germany. He could no longer cope with school (even though the boycott had been lifted with the news of his chief opponent's death), with his estranged family, with the alien values around him. Does the author mean to suggest that this is the only, or the correct, or the appropriate course of action for Jews who are subjected to anti-semitism in Germany—to adopt the simple life in an ancestral home, to return to "where they belong?" In a story appearing in 1930 the implications are worrisome.

> Hahnenschrei, Hahnenschrei, und es ist noch viel zu früh; noch ist es Nacht, eine Nacht, die gemacht ist aus Wald, Kühle und Bergesschatten, aus niedrigem Wolkenflug und einem Wind wie fliessendes Metall. Hahnenschrei, noch nichts ist anders als zuvor, es ist nur eines dazugekommen. (226)

This arresting beginning marks another Heuser story set in Africa, the setting which seems to stimulate his finest efforts. The dominant force in "Ein Feldzug gegen England" (August 1930, II, 226–44), as in his earlier African stories, is the land itself—mysterious, unpredictable, a world with its own laws. This is a story of monomania—again the white man pitted against Africa which always wins the contest. The motif in the opening paragraph of the cock crowing at the wrong time of day is carried to fruition at the conclusion of the story when natives are overheard commenting that such an animal must be possessed by evil spirits and will have to be slaughtered—a reference which relates to the protagonist's situation. The protagonist Titus Oger is a character cast in the mold of Michael Kohlhaas—a fanatic in the pursuit of his private justice.

Oger is an expatriate German who refuses to accept the British victory in World War I and the subsequent loss of German colonies in Africa. In particular he will not accept the loss of his own farm which he hewed out of the jungle under grueling conditions, and made thrive after a decade of hard labor. After the war he was forced to give up the farm which was sold to a British subject. Since then Oger has lived as a hermit on a hillside overlooking his former homestead, and spent his efforts gathering and arming a tiny band of blacks in order to wage his own private, one-man war against the British Empire to correct the injustice done to him.

Finally he descends to the farm and confronts the new owner with the alternative of giving up the farm voluntarily or being removed by force. To Oger's surprise the new owner turns out to be a reasonable, conciliatory gentleman—a soft-spoken but self-possessed retired officer who is as committed to Africa and the farm as Oger is. Having pointed out, during their all-night discussion, the irrationality and hopelessness of Oger's position (the British authorities would react with force), the officer explains that because of a disease contracted in the jungle he has only a few years to live, but wants to spend them on the farm and is willing to bequeath it to Oger. But the offer does not satisfy the obsessed man's hunger for absolute justice. He is willing to take the consequences.

As Oger departs to begin his attack he notices a manned machine gun emplacement in the underbrush facing the house and realizes that his life is in the Englishman's power. Nevertheless he whistles the signal to summon his ragtag troop. They do not respond. He goes to the appointed meeting place. They are gone. He has been betrayed, defeated (as his opponent had been through illness) by Africa iself.

Albrecht Schaeffer's "Die silberne Saite" (October 1930, II, 525–41) is the only murder story during our time period. It shows Schaeffer's penchant for sex among relatives ("Das Gitter"), although this time legally and genetically permissible since only cousins are involved. Again there is a mystical bond which is also erotic; again transcendental qualities of music play a role; there are religious undertones; there is an artist not suited to life, and again as in "Das Gitter" we have a somewhat hysterical story having to do with a creative misfit. This time, however, the artist comes to a bad end. Schaeffer's strength lies in descriptive passages which successfully evoke the morbid, claustrophobic atmosphere of a plush but decaying old house. The house, which is the scene of the events, is like a tomb—reflecting the advanced emotional and physical decay of its two unhappy inhabitants.

The narrator is Egid, a young priest who visits his cousin Idis, a shy, sickly young woman and a talented violinist condemned to live in poverty and hatred with her much older, bitter and sadistic husband who is hideously deformed by wounds received in the war. The overnight visit of her cousin, to whom she confesses her misery and with whom she sleeps, leads to Idis's death. She falls down a steep staircase—caught, ironically, by the trap which she had set for her husband (they were both insured) in the hope of freeing herself so that she might finally live. Egid finds her dying of her injuries and discovers the trap she had made with a violin string. Horrified and guilt-ridden, he departs to assume a new identity in a monastery.

Of the larger issues raised, one is the question of guilt for the horrible human consequences of war; another is the apparent separation of man from God, symbolized by the locked door of the church across the square where the narrator was to become assistant pastor. The door remains locked. Here, eight years later, is a story which in some ways is a negative version of the (chronologically) first story in the affirmative category—"Das Gitter"—with a destructive outcome.

Even the title, "Todeskampf einer Liebe" (November 1930, II, 644–64), reveals Friedrich Torberg's story to be the companion piece to Süskind's "Beginn einer Liebe" which appeared only eight months earlier. The two stories are so similar, except for the outcome, that it would seem one might have been influenced by the other. A segment near the beginning of Torberg's story almost repeats the segment near the beginning of the Süskind story when his protagonist first sees his lady love:

> Statt "Liebe auf den ersten Blick" soll es wohl richtiger heissen: Liebesahnung. Diese nun erfüllte ihn sogleich und mit so unwiderstehlicher Gewalt, dass er fühlte: an dieser Frau würde sich das Zerknitterte in ihm zur Völle glätten oder das Straffe in ihm verfallen müssen. An ihr würde er restlos genesen oder restlos ersiechen. Sie war, das glaubte er zu spüren, sein Schicksal. (647)

The subject is an obsessive love. Again the protagonist and his love object remain anonymous. In the Torberg story they are called "der junge Mensch" and "die schöne Frau." Again the anonymity is reflected in the lack of reference to an outside world. Like Süskind's characters, these two seem to exist in a vacuum, at remove from a reality beyond themselves. The young man seems to have no other interests than observing, reacting to and thinking about the (somewhat older) woman. He is preoccupied with interpreting small signals, investing even a gesture with great significance. Love relationships are a game, played with greater seriousness and intensity by the man than by the woman. The important difference between the two stories is that Torberg's is told tongue-in-cheek. The subject of irony is the protagonist, the infatuated young man through whose eyes the object of his infatuation is observed. It is he who has created out of his imagination this hothouse environment which he has invested with the intensity of his love.

His relationship with "die schöne Frau" is a product of his imagination which he nurtures and cultivates, investing the desired object with all kinds of extraordinary qualities, raising her to a pedestal and not noticing that she, in the meantime, is making herself readily available to him—the erotic plays a more obvious role than in the Süskind story. In fact, his desire is predicated upon her unavailability: "Seit er sie nicht besessen hatte, gab es keine andre für ihn." (649) His devotion is dependent upon sexual frustration. This is a different order of irony, of course, from that found in "Emilie." The latter reflects a world view and is at bottom deadly serious despite humorous moments. Torberg's irony is not richly complex like Kesten's nor full of nuances in tone, but rather monotonous, since it is a stylistic device with a single limited goal.

The Torberg story shares the image of women which is presented in Süskind's "Beginn einer Liebe" (above pp. 118–19), namely the ideal is distant, seemingly untouchable, coolly in control of herself and of her relations with the men by whom she seems always to be surrounded. The description of "die schöne Frau" resembles a somewhat older, more jaded version of the young girlfriend in Süskind's story:

> Die Art, wie sie mit den übrigen Männern ihrer Umgebung verkehrte, war ein Gemisch von Uninteressiertheit und Erstaunen. Jene, die unbekümmerten und vielgewohnten Schritts über die Umfriedung ihres Wesens brachen, durften darin umhertappen ohne die Gefahr, enttäuscht zu werden. Denn da ihr diese Männer nichts galten, konnte sie sich von ihnen entfernen wann und wie weit sie wollte. (648)

They are both women viewed by men who are awed, mystified, fascinated, unrealistic and deluded by a number of clichés.

This paragon of womanhood (in the perspective of the narrator) possesses the physical attributes which are a common standard of feminine beauty in the stories: "Er liebte eine hohe, schmale Frau, die unter hellbraunen Haaren—manchmal spielten sie fast ins Blond—ein blasses Gesicht trug mit grossen tiefdunkeln Augen." (644) In the above Schaeffer story the foiled murderess Idis is exceptionally slender and pale, with extraordinarily large dark eyes. In fact, she looks just like Reisiger's heroine Beata in "Stehe auf und wandle" (above pp. 144–45) and like Kayser's submissive young woman in "Die Begegnung in Padua" (above p. 26). The ideal woman, a number of stories would indicate, is even in the nineteen-twenties the Virgin Mary as represented in medieval iconography. This is true also of women in the stories by Frank, Schmidtbonn and Zweig. The alternative cliché is exemplified in the athletic heroine of "Elfenbein für Felicitas" and in Heuser's tribe of amazons. Among the hardy, sinewy, emancipated types are also "Fräulein Marion" in "Raymund," Hirschfeld's heroine Fennimore and Schaeffer's Atalante, although Atalante is converted at the end to more traditional femininity. Both ideals are stereotypes; neither is realistic. (Women characters viewed from a realistic perspective can be found in the stories by Schnitzler, Lichnowsky and Brod.)

When an author draws in this fashion on the stock of available clichés it testifies to a deficiency, for he is creating only fixtures, props. "People" in those cases are only the men characters, and their appearance is generally left to the imagination of the reader.

In "Todeskampf einer Liebe" the intelligence of the "schöne Frau" is described as particularly feminine; it is definitely not the intelligence of accomplishment or wit but another kind:

> Nicht scharf war ihre Klugheit, sondern weich, ja es war, wenn man so sagen darf, eine kosende, eine zärtliche Klugheit. Still und sanft, wie eine von lauter Schwerkranken umgebene Wärterin, setzte sie ihre Klugheit in Gang und liess sie wirken, gleich als hätte sie Mitleid mit den Dingen und Geschehnissen und Menschen, die sich ja schliesslich doch nach ihr würden richten müssen. Eine trostreiche Klugkeit war das, und es tat gut, von ihr einbezogen zu werden. (645)

It is, in other words, a nurse-like or motherly intelligence—peculiarly female in its implications. One of the most noteworthy assets of the "schöne Frau," according to the narrator, is almost never found in women—awareness of her own limitations: "Sie war überdies, was eine Frau fast niemals ist: ihrer selbst gewiss; sie wusste Bescheid über das, was sie aus eigener Absicht vermochte, und war daher den andern allen, die an Überschatzung ihrer Tragfähigkeit zugrunde gehn, weit voraus." (645)

Torberg's story, in late 1930, maintains that tradition we have seen in other stories of stereotypes about women who are viewed from afar, like an exotic species, lumped together by ignorance or prejudice, and misunderstood.

In contrast to "Beginn einer Liebe," Torberg's protagonist ends amidst the shambles of his illusions. One night the young man's imagination no longer functions as he is accustomed; it no longer successfully conjures up his passion. Afraid of losing the state of being in love, he rushes over to the love object's apartment to see her, thinking that now only fulfillment will rekindle the desire which has become the object of his existence. Once in her presence, however, he cannot help remembering a pornographic story he had once read, which described the cliché of seduction by an older woman of a younger man. Suddenly this situation—alone with the older woman whom he worshipped, but who for the first time appears deliberately seductive—seems to him to come dangerously close to duplicating the cheap cliché. The relationship is spoiled for him and he leaves abruptly. It could be argued that his behavior represents the triumph of noble ideals. The thrust of the story, however, is clearly the deflating of the protagonist's romantic illusions.

"Gertrud und Bianca" by Ludwig Strauss appears in the May 1931 issue (I, 615–43), an issue which provides the greatest possible contrast with the one a little over a year before (March 1930) in which "Beginn einer Liebe" appeared. That earlier issue was apolitical or reactionary in its political tendency and escapist in mood. The May 1931 issue meets the problems of the day head-on and from a progressive standpoint. The lead essay, "Quo vadis?" (577–87) by Fritz von Unruh, is a courageous attack on militarism (by a man who himself had previously belonged to the military) and a plea to German youth to dedicate itself to a better Germany than the one whose most sacred goal was death on the battlefield, glorified by the militaristic mentality. It was a bold statement at a time when militarism was in the ascendancy. Unruh's essay is followed by "England von gestern und heute" (587–604) by Emil Lederer—a positive analysis of British society (also remarkable in 1931, in view of an upsurge in anti-British feeling), then Thomas Mann's tribute to his brother Heinrich on the occasion of the latter's sixtieth birthday, and Heinrich Mann's own brief birthday statement about the role of the writer which he believes must be that of the non-conformist. Heinrich Mann also touches upon the theme of the March 1929 essay by August Vetter, "Verzweiflung am Geist," which appears like a *Leitmotiv* throughout this issue, that is, the beleaguered position of "Geist" in contemporary Germany[2]: "Nun fehlte es aber seitdem [twenty years ago] wieder an der Schätzung des Geistigen." (613) Mann is using "das Geistige" to refer in general to the activity of the creative intellectual which is no longer held in high esteem. The theme is taken up in an essay by Fritz Heinemann, "Graf Keyserling und die Krise des Bürgertums" (643–54), bringing "Geist" again into an adversary relationship with those problematic concepts "Leben" and "Materialismus":

> Denn des Bürgertums herrschendes Prinzip ist der Geist, speziell der berechnende Verstand, die Ratio. Das moderne rationale, berechenbare Recht, den rationalen Staat, das System der berechenbaren Natur in dem gewaltigen Bau der modernen mathematischen Naturwissenschaft, die rationale Kunst hat der Bürger als bleibende Grosstaten geschaffen. Wenn sich im zweiten Drittel des neunzehnten Jahrhunderts gegen diesen Geist in den Systemen des Materialismus die Materie, im dritten Drittel das Leben erhebt, so bedeutet das einen einzigen, sich fortsetzenden Auflösungsprozess des Geistes. (644)

Heinemann uses "Geist" in a broader sense to mean the social structures based on reason—such as the state, the law, the natural sciences (even "rational art," whatever that is)—which have been erected by the bourgeois class. His assumed dichotomy between this broad concept and "life" as well as "materialism" places Heinemann in the neighborhood of Kayser's way of thinking.

To Samuel Saenger, on the other hand, in his "Politische Chronik" (700–08) "Geist" is threatened in the political arena where it has a very concrete adversary in the Nazis:

> "Deutsch oder teutsch: Du wirst nicht klug." So manchem Geistigen, der mit seinen Sympathien die Anfänge der Hitlerei beg-

[2] It is, by the way, still an issue in the Federal Republic as of 1980. An example is an essay, "Geist und Macht," by Fritz Raddatz in the 4 January 1980 issue of *Die Zeit*, Overseas Edition, pp. 14–15.

> leitet und die nationalsozialistische Gesundungskur begünstigt hat, wird beim Anblick ihrer Heldenspieler hoffentlich die Scheltrede Goethes einfallen. So sieht eine Politik aus, die die Reinigung der deutschen Seele zugleich mit der Wiederherstellung kaiserlicher Macht und Glorie auf ihr Panier geschrieben hatte und nun, durch die Sinn- und Geistlosigkeit ihrer Führung und durch die Exhibition eines barbarischen Muskelpatriotismus, das kläglichste Schauspiel der deutschen Parteigeschichte bietet. (700)

From Rudolf Kayser's idealistic point of view the concept again becomes fuzzy. The first segment of his "Europäische Rundschau" (709–14) is called "Geist und Leben" and discusses—in the context of reviewing a work by Fritz Heinemann, *Neue Wege der Philosophie*—the changing role of philosophy. Kayser's definition of "Geist" is broader than any of the above; in fact it has almost no limits and therefore is not really a definition at all. He begins: "Manchmal scheint es, die Zeit hätte den Geist aufgegeben, den Geist, der bisher als das transzendente, das formende, das sinngebende Prinzip jedes Daseins galt." (709) Like Heinemann (and as opposed to Heinrich Mann and Saenger) Kayser is making distinctions which are too abstract, too general, too unsupportable to bear any relation to actual problems. He continues:

> Ohne ihn [den Geist] nimmt das Leben die Tatsachen schweigend hin, es reiht sie aneinander, es atmet den Alltag ein und endet, ohne dem Tod einen Sinn gegeben zu haben. Man kann die Tatsachen anwachsen lassen und mit der Macht der Maschinen auch die Macht der (an Präzision und Uniformität mit ihnen verwandten) Masse ins Grossartige steigern. (709)

"Geist" seems here to be a combination of every possibility ever associated with the word and more: soul, spirit, intellect, mind, perhaps thought itself, even meaning. Kayser's use of "Geist" also has a religious connotation for it is transcendental and bears the heavy burden of giving meaning to death. Opposing forces are: das Leben, die Tatsachen, der Alltag, Maschinen, Masse. Only the next sentence is sufficiently concrete to bear a clear meaning: Kayser is condemning political violence and mindlessness, by implication the Nazis and their ilk: "Man kann den Geist ausschliessen aus dem allgemeinen Bewusstsein, man kann gegenüber den zergrübelten Gesichtern der Geistigen auf die Kraft der Muskeln verweisen und auch die politischen Probleme mit Revolver und Messer entscheiden." (709) But the last sentence of this opening paragraph once again flails about so broadly among abstractions that it loses precision and fails a target: "Dies alles geschieht und lässt eine materialistische Modernität zur Herrschaft kommen, die sich am Oberflächlichen berauscht und das geistige Erbe Europas zu verschleudern droht." (709) Added to the above list of opponents are: materialism, modernity and the superficial. Kayser continues: "Der Widerstand des Lebens gegen den Geist ist ein Zeichen der Zeit, . . ." (709)

He is not politically unaware, as his commentary on the government's prohibition of the film of E. M. Remarque's *All Quiet on the Western Front* shows. (714) Kayser exposes with eloquence the dangerous implications of such censorship. In his review of the Heinemann book, Kayser supports the reconciliation of historical opposites no longer relevant to contemporary thinking:

> . . . erleben die Überwindung alter Begriffe und Gegensätze, sehen den Einbruch des Lebens auch in die rationalen Schichten unseres Weltbildes und als letzte Folge: ein neues Totalitätsbild des Daseins, entstanden aus dem Geheimnis der menschlichen Existenz. So werden in unserer Zeit die alten Antinomien zwischen Rationalismus und Sensualismus, Idealismus und Realismus überwunden; denn diese Unterscheidungen sind für uns nicht mehr prinzipieller Art, da sie nur den Blick auf die eigentlichen Lebensfunktionen verbergen. (709–10)

This positive attitude toward the reconciliation of opposites—including the invasion of "life" into the rational sphere—certainly contradicts Kayser's presentations above and throughout the years which have consistently and adamantly insisted upon dualism. His previous remarks show neither a tendency toward totality nor an inclination to regard the "actual functions of life." In another review he maintains the familiar resistance to the mundane, the tangible, the concrete, and to that old bugaboo of the philosophical idealist, "material existence" (as if it were avoidable). Material existence, in his view, is the moral inferior of the ideal realm of "Geist." The context is a comment upon a quote from the work of John Dewey (in the course of a review of a book about America by Georges Duhamel): "Eine solche Verweltlichung des Denkens kann uns Europäern keine Erlösung bringen. Sie bedeutet die restlose Anerkennung des Primats des materiellen Daseins, unter Verzicht auf jede wirklich philosophische Erkenntnis der geschichtlichen Situation und des Menschen als ihres Trägers." (710) The enemy is the "secularization" of thought. This trait has been consistent in Kayser's thinking as expressed in his *NR* writings since 1922. Whether the quality be called transcendental, mystical, or religious, it is coterminous with Kayser's concept of "Geist."

Kayser concludes his review of the Heinemann book (above p. 173) with an article of faith in an indefinable entity, European "Geist": "Es bleibt der Glaube an den Bestand des europäischen Geistes und das Misstrauen gegenüber einer Zukunft, die für den europäischen Geist keine Zukunft hat." (711) When "Geist" is used as Kayser uses it here it is difficult to imagine what the unifying essence would be which could make it common to all Europe and still share all the properties of "Geist" indicated in Kayser's "Geist und Leben" article. The mentality which Kayser still represents in these pages, while recognizing political realities, is unprepared to cope with them. Kayser's commitment to values resident in an elevated, unimpeachable realm and his insistence upon their superiority to "secular thinking" and "material existence" indicate deep-seated resistance to the predominance of the political (in the broadest sense) in the modern world.

This issue also includes an essay on the reform of

German universities by anti-Nazi activist Hermann Heller[3] and a review by Erwin Poeschel of Jakob Wassermann's latest novel, *Etzel Andergast*, published by S. Fischer. The review concludes with a sentence which is anti-collectivist and hence has potentially anti-Nazi political implications: "Nicht Gesetz, Begriff, Konstruktionen, Verbände, Kollektive,—der Mensch, der einzelne, einzige Mensch." (700) Broadly speaking, the May 1931 issue is an opposite pole to the March 1930 issue. The contrast between the two also illustrates the gamut of possibilities which the *NR* admitted, including the political spectrum from one end (on the right, in March 1930, Carl Schmitt) to the other (on the left, Heinrich Mann).

The perceived threat to "Geist," whatever its definition, which is a *Leitmotiv* of this issue is bound to find some correspondence in the stories. The dread is both specific, in reaction to political developments, and general—a mood, a diffuse sense of menace, a feeling of being threatened. By all criteria a negative story *par excellence*, "Gertrud und Bianca" can be read as a reflection of the sense of threat to "Geist" and as a direct relative of the Kayser option: the antinomy between "Leben" and "Geist."

In a number of ways, "Gertrud und Bianca" is reminiscent of Reisiger's "Stehe auf und wandle." The Italian setting is a dominant force in the story. Again a northern European seeks (this time not deliberately) in the south salvation of his (her) soul. In a statement representative for all stories set in Italy, the narrator, speaking of Gertrud, describes the impact

---

[3] Gottfried Bermann Fischer, in *Bedroht—Bewahrt: Weg eines Verlegers* (Frankfurt am Main: S. Fischer, 1967), p. 83, mentions Heller: "Einige beherzte Männer hatten sich noch zusammengeschlossen, um in Massenversammlungen zum Widerstand gegen den Nazismus aufzurufen. Anfang 1932 kam Professor Hermann Heller, damals Staatsrechtslehrer an der Berliner Universität, zu mir, um mich um meine Mitwirkung bei ihren Bestrebungen zu bitten."

of sun and light and landscape upon visitors from Germany:

> Die Erzählerin sagte nichts davon, was Licht und Luft unserer Umgebung damals an ihr gewirkt hatten. Aber ich hatte den Blick ehrfürchtiger Dankbarkeit gesehen, mit dem sie die Aussicht umfing, und ich kannte die Schauer, zu denen die Welt des Südens den nördlichen Menschen löst, wenn er zum erstenmal in ihren strömenden Feuerhauch eintaucht. (620)

Again two people experience a mystical relationship, a transcendental love. One of the persons is Gertrud, a lonely outsider all her life, a misfit in society, set apart by her inability to make the compromises required by reality. Her life has been marked by melancholy dissatisfaction, a longing for the ideal beyond her reach. We encounter her via the narrator who has climbed to ruggedly beautiful castle ruins on a lonely hillside in northern Italy. There he meets a middle-aged German woman living in a shelter in the ruins (as are a number of other poor people) and she eventually tells him her tragic story.

After a particularly traumatic period in her failed life, Gertrud has accepted an invitation from her close and only friend, Clara, to vacation in Italy. (There are, interestingly, no male characters in this story, with the exception of Bianca's father, who appears briefly.) In Italy they meet—and Gertrud falls in love with—Bianca, an angelically beautiful six-year-old child of a poverty-stricken family. The name Bianca is significant, for the girl is reminiscent in her ethereal beauty, her delicate constitution, and mysterious effect on Gertrud, of Reisiger's Beata. In a disastrous accident, Bianca's parents and Gertrud's friend drown. Bianca becomes Gertrud's ward, fulfilling at long last Gertrud's previously insatiable hunger to give and receive love. Gertrud takes Bianca, for the sake of the child's damaged health, to live for the summer in the mountains. There Bianca soon acquires the bloom of good health and grows into an agile, daring and unrestrainable climber. At this point, as her grace and agility flower, Bianca is both in appearance and nature like a reincarnation of Goethe's Mignon—a pure spirit and creature of nature, so graceful and fearless that she seems almost to fly. Gertrud often fears for the beloved child's safety and tries as hard as she can to restrain her daring exploits. In her anxiety, it seems to Gertrud as if nature itself wants to assume Bianca: "Alle Elemente schienen mit begehrenden Armen auszugreifen nach Bianca, um sie hinüberzureissen in ihre Gewalt." (637) Gertrud cannot take Bianca back to the city they came from because in that safe but mundane environment of everyday life ("Alltag"—the parallel to Kayser's ideas is obvious) the dazzling child would atrophy in body and soul:

> Gertrud hätte dann gern den Pflegling in dichte Menge geflüchtet, ihn im Alltäglichen, als sei er seinesgleichen, vor aller Gefahr zu verstecken. Wenn sie ihn aber in der Stadt erwachsend sich dachte, verkümmert oder halb entfaltet wie die Menschen da unten, und die strahlende Erscheinung, in welcher er neben ihr ging, mit diesem Bilde verglich, so wusste sie, dass es nicht anders hätte sein dürfen, als es nun war. (637)

One day it happens: the ruin of a castle tower in which she imagines her ancestors once lived is too tempting for the untamed Bianca. Early one morning she secretly climbs it. Gertrud is awakened from sleep by the sound of a crash and finds the little girl dead among the ruins of the tower staircase. Glancing up, Gertrud sees Bianca's little apron attached as a banner to the summit and she realizes that Bianca had reached her goal and only upon her return did the staircase collapse. Inspired by her undiminished love, Gertrud sculpts a beautiful likeness of Bianca's face for her tombstone and remains to live out her days near the child's grave.

In Bianca it is justifiable to see a representation of "Geist." She is the spirit which reaches to and beyond accepted limits, which strives for the unattainable ideal, for pure freedom. She is pulled down by the forces of earth, by the unbending requirement that the rules of material existence be heeded. Such a spirit cannot realize itself on earth. And Gertrud's nameless, haunting anxiety for Bianca resembles the anxiety of authors in this issue for the safety of "Geist."

Her death reflects the incompatibility which exists, in Kayser's vision, between the mundane and the spiritual. In Reisiger's story the comparable situation was indicated in the initial disagreement between the physician and Beata about whether she should submit to illness for the sake of her spiritual health, or try to return to living in the everyday world. The attempt to have her do the latter fails, of course, because "Geist"—in the figure of Beata—is incompatible with material existence.

In September 1931 a strange story appeared which by any standard marks the low point in quality during our time period. Eduard Stucken's "König Pfauhahn" (II, 367–89) is related to "Gertrud und Bianca" and the last two stories in the negative category by virtue of the protagonist's finding and losing an ideal being. In this case, however, a cruel fate twice determines that the protagonist himself must destroy the ideal being. In the first case it is a magnificient horse (the "König Pfauhahn" of the title) which the protagonist spares the suffering of inevitable drowning by stabbing it to death. In the second case it is a beautiful young woman whom the protagonist loves but must stab to death (by mutual agreement) to save from a worse fate (coincidentally he is foiled at the last minute in his attempt to kill himself). The point of the story seems to be that the hero is condemned to administer euthanasia.

The story is a lengthy, tedious hodgepodge of outlandish characters and contrived events in an exotic setting, interrupted at intervals by irrelevant digressions and moralizing interpretations of what has transpired. The level of commentary is so banal that one might believe it to be a parody were there any hint of that possibility. After pathos, melodrama, and extensive lofty speculations about the hero's extraordinary fate, the entire enterprise fizzles out to the following lame concluding thought: "Und plötzlich wurde mir bewusst, dass mein Schicksal sich gleichblieb trotz verschiedener Gestalt: das Pferd und nun dieses Mädchen hatte ich aus Mitleid umgebracht." (389)

Gustav Regler's "Ein Lamm hat sich verlaufen" in the December 1931 issue (II, 795–811) represents the negative as the destruction of faith. This issue continues in the vein of the May 1931 issue—with deep involvement in the overriding issues of the day. The opening essay by Pierre Viénot, "Frankreich und Deutschland: Die Überbetonung des Nationalen" (721–36), is a model of reasoned tolerance. "Nationalismus und Kultur" (736–48) by Ernst Robert Curtius is a brilliant defense of the humanistic values of Western culture against the threat represented in *Die Tat*, a journal of national socialist tendency. Curtius too is manning the barricades to defend "Geist" against its attackers. "Geist" in his parlance is synonymous with rational thought and with culture and the humanistic tradition. In the course of his otherwise politically astute defense, Curtius makes the unfortunately representative error of dismissing the National Socialists as politically bankrupt and therefore insignificant for the future. Curtius homes in on the nationalists' attempt to dismiss traditional cultural values by denigrating them as "Western ideas." In his spirited resistance to these mindless attacks we see how far the *NR* has come since Kayser's nationalistic remarks of March 1923 (above p. 23) on the German crisis.

Kayser distinguishes himself in his "Europäische Rundschau" section (854–58) with an impassioned condemnation of irrationalism and "political romanticism." He recognizes and pinpoints the clear and present danger: "Es handelt sich nicht einmal um den Kampf zwischen Geist und Leben, sondern es geht um unsere menschliche Existenz." (854) It is a statement which represents a milestone in the development of Kayser's thinking. It involves a reordering of his intellectual priorities—those antinomies which he had consistently highlighted are now of a lower order of importance. The about-face is so marked and so significant in relation to the stories that the two key paragraphs of Kayser's article "Zum Thema: Irrationalismus" are quoted here. Betokening a new realism, Kayser's analysis—in the first quoted paragraph—of the roots of irrationalism and political romanticism is essentially the same as the analysis by the contemporary (present) German political scientist Kurt Sontheimer[4] on which we relied as a basis for criticizing Kayser's remarks of the early twenties (above p. 28):

> Die Herkunft der irrationalistischen Wendung aus dem Geiste des neunzehnten Jahrhunderts ist ganz deutlich. Sie bedeutet die dialektische Abwehr gegen einen Intellektualismus, der im Formalen erstarrt war, und die begeisterte Hinwendung zum Leben. Die Lebensphilosophie, die also an die Stelle der Ratio das Leben, das Irrationale, die Intuition und die Schau gesetzt hat, sie ist die mütterliche Kraft, aus der die irrationalistische Leidenschaft des heutigen Nationalismus stammt. Aber der philosophische Irrtum am Beginn bedeutet die politische Romantik am Ende. Und jener Irrationalismus, der mit Bergson und Sorel begann und jetzt mit Pareto und Gentile im Faschismus angelangt ist, findet seine Antwort in einer politischen Ideologie, die der Romantik eines Adam Müller und seiner Epigonen weit näher steht als unserer so unromantischen Zeit. (854)

In the second quoted paragraph Kayser casts off like so much extra ballast the distinctions to which he had been so firmly wedded all along. There is a no-nonsense tone, a sense that the ultimate—reason and life itself—is at sake, which is mirrored in the striking fact that there are no more affirmative stories. Now, Kayser seems to feel, there is no more time for philosophical niceties, for defending the ideal "Geist" against "Leben." Although the word "crisis" is not mentioned, the tone bespeaks crisis and urgency. In Kayser's remarks and in Regler's "Ein Lamm hat sich verlaufen" the mantle of philosophical idealism has been stripped away to expose a cold and threatening reality, with no panaceas offered:

[4] Kurt Sontheimer, *Antidemokratisches Denken in der Weimarer Republik* (Munich: Nymphenburg, 1962).

Es handelt sich für uns nicht darum, Stürzendes zu halten und junge Leidenschaften von ängstlich behüteten Ordnungen zu vertreiben. Es handelt sich nicht einmal um den Kampf zwischen Geist und Leben, sondern es geht um unsere menschliche Existenz.[5] Man kann der einseitigen Herrschaft von Abstraktion und Idee die Realität und die konkreten Erfahrungen gegenüber stellen, man kann den Idealismus durch den Positivismus, die Kultur durch die Natur bekämpfen, aber unmöglich ist es, das vernünftige Denken widerlegen zu wollen durch einen Irrationalismus, der seiner eigenen Definition nach auf jede Vernunft verzichten muss. Mag das Leben mehr sein als nur Vernunft, so ist eine Existenz ohne Vernunft unmöglich. Und wenn es sich um die Existenzformen der Gemeinschaften handelt, so können Gefühl und Trieb nur der Motor sein, der unser Denken und unser Tun in leidenschaftliche Bewegung setzt, nicht aber die Formungsprinzipien der menschlichen Gesellschaft selbst. (855)

"Ein Lamm hat sich verlaufen," which deals with confiicts of a Catholic conscience, reflects these changed sensibilities.[6] A desperate man seeks out a priest in order to confess a terrible crime and the reasons for that crime. The structure of the story consists of the visitor's narrative alternating with a paragraph of the priest's thoughts in reaction to what he is hearing. The priest, who is the interpreter of the narrative, bears the symbolic name of Loup. In his case the name might rather connote "lone wolf" than wolf among a flock of sheep, for this Loup is a lonely, independent thinker. He considers deeply the meaning of his tasks as priest and is skeptical of their efficacy. As a result of hearing his visitor's story, he will decide to give up the priesthood.

---

[5] Bermann Fischer (*Bedroht—Bewahrt*, p. 85) gives a moving description of what the phrase "es geht um unsere menschliche Existenz" meant to people like himself (like Kayser, a Jew, liberal and humanist): "Eine Welt, die Welt meiner Kindheit, meiner Jugendjahre, die Welt des Rechts, der Moral, der Achtung vor dem Nächsten, war zusammengebrochen. So sicher hatten wir uns in ihr gefühlt, dass auch die schweren Erlebnisse des Ersten Weltkrieges, der Inflation, des Hungers und der Armut, den Glauben an ihre Unzerstörbarkeit nicht hatten erschüttern können."

[6] And a complete reversal of the world of Catholic faith and orthodoxy represented in Regina Ullmann's 1923 story "Die Barockkirche," above pp. 46–47.

The visitor had adopted his orphaned twelve-year-old niece, Lucile, whose mother (his sister) had committed suicide because her confessor had convinced her of the sinfulness of her feeling of relief at the death of her brutal and tyrannical husband. The uncle vows to keep Lucile away from priests, but unknown to him a young monk has been seeing the girl while she was alone outside. He has been frightening her with tales of hell where her mother is condemned, as a suicide, to suffer forever. Lucile is transformed from a carefree, blithe spirit to a unhappy child. She becomes ill, has faints and hysterical attacks, and eventually dies.

The uncle in the meantime had learned of the monk. He realized fully the effect the monk was having on the child when one night Lucile is transfixed by hearing the screams of a cow trapped in a burning stable and asks whether her mother screams like that in hell. Once Lucile's sickbed caught fire from an overturned lamp and the young monk happened to arrive on the scene (the uncle was out) and rescued her from the burning bed, but only after first stopping to impress upon the child that her mother was burning that same way in hell because she had died without confessing her sins.

After Lucile's death the uncle wreaks revenge. He sets fire to the monk's cell, making sure first that he could not escape. Then the uncle begins a campaign of revenge against all priests by going from town to town and church to church to tell his story and to threaten the priests with death. But he is unable to carry out this continuing revenge as he had intended. He is still trapped by his faith. Priests still have power over him. Now he expects to take them before the divine judge in the afterlife when he will meet his beloved niece and will accuse the dead monk.

The story exposes the cruel potential of religious fanaticism. But more than that it bears the familiar message that the Church has been corrupted by its representatives on earth, that it has distanced itself from its Christian purpose. Priests are divided here into three groups: the dangerous ascetics such as the monk responsible for the death of the child; the useless epicures such as those who pass Loup's refectory window as he is listening to the story and remind him that it is aperitif or coffee break time; and the conscience-stricken doubters such as Loup. The visitor accuses Loup: "Wölfe seid ihr, Seelenwölfe, stürzt aus dem Wald in die harmlose Herde, Kinder tötet ihr. Und uns beherrscht ihr. Wir zittern vor euch, . . ." (809)

Faith is torture and there is no relief from it. The priest Loup himself comes to believe that in the end. It is a bitterly anti-Catholic (Church) story, as is obvious in the description of the refectory:

> Im Halbdunkel daneben bleicht im Mosaik ein Lamm. Ringsum auf den Brettern und Absätzen blinkt matt das rituelle Kultgeschirr; aus den Schränken geistern die gestickten Blumen und die Gesichter des toten Kultstifters. Eine Robe neben der anderen, die Kleiderkammer eines kleinen Provinztheaters. (796)

The bitterness which is conveyed by such a passage leaves the same impression as the bitterness of the despairing visitor—that it is the product of faith which has been denied but not yet become indifferent; otherwise there would be more detachment.

On yet another level, the story is about the unbreachable aloneness of every individual. Loup wants desperately to help his visitor but cannot. The priest knows that even those whom he watches depart from the confessional booth ostensibly comforted, have not really been helped:

> . . . es ist ein lautloses Weggehen in den Alltag hinein, der ihnen für einige Stunden freier scheint.
>
> Aber was ist das schon für eine Freiheit? frage ich euch. (811)

The last of the negative stories, Schmidtbonn's "Der Vater" (December 1932, II, 774–92), is the third about the loss of a child. The Schmidtbonn story, in the predictably unimaginative style and the predictably conventional mentality, this time also has racial overtones. It is the tale of an adoptive father who develops an obsessive love for his adopted baby girl, Lo, whose life he consequently warps until he and his wife decide that the only way to save the teenaged Lo from a good-for-nothing boyfriend is to send her to live with her real mother (the wife's sister who had been forced by economic necessity to give up the child) in Prague. It is the only way to make good, the father believes, for the "sin" they committed of living the lie that Lo was their own child by birth. In Prague Lo finally finds contentment because she is with her "blood" relative. Lo had always seemed less than completely attached to her adoptive father, which he attributes to her yearning for her real father (who died shortly after her birth): ". . . und hatte ihr in dumpfer Ahnung des Blutes das Gesicht ihres wirklichen Vaters vorgeschwebt?" (783) The adoptive father comes to feel intense jealousy of the dead real father and even hides a photograph of him so that Lo will not see it. The entire story revolves around these pseudo-issues of "blood" relationship or lack thereof. In the background there is war, inflation, an encounter with benighted Bavarian villagers who discriminate against the child because she is adopted, and an example of unemployed, apathetic and amoral youth (Lo's boyfriend). But these problems are not explored; they remain shadowy and distant compared to the overriding theme of the father's all-consuming love for his adopted child. Once Lo is gone from his life the existential emptiness returns. His yearning could be satisfied only by a child of his own "blood":

> Mein eigenes Kind, das mir vom Leben nicht gewährt wurde—wo im Weltraum ist es versteckt? Es kann nicht kommen. Es ruft vergebens wie ich.
>
> Daher die Qual. (792)

Loss has been a *Leitmotiv* throughout the negative category, but it is remarkable that in three of the four negative stories which appeared in 1931 and 1932 the loss should be a child. In all three cases that child is a girl and the object of an all-consuming love. The child is more ideal than real, symbol of a pure spirit, and in two cases its exceptional beauty is stressed. In all three stories the love which the adult in question feels for the child has elements of the pathological. The child fills an otherwise emotionally empty life and becomes the exclusive object of the most intense feelings. She answers some kind of deep-seated need in the adult for a mystical bond with the unsullied spirit of a child. When the child, around which the existence of the adult is built, is lost it signifies the loss of meaning and purpose in the adult's existence—a loss which cripples and for which there is no compensation. The result is a void which cannot be filled.

In view of the frequently symbolic role of the child in literature there would seem to be a relationship between the striking common theme of the three stories and the mood of apprehension we find in these three issues, that is the fear for "Geist," the survival of which in Germany is threatened by mindless barbarism. This parallel is reinforced by the fact that the three children are all female. We have seen that in a number of the earlier stories women characters represent more than themselves. They are also (to the narrator and male characters) distant, enigmatic spirits, in closer touch with the elements, inferior to men in some ways, superior in others, but essentially foreign to the male and untouchable in a figurative sense. It is consistent with these attitudes that the three children who represent more than themselves, whose essence seems to be the spirit which flees the attempt to grasp and hold it, should be female. Why should a child, in particular, be a symbolic proxy for the endangered "Geist"? These three children are imaginative products of the Rousseauean heritage—uncorrupted by material existence. Here we see the parallel to Kayser's dichotomy between "Geist" and "materielles Dasein" (above p. 175). The children and "Geist" in those times are fragile and vulnerable.

In the opening essay of this last issue of 1932, "Das

Bekenntnis zum Übernationalen" (721–46), Heinrich Mann is making a courageous political statement on behalf of "Geist" and the spirit of international understanding against nationalism. His "Geist" is synonymous with "das Denken" and "die Vernunft." The essay is full of impressive insights into the political and spiritual predicament of Germany. As Heinrich Mann sees it, there has long been a fateful separation between the realm of thought and reality in Germany, and the consequence of this separation is political dictatorship[7]:

> Der klassische Friede zwischen der Wirklichkeit und dem Gedanken war immer schwerer zu schliessen. Das Reich jedenfalls, das 1871 anfing, hat ihn nie erlebt, keinen Augenblick, weder als es Kaiserreich noch als es Republik war. Hauptsächlich darum verfiel es dann auch endlich der Diktatur. Die Diktatur ist der gegebene Zustand für gesellschaftliche Gebilde, in denen Gedanke und Wirklichkeit einander überhaupt nicht mehr kennen. (721)

Undeniably, that separation which also had marked the thinking of men of good will such as Kayser is fundamentally apolitical and therefore tends to grant the sphere of public affairs to those groups which do not mind being sullied by everyday politics, and potentially to those who do not hesitate to soil their hands by seizing power. The problem is the political vacuum which is left by preoccupation with ideals on the

[7] This insight of Heinrich Mann's is at bottom the same as Sontheimer's (*Antidemokratisches Denken in der Weimarer Republik*) interpretation, although Sontheimer—justifiably—criticizes the intellectuals of the left such as Heinrich Mann for couching their critiques in the same irrational tone as their rightist opponents: "Gewiss verherrlichten sie mit Heinrich Mann die Ideale der Aufklärung und der französischen Revolution, teilweise angereichert durch sozialistischen Utopismus, aber *wie* sie die Vernunft verherrlichten, die Freiheit des Geistes und des Menschen von den angeblichen Fesseln einer obrigkeitsstaatlichen Verfassung und Kultur priesen, das war bar jeder trockenen Vernünftigkeit. Das war kaum minder rauschhaft als die ekstatischen Verherrlichungen des Lebens um des Lebens willen, die auf der gegnerischen Seite wucherten." (392–93) Sontheimer's quarrel is that the intellectuals of the left thereby also contributed to the downfall of the Republic.

part of men of reason and moderation who would have the intellectual and ethical prerequisites—if they thought the game worth the candle—to provide an articulate and fighting democratic opposition.

Heinrich Mann, like Curtius before him, cannot be blamed for making the mistake of looking too optimistically toward the future: "Das Zeitalter des Irrationalen wird gegen 1940 ablaufen. Die Vernunft darf sich vorbereiten, wieder einzuziehen." (726) Mann and Curtius cannot be expected to have already anticipated the second World War.

Another example of an optimistic look toward the future is an essay by Wilhelm von Scholz, "Ende der Grösse" (807–15), which harks back to an earlier way of thinking in the *NR*. In fact, in view of the trends of the times, it is frighteningly reactionary. Scholz bemoans the contemporary lack of great men. They have been replaced by the egalitarian collective. The current crisis is "seelisch" rather than "wirtschaftlich." It could be overcome if a great man took the helm and inspired the people. The contemporary world moves too fast to provide the proper environment of slow nurture which is necessary to develop the great individual. Scholz closes with the hope that the future will bring a slowing of the pace of life and therefore conditions for the appearance again of greatness. The Nietzschean cult of the superior individual is reminiscent of Kayser's early thinking and of the early affirmative stories. It seems strangely out of place and dangerously naive in December 1932. The simplistic theory proposed by Scholz (whose call for a political savior will be answered in reality by a Hitler) in the same issue with Heinrich Mann's thoughtful essay shows the range still possible in the *NR*. One questions why a mentality such as Scholz's should still be represented. Perhaps it is the result of political pressure, or poor judgment. Or perhaps to some sincere but politically naive thinkers such an alternative was the only one they saw for staving off the looming threat of barbarism.

By this time Kayser, in his own way, is manning the barricades. Heinrich Wiegand, who in this issue reviews Kayser's newly-published biography of Spinoza (*Spinoza* [Vienna: Phaidon, 1932]), sees in the Kayser book a political statement relevant to the contemporary crisis:

> Durch die Universalität seines Helden, der als Politiker beim Bankrott der niederländischen Freiheit ein Volksfeindschicksal erlitt, wird Kaysers Buch auch zur politischen Schrift. Es macht in den Tagen, da der Geist zugunsten der Roheit und des Blutrausches geschmäht wird, die Vernunft als menschenfreundlichste und auch Nationen gründende Macht sichtbar. (830)

And in the July 1932 issue Kayser wrote a courageous statement under the title "Kulturbolschewismus" (140–41) (in the "Anmerkungen" section) which exposes the hollowness of this Nazi expletive and condemns its implications in the strongest terms. With the crude expression "Kulturbolschewismus" the Nazis dismissed modernist culture which was alien to their ideology.

Yet by the fall of 1932 Kayser had already received his notice as editor of the *NR*. According to Gottfried Bermann Fischer who made the decision to replace Kayser with Peter Suhrkamp, Kayser's temperament was unsuited to the more aggressive political direction which Bermann Fischer wanted the *NR* to take.[8] In view of Kayser's increasingly direct and uncompromising defense of the values for which the *NR* stood and against the growing political threat, it would seem difficult to justify letting him go at this juncture. He remained responsible for the issues through March 1933[9]; after that his name was replaced as editor by Suhrkamp's.

---

[8] For Bermann Fischer's explanation of this decision, see above, Introduction, p. 6, n. 24.

[9] Referring to the March 1933 issue with its daring—in the political context—tribute to Jewish author Jakob Wassermann, Peter de Mendelssohn (*S. Fischer und sein Verlag* [Frankfurt am Main: S. Fischer, 1970], p. 1271) explains: "Natürlich war das Heft seit längerem (noch von Kayser) vorbereitet, die Beiträge Heinrich Manns und Döblins waren noch vor dem Umsturz geschrieben."

Chapter V

I. Stories in the Non-Judgmental Category

A dialectic between two alternative conditions, forces or directions is a typical feature of the stories which can be categorized as non-judgmental. In contrast to the affirmative category on the one hand and the negative category on the other, the dialectic remains unresolved. The basic posture appears to be balanced objectivity rather than protest or affirmation. Concepts of good, evil and fate do not seem to be as important or clear-cut as they were in the stories grouped in the two previous categories. Often a situation is presented whose hallmark is not development—movement forward or backward—but a treading in place. It is then a fundamentally static portrait of a condition. Both features—the attitudinal (objectivity) and the structural (either undecided conflict or static portrait)—result in a more distant perspective on the subject.

The last of the stories appears in July 1931. Otherwise they are scattered throughout the time period, the only noteworthy cluster being five stories in 1922–23, which is a larger number than in any other two-year period. There are only fourteen stories in all—far fewer than in the first two categories—which might hint at a more problematic, perhaps more difficult nature of this posture. Some of the same authors are represented. It is significant that the non-judgmental stories by Zweig, Süskind, Schaeffer and Flake represent a notable change in sensibility from those authors' earlier, affirmative stories.

Variations of the previously noted "Geist" versus "Leben" theme play a role in the non-judgmental category. Here, however, their conflict remains undecided. An example is the earliest story, Ponten's "Unterredung im Grase" (February 1922, I, 182–94). It appeared close in time to Schaeffer's "Das Gitter" (March 1922) and Stefan Zweig's "Phantastische Nacht" (May 1922) both of which drive the supposed dichotomy to an extreme and take without reservation the side of (their interpretation of) "life." Ponten's treatment is more sophisticated.

The story is confined to one brief scene: a conversation between a boy and a girl of different social classes which takes place in the garden of a country estate situated outside of an ugly mining town. Felix, the son of a miner, is raised above his station by his brilliance in mathematics and his refined manners. Consequently he is permitted to enter the mine director's estate garden and converse with his lovely daughter Viktoria. Felix is in love with Viktoria and uses the opportunity of their being alone to manipulate her by his wit into revealing that she is attracted to him and vulnerable to his erotic insinuations. During the course of their banter, the relationship reverses itself. Viktoria, who is in control at the beginning, becomes by the end emotionally the willing tool of young Felix. "Geist" has briefly triumphed over the prerogatives of wealth and power which Viktoria represents. Viktoria, whose philosophy is "Wir müssen fest auf der Erde stehen" (193), calls herself a "plebeian" compared to Felix who is an "aristocrat." However, crass reality asserts itself; social barriers will not be breached. Despite her fascination with Felix, Viktoria is and will remain engaged to a humdrum bureaucrat of her own social class. Her father appears in the garden and whisks Viktoria away. Felix is never again permitted to visit. Their intense moments together have not changed anything.

As is characteristic of the three Ponten stories in this category, the crux is erotic tension between man and woman. There is charm and humor in their interaction which is portrayed with convincing psychological insight. But the young people's brief idyll is set against a background of implied social criticism which is more apparent than in any of the other Ponten stories. "Unterredung im Grase" opens with a description of the contrast between the ugly destructiveness of the mines on the one hand, and the director's magnificent estate and Viktoria with her pristine white dress on the other. But the foundation of the estate—with portentous symbolism—has begun to develop cracks from earthquakes which result from the mine shafts underneath it. And Felix is able to trick Viktoria into showing him her garters by insisting that from his vantage point in the mines and by means of the underground cracks in her house, he was able to observe her dressing. Both his metaphor and the color of Viktoria's garters which, it is emphasized, are "mouse gray," are part of the symbolism for impending social change.

In September 1922 Ponten's second story, "Das Autodafé" (II, 902–12) appeared, followed by a significant review by Rudolf Kayser ("Dramen-Rückschau," 912–20). Kayser prefaces his discussion of five plays with the judgment that "Geist" and creativity in general are endangered in the contemporary world: ". . . was vor einem Jahrzehnt noch unmöglich erschien: die Entwertung des Geistes, die Ohnmacht der Schöpferischen in der Welt. . . . geistige Wirklichkeit, . . . scheint heute gestört, in seinem geheimsten Wesen beunruhigt zu sein." (912) Expressing once again his characteristic resistance to what he regards as products of the debasement of "Geist" on the contemporary cultural scene,

Kayser maintains that the generation of idealistic artists is gone, or has foresworn its "ideale Revolte." (912) Those who are left are bound to squander themselves on that representative manifestation of the times—the film industry. Yet, as is typical for Kayser at this time, he refuses to despair: "Man möchte verzweifeln, wenn man nicht wüsste, dass auch die feindlichste Situation den Geist nicht zu vertreiben vermag." (913) Built around the catch-all term "Geist," these abstractions are representative for a cast of mind which is manifested in Kayser's style.[1]

His style and point of view are inseparable. The style of this essay (which is characteristic for Kayser at the time) is effusive to the point of lacking substance. There appears to be a striving for spontaneity at the cost of clarity and even of meaning. A typical example is an excerpt from his definitions of genres: "Die Epik gestaltet formloses Leben zur Form. Das Drama ist die Tat dieses Lebens, Aufhebung seiner Zeitlichkeit, Umsetzung aller Energien in gegenwärtige und selbständige Welt." (913) The punctuation is characterized by overuse of the dash for emphatic pauses. At times the style seems more a vehicle to test the author's stylistic limits than to communicate with the reader. It is very difficult to learn any-

---

[1] Jost Hermand and Frank Trommler (*Die Kultur der Weimarer Republik* [Munich: Nymphenburg, 1978], pp. 140–41), who see a turn by artists to political concerns in the postwar period, call the prewar interpretative viewpoint the "ästhetische Attitüde." It is one possible way of describing Kayser's approach as he expressed it in this essay and other *NR* contributions in 1922: "Die ästhetische Attitüde, vor 1914 notwendige Voraussetzung einer breiteren öffentlichen Wirkung, trat zugunsten direkt politischen Engagements zuruck—ohne jedoch ganz zu verschwinden. . . . Demgegenüber [in comparison to the *Weltbühne*] geschah bei der wesentlich konservativeren literarischen Zeitschrift *Die neue Rundschau* erst 1925 eine umorientierung ins Politische. Auch nach dem Krieg, angesichts der, wie es schien, chaotischen Umbruchszeit, konzedierte ein Grossteil des Publikums der ästhetisch-künstlerischen Perspektive noch eine Weile spezifisches Gewicht für die Analyse der Gegenwart."

thing specific about the plays from Kayser's reviews. The term "Schicksal" appears frequently. The mystical implications of that concept, its amorphous quality, are indicative of the tenor of the whole. The style is a kind of free-form impressionism, romantic in tone, idealistic in tendency. An example are his concluding remarks on Moritz Heimann's play *Das Weib des Akiba:* "Diese menschliche Tragik, die doch an Übermenschliches rührt; dies freie Auftreten der Gestalten und Hinsinken in ein Sterben, das . . . ein letztes und tiefes Erkennen ist—hier spricht ein ganz grosses Werk zur hilflosen, müden Zeit." (917) The pathos goes hand in hand with a semantic carelessness which leads the reader to conclude that dying is an appropriate ideal in difficult times. The style illustrates a cast of mind which seemed to withstand successfully the intrusion of empirical reality and resist the strictures of rational discourse.

With "Das Autodafé" Ponten strikes out in a different stylistic direction from his other *NR* stories. The point of view switches at short intervals and without transition from a narrative voice to modified stream of consciousness in the minds of the two characters. The technique creates a rapid-paced, dramatic tale, characteristically vivid and laced with humor. The dominant device is irony. At its most humorous it rests on the discrepancy between the impression a visitor believes he is making and his actual impression as revealed in the disdain which his hostess's silent thoughts express. On a larger scale the subjects of irony are the fading caste of impoverished minor aristocracy, the affluent but crude rising commercial class, and the interaction between typical examples of both. Erotic tension is central, as is the victimization of a woman by an outmoded, exploitative social code.

A middle-aged, lonely spinster—the baroness Klotilde—waits for the mail to arrive and hopes for a letter, any letter as a sign of interest from the outside world. She is pleased even with a letter which merely announces the annual visit of the wine merchant. Although she regards him with haughty disdain, the baroness grooms herself elaborately for the visitor. She is an unhappy example of a woman of passion and determination who has no outlet for these qualities in the prison to which patriarchal custom has condemned her. On the one hand she resents men. On the other hand she is a victim of the training of her caste which has instilled in her the conviction that only men are worthwhile and significant:

> Niemand hatte sie besucht.
>
> Niemand, das war gleich: Kein Mann. Denn Frauenbesuche der einen oder andern Dame von den Landschlössern zählten nicht. Kann eine Frau von Geist etwas an Frauen finden? Vertrauen unter Freundinnen? Ah bah, Neid, üble Nachrede! Würde aber ist beim Manne! Ruhe geht vom Manne aus (ob in geheimer Weise auch Aufregung). Etwas Bedeutendes ist der Mann! Kommt es daher, dass man nur Männer auf Denkmälern sieht—? (903)

Late that night, having drunk vast quantities of wine, the baroness and the merchant lounge before the blazing fire—the merchant in a drunken stupor, the baroness sober, maintained as always by unyielding pride and self-control. In a fiendish scene, while the salesman drifts from a paroxysm of fear into unconsciousness and bats, moths and owls fly in through the window, a cat and mouse cavort as the baroness melts cheese over the fire, twisting it—by way of revenge—into the imaginary forms of her brothers who by their extravagant ways have destroyed her life, leaving her nearly destitute and unable to offer a dowry to her many suitors. Brought up to believe she must serve men, she has carried out even the most degrading tasks in caring for her brothers. Finally, through an unhappy coincidence her last suitor is lost to her and she is condemned to a life of permanent loneliness and deprivation. These past events are only revealed in her midnight monologue before the fire. The next morning at a sumptuous breakfast the traveling salesman must express his admiration for his triumphant hostess who had been able to "drink him under the table." The story closes with the baroness continuing to maintain the self-possession and show of magnificence to which she believes her status obliges her.

Kafka's "Ein Hungerkünstler" (October 1922, II, 983–92) appeared only a month later. It is included in the non-judgmental category because it lends itself to being viewed as an example of a "Geist/Leben" confrontation in which the downfall of "Geist" and the triumph of "Leben" is neither celebrated nor mourned. "Life"—in the guise of the young panther—appears as elemental sensuality, untamed physical power, and unequivocal survival capacity. "Geist"—in the guise of the "Hungerkünstler"—is cynically viewed as a pseudo-artistic activity of dubious merit and sideshow qualities, the consequence of an inner deficiency on the part of the artist—a self-imposed martyrdom with no higher justification than obsessive exploitation of the personal deficiency to gain recognition and applause. The dead "Hungerkünstler" is replaced in his cage by the panther who exercises an irresistible attraction over the public. The trend of the times has moved away from titillation at the sight of the emaciated, almost disembodied fasting figure to fascination with the life-exuding animal in its unadulterated vigor. This change and the ultimate disappearance of the "Hungerkünstler" are not subjected to a moral judgment. Both creatures are spectacles by their very nature which neither can escape.

Irony in "Ein Hungerkünstler" as well as in the two Ponten stories underscores their non-judgmental character. By contrast in Eugen Hoeflich's "Der Meister" (January 1923, I, 44–68) there is no trace of irony. Chronologically it is in close company with Hirschfeld's "Die Insel des Verbrennens" (February 1923), Ullmann's "Die Barokkirche" (May) and Werfel's "Cabrinowitsch" (June)—all stories to which the ironic style is foreign. Like these affirmative stories "Der Meister" is a moral tale and treats questions of the spiritual welfare of its characters. It also shares transcendental concerns. It departs from the affirmative stories, however, in that it does not resolve the dilemma which it presents.

The setting is China. People are starving because of the greed of rice merchants who are hoarding the rice for a higher profit. Unable to bear the suffering which he sees, a civil servant—not fully aware of what he is doing—beheads the wealthiest and most ruthless of the rice traders, thereby precipitating a revolution. The civil servant is approached by a conspiratorial group, two members of which represent conflicting approaches to effecting social change. The revolutionary demagogue, with his simplistic solutions, sways the group and the crowd which the next day storms the rice warehouses (wasting most of the rice in the process). In its frenzy the mob kills the conciliatory figure who had advocated spiritual renewal instead of mob violence. The civil servant, disillusioned with the brutal, mindless turn of events, escapes the mob. On the road away from the city he meets his old superior who is also fleeing and who teaches him more about the moral dilemmas which revolutions raise and the various possible responses to them. The two men part and the civil servant, burdened by a sense of guilt for his actions (and his inaction), contemplates suicide. He is prevented by a vision of a wise monk who preaches acceptance of life as it is. The civil servant comes upon a Taoist monastery which he enters, thereby accepting the motto engraved over the entrance (which is also the concluding sentence of the story): "Alles besitzt, der hier eingeht und alles draussen lässt." (68)

The story is a parable. It opens with the motto: "Der Mensch erkennt seinen Geist als Geist, aber er erkennt nicht, wodurch sein Geist Geist ist." (44) At issue is the role of "Geist" which seems to have no place in a political upheaval. The protagonist is unable to accept the requirements for being an active partisan on either side of events. The only alternative for him is a life devoted to the spirit in isolation from the world.

The narrative voice does not pass judgment on this choice. It is an alternative to involvement chosen by a particular type of individual who is a representative of "Geist."[2]

The setting and mood of Annette Kolb's "Geraldine oder die Geschichte einer Operation" (December 1923, II, 1122–30) are modern, its conclusions the contrary of "Der Meister." A young woman is admitted to a hospital for minor surgery. Soon the hospital becomes a haven from the world for her. She thinks of it as an ark. The solicitous care she receives, the release from responsibility which being ill permits, makes it justifiable for her to concentrate on herself. Escape in the mind is made complete by an occasional dose of morphine to combat post-operative pain. However, reminders of the world intrude unavoidably upon her. By soliciting her physician's comments on some new French books she is reading, Geraldine discovers his anti-French feelings and is reminded of the apparently insurmountable difficulty of overcoming the barriers of prejudice between nations. She thinks also of the suffering and deaths of friends in wartime. Finally the day of her discharge from the hospital arrives. Geraldine forces herself to accept the necessity of reentering the outside world, but with great reluctance and dark uncertainty about the future.[3] The metaphor for her departure is the dove sent out by Noah to see whether the flood waters had receded: "Und wie die Taube, der Arche entsandt, die vergebens spähte, ob die Wasser noch nicht fielen, und die nicht wiederkehrte, so flog sie aus." (1130)

---

[2] The implications inherent in such a conclusion—the survival of "Geist" by withdrawal from the fray into a supposedly purer realm—have been discussed in earlier chapters. (Cf. Kayser's early essays and Flake's "Die zweite Jugend" above pp. 58–60.) Realized in the political realm, non-involvement means death to the fragile beginnings of democracy.

[3] Her feelings reflect the disillusioned mood of this December 1923 issue (cf. above p. 127).

The story is the portrait of a state of mind which is the opposite pole from "Der Meister." Although she is tempted by the sweet pleasure of escape, Geraldine greets the temptation only as a temporary respite from duty. By no means naive—"Aber auch Geraldine kannte die Welt" (1123)—she accepts her responsibility to assume a role in the real world,[4] however great the suffering and the injustice she has seen and will continue to see. Geraldine is the same illusion-free person with the same world view and approach to life at the end of the story as she was at the beginning.

Hermann Hesse's humorous little parable "Üble Aufnahme" (I, 266–71) appears to play the role in the March 1925 issue of providing a light-hearted contrast to Heinrich Mann's macabre satire of capitalist society, "Kobes" (below p. 225). "Üble Aufnahme" is a tale of two mendicant Franciscan friars in thirteenth-century England who are seeking shelter one stormy night. One of the friars is young and merry, the other middle-aged and somber—a self-righteous pessimist. Eventually they gain entrance to a monastery, but are uncharitably tossed out again by the prosperous, feasting monks as soon as it becomes clear that the wayfarers are friars and not traveling entertainers. Years later each of the two friars relates entirely different versions of the event. The younger friar's version is rational and mundane, the older's a tale of a miracle of God's vengeance. The contrast between the two seems to expose the possibilities of religious mystification. But the narrator

---

[4] An earlier story-essay, "Varramista" (July 1923, II, 639–52), shows Kolb's insight into political reality and the necessity of involvement: "Wo aber sah ich den Weisen, ach, der noch Hoffnungen fröhnte? Er kehrt sich ab, begibt sich seines Anteiles, und glaubt nicht mehr an diese Welt. Doch wehe, sie ist die unsere!—Wie ihr heutiger Zustand Werk und Schlagwort Einzelner ist, so könnte nur Wort und Tat Einzelner ihre Rettung bereiten." (651) The statement sounds like a direct reply to the protagonist of "Der Meister." More specifically she remarks prophetically in this *1923* essay: ". . . während die Hitlerleute und Hakenkreuzler ihr Land dem Chaos entgegendepeschieren." (641)

(though his tongue may be in his cheek) refuses to take sides between the versions and presents both with equal conviction.

The June 1925 issue is devoted to Thomas Mann on his fiftieth birthday. His own contribution, "Unordnung und frühes Leid" (I, 578–611), is exemplary for the non-judgmental category[5] because of its dialectic between tradition and social change.[6] Both sides are portrayed with ironic sympathy: the representatives of social upheaval in the guise of the story's cheeky young people and the relic of traditional mores, history professor Cornelius. The theoretical musings of Prof. Cornelius, who stands for "Geist" as well as tradition, center on what to the reader are obvious parallels to the contemporary situation: he plans, for example, a lecture to his class ". . . über den sachlich aussichtslosen Kampf des langsamen Philipp [Philip II of Spain] gegen das Neue, den Gang der Geschichte, . . . über diesen vom Leben verurteilten und also auch von Gott verworfenen Kampf beharrender Vornehmheit gegen die Mächte des Fortschritts und der Umgestaltung." (591) Philip represents the professor's own struggle, symbolized with ironic humor in his resistance to the young servant Xaver's tearing the daily page off the professor's desk calendar

---

[5] An insightful review by H. E. Jacob which appeared in the January 1927 issue (I, 106–07) supports the non-judgmental categorization of "Unordnung und frühes Leid": "Die Komödiengöttin dieser holden und elegischen Vaternovelle ist die Unordnung: ein Shakespearischer Troll, der hinter jedem Satze reflexiv aufspritzt, ein Kobold, der alles verrückt, umspukt und verstellt. Thomas Mann hasst diese Göttin nicht, er klagt sie nicht an als blutige Fresserin; er fragt nicht, wer in der Welt den Kindern Wasser statt Milch gab, wer das Falschgeld druckte und wer aus dem Faulen das Faire machte. . . . Er tut es nicht—und dennoch erscheint es mir schön! Wie mir an andern Dichtern über alles der Zorn schön scheint und der männliche Gegenstoss gegen die Zeit—so hier das freie und lächelnde Tragen, so hier des Dichters unzornige Weisheit. . . .Diese Novelle ist das erste Werk, in dem Thomas Man auf sein stärkstes Kunstmittel verzichtet: auf die Erregung moralischer Vorurteile." (107)

[6] For a darker view of the same society in transition see "Der Beamte" (May 1925), above p. 129.

because Xaver invariably tears off the next day's page as well: "Er soll das Kalenderblatt in Ruhe lassen, Doktor Cornelius hat es ihm oftmals anbefohlen, da dieser dazu neigt, auch das nächste noch abzureissen und so Gefahr läuft, aus aller Ordnung zu geraten." (601) While Xaver, a representative of the new, young, impatient, fast-moving generation, cannot wait for time to pass, does not, in fact, have a sense of (historical) time at all, Cornelius resists change which is more rapid than necessary. In the midst of the general upheaval he clings tenaciously to proof that at least one day still follows the other and each day matters. As the standard–bearer of "Geist" he maintains the historical perspective which denies that time can slip away without notice, meaning or significance. The professor's thoughts on the impartiality which he believes is required of the historian mirror the narrative perspective of the story as a whole: "Aber Parteinahme, denkt er, ist eben auch unhistorisch; historisch allein ist die Gerechtigkeit." (605)

The pragmatic victory is carried off by the counterforce: Xaver and company. It is the servants and a young guest who—due to their lack of inhibition and their closeness to life, compared with the over-refined and inhibited professor—are able to comfort successfully Cornelius' distressed little daughter Lorchen. In this sense the conclusion is analogous to "Ein Hungerkünstler." Practically speaking, the representatives of life, with their creaturely health and survival capacity, triumph over the weaker representative of "Geist." But the victory is confined to the practical sphere; it is not a moral one. In that sense there is a victory but no defeat.

Ponten's last story in our group, "Frau im Süden" (II, 1145–56), appeared in November 1925. Like "Das Autodafé" it is an examination of a woman's psyche and a static portrait of her situation. A German woman, who lives in Italy, is caught between two men. One is her husband—a tall, dark, handsome, charming, gallant, loving, loyal, considerate, intelligent, successful, wealthy Italian count. Despite all these virtues—he has no faults—his wife does not love him. Instead she is in love with a physican who lives as a recluse in southern Germany where she spends three months every summer to assuage her homesickness. The German physican is wooden, distant, unapproachable, unyielding in character, austere in personality and appearance. He bears the same first name as the Italian count, indicating that they represent two equally compelling alternatives. The woman's devotion to the German can be explained only in terms of her longing for Germany. Despite the love, security and privilege which she enjoys with her husband, she longs with such intensity for the forests and landscape of Germany that she becomes physically ill. All good, in her eyes, is there; all that is distasteful is in Italy. The contrasting landscapes represent antagonistic mentalities and life styles. To the protagonist north and south stand respectively for young and old (although in fact the German is older than her husband), for pure and corrupt, clean and dirty, quiet and loud, cool darkness and brilliant heat, green and brown, moist and dry, mountain and desert, home and alien territory. In her mind the qualities of the south are always the negative ones.[7] However, out of a sense of obligation to her husband, she will continue to divide herself between the two worlds.

Ponten's own view of the German landscape appears in an essay, "Deutsche Landschaft," in the May 1923 issue (I, 406–19), which is devoted entirely to various aspects of Germany. The essay presents the standard folkish, nationalistic view which equates Germany with "Kultur" and other

---

[7] The north/south dichotomy is a familiar theme in stories such as Schaeffer's "Das Gitter" (1922), Kayser's "Die Begegnung in Padua" (1924), Reisiger's "Stehe auf und wandle" (1926), and Strauss' "Gertrud und Bianca" (1931); however in those cases the favorable qualities are associated with the south. This is, of course, a tradition of long standing in German literature in general, as for example in the works of Goethe and Thomas Mann.

countries with inferior "Zivilisation." Like his protagonist in "Frau im Süden" Ponten glorifies Germany and its landscape to the point of chauvinism.

There could hardly be a greater contrast between Ponten's earthbound stories and Stefan Zweig's "Rahel rechtet mit Gott. Eine Legende" (March 1927, I, 260–73) which is set in heaven and exclusively concerns spiritual and moral issues. Despite its biblical context the story must be considered an example of the non-judgmental. Rachel begs God not to destroy the Jews despite their idolatry. Her argument is interesting: it is based on the example of her own mercy during her lifetime toward her father and her sister Leah in the face of the great wrong they did Rachel. Rachel argues that if she, a weak mortal, was able to find the strength to show mercy under the most trying circumstances, how much sooner ought almighty God to find it in his power to exercise such mercy. When God does not immediately reply, Rachel dares to accuse him of being a servant of his anger and therefore not God almighty. But the power of her words and her example succeeds and God shows mercy toward the Jews. What appears at first glance to be an affirmative story is actually non-judgmental because the resolution has taken place entirely outside of the earthly and human sphere. God's mercy is just as distant and incomprehensible to people on earth as his wrath: "Die Menschen aber tief unten, ewig dem Ratschluss der Himmlischen fremd, sie ahnten noch immer nichts, was ob ihren Häupten geschah." (273) The people on earth have merely been permitted by divine mercy to survive longer irrespective of their own merits or lack thereof.

There is a significant contrast in attitude between this story and Stefan Zweig's "Phantastische Nacht" (1922). In the earlier story an individual—the hero—transformed himself on his own power. Here the group—no individuals are singled out—is powerless to control its fate. The hero of "Phantastische Nacht" consciously abandoned (his concept of) "Geist" in favor of (his concept of) "Leben." The argument of Rachel which successfully persuaded God is the opposite: her example from life was one of "Geist" (her moral and spiritual character) overcoming the most powerful force of "Leben" (her long-frustrated passion for Jacob).

The contrast between the two Zweig stories is indicative of a change of sensibility over time which can be seen in the contrast between the affirmative and non-judgmental works of several authors. The change is indicative of a general trend in the *NR* stories between the beginning and the end of Kayser's editorship—toward greater sobriety and toward less easy distinctions. The biblical style of "Rahel rechtet mit Gott" makes a more disciplined and far more restrained impression than the style of "Phantastische Nacht." The non-judgmental posture—as opposed to the affirmative—implies a greater sense of the relativity (moral or otherwise) of contending forces in the human condition. It implies that outcomes do not seem as clear as they once did and that it is not possible as facilely to assume a standpoint. The non-judgmental category shares the posture consequent on Einstein's theory of relativity: it is impossible for an observer who is outside of a system to accurately judge its motion. Judgments of human affairs therefore cannot be conclusive. Broadly speaking, Einstein as the intellectual progenitor of the non-judgmental stance is the equivalent of Freud as the progenitor of the affirmative.[8]

---

[8] As authors of the two prime intellectual currents of the time their influence could hardly be escaped. In an article and review entitled "Das Weltbild der Physik" ("Europäische Rundschau," October 1931, II, 568–69) Kayser comments on his sense of the influence of the new physics: "Die neue Physik hat unsere Denkvorstellungen in einer Weise verwandelt, dass es manchmal fast scheint, als ob Unsinn Sinn geworden wäre. Desto grösser ist die pholosophische Bedeutung, und desto mehr können wir von einem 'physikalischen Weltbild' sprechen, dessen Perspektiven bis ins Psychologische reichen und ebenso den metrischen Kosmos wie den metrisch bauenden Menschengeist umschliessen." (568)

"Phantastische Nacht" is the most obvious example of a direct assumption into fictional discourse of Freudian concepts. But they provide the basic direction and impetus to the affirmative category—the individual and his struggles with inner forces, resolution by introspection and self-analysis, or the style which creates characters by means similar to psychoanalysis transferred to fiction (the stories by Schickele are examples).

Robert Musil's short story contribition is the enigmatic tale "Die Amsel" (I, 36–51) which appeared in January 1928. There are two unnamed characters, "Aeins" and "Azwei," who had been friends in childhood. "Azwei" was a boy who had liked to tempt fate; his friend was a more practical type. "Aeins" grew up to lose his ideals and become a financial and career success. "Azwei" had seen hard times but was surviving tolerably well. "Azwei" tells "Aeins" about three transcendental experiences which marked crises and turning points in the former character's life. Two of them involve the sudden appearance at his window of a blackbird with a message. The style of the story is direct, matter-of-fact, restrained—a sharp contrast to the nature of the events related. "Azwei" accepts the experiences, however bizarre, and does not try to undertake an inevitably fruitless search for meaning. His listener, a conventional type to whom such experiences and such an attitude toward them are clearly foreign, remains skeptical. The non-judgmental stance is revealed in the concluding paragraph: "Du lieber Himmel—widersprach Azwei—, es hat sich eben alles so ereignet; und wenn ich den Sinn hätte, so würde ich dir wohl nicht zu erzählen brauchen. Aber es ist, wie wenn du flüstern hörst oder bloss rauschen, ohne das unterscheiden zu können." (51)[9]

---

[9] Wolfgang Rothe, in his article "Metaphysischer Realismus. Literarische Aussenseiter zwischen Links und Rechts," in *Die deutsche Literatur in der Weimarer Republik* (Stuttgart: Reclam, 1974), p. 259, discusses Musil's *Der Mann ohne Eigenschaften* (as well as Alfred Döblin's *Berlin* *(continued on page 206)*

Wilhelm Lehmann's "Verführerin, Trösterin" (February 1928, I, 153–71) is the story of an encounter between two people and the ultimately incompatible attitudes which they embody. Profound in implications and stylistically one of the most beautiful of the stories, it is cast in a style reminiscent of the lyricism of von der Vring's "Aube." An example is the introductory paragraph which, making use of an unusual device, interprets in poetic abstractions the central events to come; but because of its condensed, cryptic form the story is not robbed of natural suspense:

> Der Tod war immer und überall gleich nahe und hatte durchaus nicht nur in den Granaten gesessen. Er stand auf dem Grunde des Meeres, und der Scheitel seines Hauptes war der Scheitel des Wassers, das der Ostwind mit breiten Händen kämmte. Er stand und wartete. Die Seele aber, wiewohl sie nicht wusste, was sie war, wollte sie selbst bleiben. Sie rollte sich ein wie Igel, schloss sich ab wie Auster, wenn jemand ihr zu nahe trat. Und wer trat ihr nicht zu nahe? Hingabe und Flucht vor dem Sturm der Zeit, wehrte sie ab, verpuppte sich, wehte auf, stellte sich tot, liess sich fallen und flog weiter. (153)

Paradoxically, "der Tod" will present itself in the form of an attractive young woman, blooming with good health and vigor, vivacious and charming. For it is not the threat of physi-

---

(continued from page 205) *Alexanderplatz* and Hermann Broch's *Die Schlafwandler*). Rothe explains the metaphysical level in these works in terms which also explain the role of the transcendental in "Die Amsel": "Das Transzendieren, nicht die Transzendenz stellt das Primäre dieser Metaphysik dar. Da aber jedes Transzendieren als Loslösung, Abstoss von einem Vorhandenen—hier von einer 'mechanischen' Zivilisationswelt und ihrem funktionalen, operationalen, instrumentalen Rationalismus— logischerweise sich auf diese vorgegebene Faktizität bezieht, ist eine negative Definition solcher Meta-Physik nicht nur leichter, sondern auch angemessener als eine positive. Dessenungeachtet wirkt sich ihr Überschreiten der just gegebenen Realität in durchaus positiver Weise aus, etwa bei der Selbstbehauptung des Einzelnen gegenüber einer sich absolut setzenden System-Wirklichkeit und der Relativierung derselben, generell bei der Bewältigung der Existenzprobleme des Ichs in der zeitgenössischen Welt. Nach Musil muss diese Metaphysik auch der moderne 'Erfahrungsmensch' erleben—als 'beginnende Überwirklichkeit.' " The whole statement describes the situation in which "Azwei" finds himself.

cal death which she brings, but the threat of death—in the form of distortion—for a sensitive soul. The soul belongs to a gentle, poetic, intellectual school teacher named Mengs.[10] Hiding his unconventional thoughts and putting on the public mask required by his job and dealings with the philistines around him means continual suffering, which he has learned resignedly to accept. The story also concerns the incompatibility of the life of the soul with the prosaic and often hypocritical demands of the world. Coping with the trappings of daily life is difficult for Mengs: although he is an excellent and popular teacher he has not received the normal promotions and salary increases, must support his wife and three children with a fourth on the way, must in short live not merely modestly but frugally. Mengs is the kind of melancholy, introspective, contemplative protagonist more appropriate to the earlier categories.

A naturalist at heart, Mengs participates with his whole being in the life cycle of the natural world around him. The author achieves this integration as well in style. An example is a type of paragraph which proceeds by uninterrupted flow from a departure point in contemplation to mystical union with nature, interrupted again by prosaic thought which draws Mengs back to his official world:

> Wer sich so über eine einzelne kleine Pflanze bückte und sich mit Aufbietung aller Kräfte auf sie besann, dem könnte es dann auch mit den Menschen glücken. Wer dachte, kam ins Flache, wer sah, rückte ins Geheimnis. So sass Mengs lange, flüsterte, lockte. Aus zarter Geduld keimten ihm Flügel, sie wurden gross und mächtig, er konnte über den Pflanzen kreisen und jede ihrer Bewegungen sehen—bis sie sanken, die Flügel, da Gedanken sich in den Blick mischten, die Empfindung einschrumpfte wie Wasser im heissen Graben, Enttäuschung hastig auffuhr, dem Verlorenen

[10] He is a character typical for Lehmann—the teacher who is a sensitive outsider and not very successful, in a worldly sense, in coping with the exigencies of career and survival. (Peter de Mendelssohn, *S. Fischer und sein Verlag* [Frankfurt am Main: S. Fischer, 1970], p. 737.)

> nachzupoltern—vergebens, Kanten nur, Ecken von Gesehenem blinkten. Geduld verwilderte, Ruhe verfiel, nichts wollte sich breiten. Und Mengs dachte an sein Amt. Morgen früh begann es wieder—es war immer da. (155)

To Mengs "Geist" and nature are integral to one another. The distinctions which others make are foreign to him. Where they separate and divide he sees unity at the heart of things. Contemplating the metamorphosis of color in a flower he thinks: "Das Rot und das Blau gelten. Sie sind wie Geist und Natur: eins bewegt sich im anderen wie das Knie im Gelenk, vom Kniewasser umspült." (157) This outlook is a variation of the striving of the sensitive individual for unity with nature and the search for a sense of universality, of the whole of existence rather than separate parts which marked a number of the affirmative stories, in particular Schaeffer's "Das Gitter." The significant difference is that Lehmann does not merely state these concepts but reveals them in structure and style.

One day Mengs is visited in his office by Margot Föh, the mother of one of his students and the wife of a well-to-do fish merchant.[11] She is a vibrant, completely natural and unaffected, emotionally sturdy woman whose life centers on the well-being of the body[12]: "Das ist ja alles selbstverständlich.

---

[11] The contrast between Mengs and Margot—humorously underscored by her husband's occupation and name—is reminiscent of the contrast between Thomas Mann's sensitive-aesthetic characters and his bourgeois-worldly characters, particularly in "Tristan" and "Tonio Kröger."

[12] Margot is in tune with the contemporary emphasis on sports and the body. A representative statement is the essay by Frank Thiess, "Die Geistigen und der Sport," which appeared in March 1927 *NR* (I, 293–305). In this widely quoted essay, Thiess sees the fitness of an athlete as an absolute requirement for the "geistiger Mensch" in modern times. Walter Laqueur, in *Weimar: A Cultural History 1918–1933* (New York: G. P. Putnam's Sons, 1974), p. 34, paraphrases this essay, as do Hermand and Trommler, *Die Kultur der Weimarer Republik*, p. 79. These two books, as well as, for example, John Willett's *Art and Politics in the Weimar Period. The New Sobriety, 1917–1933* (New York: Pantheon

Mein Mann ist ein Herkules, unsere jungen Leute beim Rudern und Segeln—natürlich. Man fühlt sich mit dem Körper wohl dabei—wir stecken ganz gern in unserer Haut, und das andere muss man nicht so wichtig nehmen, geht ja auch—." (161–62) Margot is an accomplished and graceful tennis player and Mengs, who inadvertently notices her on the tennis courts, cannot help but admire her for the confidence and physical well-being which she projects. Margot in her turn is intrigued by Mengs and makes an effort to attract him. They converse easily together and share the same skeptical attitude toward human nature. Mengs, bowed as he is under the burdens of existence, is stimulated and refreshed by Margot's presence.

But Margot is also a destructive force, represented by her insensitivity toward nature. Compared to Mengs she is, in a carefree way, brutal. On one of his regular walks in a park Mengs sees from a distance someone, who he does not yet realize is Margot, lying in a bed of flowers: "Den Hügel hinauf aber sah Mengs jemand liegen, der den Kopf rücksichtslos in die geliebten Blüten drückte." (165) "Rücksichtslos" is the appropriate description of Margot; she is in every way successfully in tune with her times. Mengs finds her disturbing. Her well-adjusted, untroubled self exudes a force he would like to resist: " 'Ja, Sie haben gut lachen. Sie brauchen bloss da zu sein. Und wir—wir qüalen uns und müssen uns verbergen.' Er wurde plötzlich böse. Er wollte sich mit Gewalt von ihrer Nähe befreien." (166) Her healthy rationality insures that Margot will cope well with life: "Ich will nicht träumen. Ich brauch' keine Träume." (170)

Books, 1978), pp. 102–03, stress the central role of sports in Weimar popular culture. Cf. also Klaus Mann's essay "Fragment von der Jugend" (March 1926, I, 285–95), above p. 132, and Kurt Heuser's story "Wiederkehr der Amazonen" (April 1928, I, 347–65), above p. 152.

The culminating scene takes place on a little island to which Margot has taken Mengs in a rowboat.[13] It is a scene of potential seduction, Margot having pushed the boat away so that they are stranded. But Mengs remains thoughtful and distant; he thinks of Nausicaa and Odysseus. The break comes with her reaction to the realization that Meng's real concerns lie elsewhere. It is a blow to her ego for which she will punish him:

> Er hob vorsichtig mit zitternder Hand eine Schnecke vom Sande: "Die hätten Sie gleich zerdrückt!" Sie sah, wie er bebte. Sie sprang auf: "Was hat die Schnecke vor mir voraus? Warum lieben Sie mich nicht?" "Ich liebe Sie ja schon tausend Jahre," er murmelte es nur.
>
> "Immer solche Übertreibung! Was sollen mir tausend Jahre? Jetzt, jetzt, jetzt und hier!" (170)

The contrast between her carelessness and his sensitivity toward nature gives the story particular relevance to the ecological concerns of the present. Margot's revenge is to take off her clothes and swim away, leaving Mengs stranded on the island.

Months later Mengs (who has not seen Margot in the meantime) is standing at the gate to his garden when a large automobile full of passengers fresh from an excursion zooms by with the fish merchant Föh at the wheel. In passing Margot leans out of the car to yell at Mengs: "Heute ist immer!" (171)—a point of view which Mengs had taught her to articulate. For his students he had compared this point of view to classicism which is concerned with the present as opposed to romanticism which is occupied with longing for another time. Whereas Margot has interpreted the idea in her own way, as support for hedonism, Mengs had meant reverence for the moment in nature and the soul.

---

[13] See introductory paragraph, p. 206, about "death" lurking in the sea.

Neither side has won or lost the case; nothing has changed. Margot and Mengs go on living their disparate lives as they had before they met. This conclusion means that "Verführerin, Trösterin" cannot, as were earlier stories with related style, themes and protagonists, be grouped in either the affirmative or negative category. It is the tale of an encounter between two mutually exclusive possibilities whose paths crossed briefly, intermingled and then continued on in opposite directions.

The next non-judgmental story does not appear until over three years later. Süskind's third story during our time period—"Das Leben zu dritt" (March 1931, I, 366–90)—is the tale of a young physician's stay in a strange city where he is substituting in a general practice for a year. There he encounters two odd women who live together: twenty-three-year-old Ella, who is a circus dancer and the mother of a ten-month-old boy, and her protector, the masculine Pauline. Pauline controls Ella and takes care of her and her baby. A relationship develops between the three—Dr. Rückert appears to be in love with Ella—but dissolves after several months when the baby becomes ill and Ella rejects the assistance of Rückert in whom she has, rather arbitrarily, lost confidence, and calls another physician. From then on she has lost interest in Rückert and two weeks later she and Pauline leave for another city with the circus. Two months later Rückert returns home much altered by his experience.

Like both previous Süskind protagonists, the twenty-six-year-old Rückert is thoughtful, observant and sensitive. At the same time, he is a somewhat conventional, hesitant and inhibited man who is more swept along by circumstances than appearing to control his own life. Like Raymund, he is not one to take matters into his own hands. These qualities lead to a reversal of expected relationships in the story. According to social conventions the young doctor would have the upper hand in a relationship with women of the social class, life style and type of Ella and Pauline. In "Das Leben zu dritt" it is the reverse. The women are self-reliant and in control of the relationship. This is particularly startling in the case of the shy, fragile and obedient Ella. In contrast to the two affirmative Süskind stories, the women are characters as substantial as the male protagonist, equally realistic and equally significant. The weight of the story is borne jointly by all three.

Rückert suffers from ineffectuality and paralysis of will. He never knows how to react to the unexpected and therefore does not act at all. One evening, sitting in the women's parlor opposite Pauline who is engrossed in reading a newspaper, Rückert ". . . fühlte sich in einer sinnlosen und entsetzlichen Weise an sie gebunden wie im Traum." (378) Though it is Ella to whom he is matched, he is equally under the sway of her stolid partner. The women and their relationship bewilder him and the many questions in his mind, about Pauline in particular, remain unanswered. About the reasons for the mysterious fascination which the two women hold for Rückert the reader must speculate. They have of course an exotic quality for him—their connection with the circus, their gypsy-like travels, the odd interpretations which they give their experiences. That Ella is a thoroughly good person is mentioned several times; both Pauline and Rückert recognize and appreciate her good character. Rückert also seems fascinated by the very incongruity of the women—their unconventional (and for him probably brand new) relationship in a conventional home setting; the women's tastes and habits are those of an average lower middle class German family. Finally, it is a time in Rückert's life when he feels open to new influences. At the beginning of his year in the strange city he thinks: "Dies, . . . wird eine Zeit werden, in der ich viel lernen muss." (367)

Rückert's entire situation is condensed in the picture of his regular visits with Ella to the movies. Once in the theater, Rückert ". . . [suchte] . . . dem irren Schein der Taschenlampe nach seinen Platz . . . unsicher, wie auf dem Rücken eines nächtlichen Dampfers—. . ." (378) It is also the situation of his compatriots in the real world—trying to find their way uncertainly in darkness with only small, uncertain light.

The last article in this March 1931 issue of *NR* is "Mordprozess und Gesellschaft" (431–32) by Siegfried Kracauer. The author links the murder conviction of three teenagers and the generally high rate of violent crime in Germany to social conditions, and in particular to the demoralizing effect of widespread unemployment—five million unemployed is the figure he uses. He explains that what has happened in Germany as a result has not happened elsewhere, despite similar economic troubles, i.e., a total collapse of moral standards along with the economic collapse. It is a time of social anarchy: ". . . das Fundament der Sitten ist zugleich mit dem ökonomischen erschüttert, und neue Verfestigungen stehen einstweilen aus." (432) The traditional relationships between the social classes have gone by the board: ". . . das Schwinden der gesellschaftlichen Hierarchie. Längst hat die Oberschicht aufgehört, das echte Vorbild der sogenannten Unterschichten zu sein, . . ." (432) Such a breakdown is illustrated in the topsy-turvy relationship of Dr. Rückert with the two ladies who dwell at the fringe of society. Rückert's own insecurity, his lack of firm guidelines for reactions and behavior, reflect a more general insecurity described by Kracauer: "Das Mass dieser Unsicherheit kennzeichnet den gewaltigen sozialen Umbildungsprozess, in dem wir uns seit dem Weltkrieg befinden. Bevor nicht die neuen Konturen festliegen, werden Blut und Tränen zu den Wegspuren gehören." (432) The lead essay in this issue of *NR*, by Robert Wilbrandt, is "Arbeitslosigkeit und Wirtschaftskrise" (289–300)—an examination of the disastrous conditions with suggestions for possible ameliatory measures.

Social upheaval is also reflected in the theme of a lesbian relationship. There is evidence of the post-World War I sexual emancipation in a number of *NR* stories whose themes include homosexuality and incest. "Moden der Liebe" is the title of an essay by Aldous Huxley (397–406) which is a companion sociological study to the fictional study "Das Leben zu dritt." Huxley examines fluctuating traditions of "love" in relation to the constants of human nature, and ascertains that two conflicting concepts of love dominate the contemporary scene. One is the love of Christian and Romantic tradition—mystical, all-consuming, monogamous, restricted by religious myths and ideals. The other is the new direction of total freedom—tossing overboard of all taboos and inhibitions, becoming an everyday form of recreation and relaxation (as a result of the possibility of contraception). He sees negative aspects in both views of love and recommends an alternative philosophy—a mythology of nature such as described in the writings of William Blake, Robert Burns, and D. H. Lawrence. In contradistinction, however, to the emancipatory aspects of the "love" triangle in "Das Leben zu dritt," Süskind's hero still manifests that superstitious feeling which almost amounts to fear of women as basically unfathomable creatures whose essence remains distant and unapproachable. Of Ella, for example, he thinks: ". . . sie glich etwas Blankem, in das man nicht hineinsehen kann, einem polierten Metallschild." (378) These contradictions in all three of Süskind's stories between the modern and the traditional in relations between the sexes—in particular the conflicts in the heroes' attitudes—can perhaps be explained in terms of Huxley's analysis. It is a time of transition, when attitudes toward relations between the sexes are in flux, and neither the one nor the other direction has become dominant.

In the last sentence of the story the reader learns that Rückert has been altered by his experience. Upon his return home old friends whom he had almost forgotten welcome him into their midst again: "Augen, die er kannte und liebte, ruhten prüfend auf seinem Gesicht. Viele, nachdem sie sich besonnen hatten, sagten, er habe sich sehr verändert." (390)

This comment remains cryptic, however, for there is no indication of how he changed or in what direction. In contrast to Süskind's affirmative stories there is no epiphany and transformation followed by a vision of harmony. Rückert has merely "changed," a term which by itself is neutral. Therein lies the non-judgmental nature of the story, and in the fact that the male protagonist shares the center state with the two very unlikely women characters who rejected him because they found him wanting in substance. Unexpectedly, they proved stronger than Rückert, more dependable, more devoted to each other and the baby, more sure of what was right for them. The relationship between the two sides ends in a draw: Rückert does not react with the firmness which might hold Ella, and the women erect obstacles to his doing so. Implied is a challenge which Rückert did not live up to:

> "Und Sie werden bei ihr bleiben?" quälte sich Rückert zu fragen. Er spürte abscheulich, wie ein herzlicher, ein fürsorglicher, ein Pfaffenton in seine Frage kroch.
>
> Pauline blickte ihn kurz an. "Nun ja," sagte sie und liess den Zigarettenrauch in breiter Schwade aus dem Mund quellen, "bis dass der Tod euch scheidet—wie der Pfarrer sagt. Bis einer kommt, der noch fester hält als Sie, Rückert." (390)

But it is not at all certain that he ought to have lived up to such a challenge.

The last three non-judgmental stories appeared in close succession: Süskind in March 1931, Schaeffer in June and Flake in July. The non-judgmental stories represent a distinct change from the three authors' earlier, affirmative contributions. Schaeffer's "Der Major" (I, 786–804) is a character study of an eccentric retired army officer who lives alone and in nearly total self-sufficiency in his modest Bavarian homestead. The narrator is a young man who has been taken by a mutual friend on a visit to the major. After the brief visit the two young men, alone again, discuss the major and what they learned of his past. In a sense it is the quintessential non-judgmental story because not only is it a static portrait, but it also bears a message (all the Schaeffer stories conclude with a stated message)—derived from the example of the major's shattering experiences in wartime as well as his peaceful life in retirement—which views human affairs from the perspective of eternity, by which in the long run the contradictory extremes compose a relative equilibrium. The message is conveyed by the friend who introduced the narrator to the major: (after bemoaning the predominance of "Wirtschaft" in the modern world and extolling a former time when that was not the case)—

> Er hob die Hand zu den Sternen, die über dem Dunkel helle funkelnd erschienen waren, und sagte andächtig:
>
> "Aber nur getrost. Auch dies muss sein; auch dies sind Lernjahre; auch dies geht vorüber. Einmal werden wir Meister werden. Dafür sorgen die Götter, die auf uns sehn, sieht auch niemand auf sie, so wie diese Sterne ihre Strahlen auch auf das unscheinbare Haus da unten hinabsenken." (804)

Flake's "Der Selfmademan" (July 1931, II, 103–20) is a superficial tale marked by Flake's usual inconsistencies, awkward style, scattered threads of themes begun and then dropped, and the inevitable *idées fixes* about women and man/woman relationships, to which are added this time clichés about the United States. It revolves around a stereotype in the person of an unconvincing macho character named Pokorny who is the "self-made man" of the title—a wealthy, naturalized American businessman of obscure Polish origins. The Pokorny character represents that well-adapted survivor type which is one half of the equation we have seen in a number of other non-judgmental stories: "Ein Hungerkünstler," "Unordnung und frühes Leid," above all "Verführerin, Trösterin," and to a certain extent Pauline in "Das Leben zu dritt." In the persons (and in one case,an animal) of these characters as foils to the more sensitive protagonists the non-judgmental stories are also portraying a society in which the qualities of the former spell success. They are typically self-confident, strong and healthy, very practical-minded, with their emotions under control, and a tendency to be less scrupulous, possibly a little on the brutal side.

The fable is about a young man who grows up and becomes more realistic as a result of his encounter and disillusionment with two characters who represent his ideals. The protagonist is a student named Erwin who works part-time as a reporter in a German spa where he meets the newly arrived Pokorny, finds a potential role model in him and eventually accepts a job as Pokorny's private secretary. Erwin both admires Pokorny for his self-assurance and success, and despises him for his ruthlessness. The plot involves a lovely but poor girl named Lily with whom Erwin is infatuated without daring to reveal his affection to her. Eventually, after many discussions between Pokorny and Erwin about effective methods of "handling women" and glimpses into what the author apparently imagines is the typical conduct of business by a nouveau riche American tycoon, Lily ends up as Pokorny's sumptuously kept mistress and Erwin philosophizes without bitterness about women in general:

> Statt Schmerz über sein Erlebnis empfand er Dankbarkeit, weil er noch frei war. Solange eine Frau sich für ein Wagnis nicht entschieden hat, wühlt es auf, zu denken, dass sie falsch wählen wird, denn sie trifft die Entscheidung für alle, die ihres Geschlechtes sind. Hat sie gewählt, so tritt sie zurück, sie ist nun eingeordnet, und die Entscheidung in die Hand einer anderen gelegt—ewige Erneuerung. (120)

This attitude makes the story a non-judgmental one. Life for the protagonist continues fundamentally unaltered. Instead of concluding with the pained disillusionment of the hero, it finds him with a non-judgmental perspective on events; life is seen as a cycle rather than as a progression. The attitude of resignation and view from a superior vantage point of the path of human affairs as cyclical rather than linear coincides with the point of view of the Schaeffer story. All three non-judgmental stories of 1931 share the mood of resigned acceptance of the ways of the world.

The lead essay of this July 1931 issue is "Die Krise der bürgerlichen Ideologie" (1–13) by Ernst von Aster. It is characterized by uncompromising political and historical realism, close reasoning and astute political diagnosis. Aster puts his finger on the attitudinal obstacles to realism in German political thinking and action. One is fatalism:

> Ein historischer Schicksalsglaube, andern Völkern in dieser Form gänzlich fremd, beherrscht heute weite Kreise unserer Gebildeten. Er ist etwas ganz andres, als die klare Erkenntnis historisch-psychologischer Ablaufsgesetze. Solche Gesetze (wie sie z.B. der "Geschichtsmaterialismus" sucht und aufstellt) lassen immer Punkte im geschichtlichen Geschehen frei, an denen der Hebel individuellen Wollens und persönlicher Wirksamkeit angesetzt werden kann. Der Schicksalsglaube dagegen lässt nur die Wahl zwischen Fanatismus und Fatalismus. (12)

A kind of fatalism is inherent in the 1931 non-judgmental stories, in particular "Der Major" but also in many of the other stories in this category (a strong example is Hoeflich's "Der Meister"). To a certain extent fatalism, in a modified form, is inherent in the non-judgmental posture.

Aster, of course, is critical of its political manifestations. It is related to the emotionalism and lack of clarity which he sees as characteristic of German thinking: ". . . Neigung zur Verschwommenheit und Unklarheit des Denkens, . . . Neigung, affektgeladene Platzpatronen an die Stelle deutlicher Begriffe zu setzen . . .—ein Fehler, der dem Deutschen an sich nahe liegt . . ." (11) An example of both errors—uncontrolled use of the term "Schicksal" in a bed of vague, emotionalized language—was Kayser's 1922 play reviews (above p. 192 ff.). By this time, however, Kayser's approach to the term "Schicksal" has changed and his thoughts are expressed clearly in a more controlled and disciplined style.

In his "Europäische Rundschau" (136–41) under the title "Das Weltbild des Nationalismus" Kayser uses his review of a book (*Das Reich* by Friedrich Hielscher) as a point of departure for exposing the ideological foundations of extreme nationalism. Kayser's analysis defends reason as the necessary foundation of affairs of state and society, and condemns the rejection of rational thought by the forces of nationalism which he accuses of falling prey to the twin dangers of irrationalism: mysticism and romanticism. Kayser proposes a pragmatic, realistic definition of the "nation" and in a near duplication of Aster's thinking accuses the nationalists: "Statt aber den Willen zur Nation an den Realitäten der Gegenwart zu bilden, ihn 'zeitgemäss' zu machen, werden Gott, Schicksal und Gefühl beschworen und das deutsche Wesen aus einem Jenseits hergeleitet, das niemand erkennen kann." (136) He contends: ". . . sie bedrohen durch solche Überzeugungen alle Emanzipationen und sozialen Fortschritte, die das letzte Jahrhundert geschaffen hat." (136) In the course of the decade since 1922 Kayser has moved in his writings from a position of basic rejection of the contemporary world to one of basic acceptance. Of the author of the book which is the subject of the review Kayser asserts: "Alles ist für ihn 'Schicksal' und das Volk die Einheit des 'Bekenntnisses' und des 'Schicksals,' eine Auffassung, die, einmal in die Politik getragen, jeder Willkür und Sinnlosigkeit die Tore öffnet." (137) The reviewer's voice is that of a political realist. Of particular interest is the pejorative emphasis on "Schicksal." The about-face from Kayser's own free and unchecked use of this term in 1922 is striking. The change in his treatment of such a representative term stands for the change in his thinking over the preceding ten years.

Kayser goes so far as to say: "Man möchte zum extremsten Rationalisten oder Materialisten werden, um dieser Romantik entgegenzutreten." (137) However, this possibility remains in the subjunctive, for it is an alternative foreign to Kayser. Evidence is the opening paragraph of the review where he is willing to concede to non-extreme nationalists the virtues of "idealism" and "revolutionary élan." (136) Most telling is his further concession: "Diese Gesinnung hat insofern einen geistigen Charakter, als sie aus den Vordergründen der Zeitgeschichte herauskommen und einer unerträglich ideenlosen Gegenwart ein Ideal geben möchte: das der Nation." (136) This point is particularly pertinent because it shows that at least in July 1931 Kayser still automatically equates "geistig" with profound—the opposite of "Vordergründen der Zeitgeschichte"—and above all with the attempt to supply an ideal to banal times.

This conclusion is supported by other remarks in the same "Europäische Rundschau." In another review Kayser describes the author's standpoint in a pointedly neutral or even distant manner: "Es ist für ihn wichtig, Antimetaphysiker zu sein und zu betonen, dass wir keine geistige Welt ausserhalb der wirklichen besitzen; . . ." (139) The words "es ist für ihn wichtig" show the reviewer to be disassociating himself from the anti-metaphysical point of view. His real, contrary feelings are expressed without reservation at the close of another review: "Das Buch ist ein Dokument, nicht einer politischen Gesinnung, sondern der harten, unverleugbaren Wirklichkeit. Diese Wirklichkeit aber widerlegt am besten jene Gesinnung, die wieder und wieder sie preist und verherrlicht." (141) Alongside his developed political perspicacity, his new directness and precision, and his avoidance of the kind of thinking which the term "Schicksal" represents, Kayser remains an idealist.

II. Satirical and Grotesque Stories

Related to the non-judgmental category are five stories which are satires of one form or another.[14] Distortion and

[14] Generally speaking, the stories—with the exception of Heinrich Mann's "Kobes" which lacks humor and evokes horror and revulsion—fall into M. H. Abrams' broad definition (from his *A Glossary of Literary Terms*, 3rd

humor are stylistic devices which establish distance from the caricatured object, a distance which is similar to the non-judgmental stance. It is remarkable how few stories there are of the satirical type. Apparently the satirical posture was foreign to the *NR*'s sensibilities.[15] Other stories have elements of satire, humor and caricature, or grotesque qualities,[16] but only in these five do some or all of those elements dominate, creating a separate idiom. While absolute distinctions cannot be made—nor are they relevant to this study—it is nevertheless possible to describe more closely the first story, Ungar's "Colberts Reise," and the last, Vietta's "Der Registrator," as grotesque for they lack the obvious didactic element of *Zeitkritik*.[17] This element qualifies the other three stories as more typically satirical.

---

ed. [New York: Holt, Rinehart and Winston, 1971], p. 153): "SATIRE is the literary art of diminishing a subject by making it ridiculous and evoking toward it attitudes of amusement, contempt, indignation, or scorn. It differs from the *comic* in that comedy evokes laughter as an end in itself, while satire 'derides'; that is, it uses laughter as a weapon, and against a butt existing outside the work itself."

[15] It is an interesting reflection on the *NR* that Wolfgang Rothe, in "Metaphysischer Realismus . . . ," p. 256, equates this posture with twentieth-century literary realism *per se*: "Während der Realist des 19. Jahrhunderts die Welt so, 'wie sie ist,' nachahmend zu schildern unternahm oder gar 'wissenschaftliche' Wirklichkeitstreue anstrebte, hat der realistische Schriftsteller des 20. Jahrhunderts die Zielwerte Ähnlichkeit, Entsprechungen, Analogie aufgegeben, als simplen ästhetischen Denkfehler fallengelassen. Nicht um eine Deckungsgleichheit von Wirklichkeit und Kunstgebilde, den Zusammenfall von dichterischer Subjektivität und realer Objektivität ist es ihm zu tun, sondern um die *Enthüllung der Wirklichkeit* mittels Groteske, Ironie, Satire."

[16] An example is the protagonist in Leonhard Frank's "Der Beamte," above p. 129.

[17] According to Ivo Braak (*Poetik in Stichworten*, 4th ed. [Kiel: Ferdinand Hirt, 1972], p. 165), *Zeitkritik* is intrinsic to satire: "Satire dient der *Zeitkritik*, ist immer Richterin, hält einer in Sitten und Anschauungen auf Abwege geratenen Zeit den scharfgeschliffenen Spiegel vor." According to Philip Thomson (*The Grotesque*, No. 24, The Critical Idiom, ed. John D. Jump [London: Methuen, 1972], p. 42), the absence of this didactic ele- *(continued on page 222)*

Hermann Ungar's "Colberts Reise" (August 1922, II, 834–48) maintains the somewhat bitter mood of the fiction in the latter half of 1922. It is the only story in the August issue, which is a memorial issue for Walther Rathenau. The object of derision is the protagonist, retired grocer Josef Colbert, who is a victim of monomania. On the serious level there is an implied criticism of petit bourgeois mentality and, indirectly, a study of the psychology of class conflict. The grotesque mode is apparent in the opening lines:

> Colbert begann seine Reise 1910. Er starb 1911 infolge der Erregungen, die sie mit sich gebracht hatte. Modlizki hatte ihn zu schwer enttäuscht. Man kann Colberts Grabmal auf dem Friedhof der Stadt sehen. Es besteht aus einem weissen Marmorkreuz und trägt die einfache Inschrift:
>
> Hier ruht Josef Colbert, geboren am 14.III.1859 hier, gestorben am 7.V.1911 ebendaselbst.
>
> Er wurde demnach zweiundfünfzig Jahre alt.
>
> Der Reise geschieht in dieser Inschrift nicht Erwähnung. (834)

The stilted language, clipped sentences, matter-of-fact tone, lack of logical connection between statements of fact alert the reader to suspend the usual expectations. This death is not meant to elicit sympathy.

The next sentence introduces the potential conflict: "Die Enttäuschung Colberts war um so schwerer, als Modlizki von

---

(continued from page 221) ment distinguishes the grotesque from satire: "Unlike the satirist, the grotesque writer does not analyze and instruct in terms of right and wrong, nor true and false, nor does he attempt to distinguish between these. . . . The grotesque is . . . *anti-rational* and not conducive to the grasping of satiric points." Thomson admits that his distinctions are somewhat overdrawn for purposes of clarity. Certainly, these forms—as in the case of the five *NR* stories—are often not clearly distinguishable. However, Thomson goes on to make a point which is particularly apropos to Heinrich Mann's "Kobes," a story which in my opinion fails for precisely this reason: ". . . it should be clear that the satirist who uses the grotesque as a tool, a shock-weapon, must be careful. There is a danger that the didactic point he wishes to make may be obscured for the reader by the nonplussing, disorienting and generally overwhelming effect of the grotesque."

frühester Jugend an in Colberts Hause aufgewachsen war. Modlizki nämlich war niederer Herkunft." (834) Both humorous and serious implications of class conflict are contained in the contrast between the names "Colbert" and "Modlizki"—as codes, respectively, for western versus eastern origins, or pretended social elevation versus inferior social standing. Colbert is an extreme francophile whose goal is to model his life upon what he regards as the superior culture of France[18]:

> Colbert hingegen rühmte sich französischen Blutes. Sein Urgrossvater, erzählte er, sei aus Reims eingewandert. Colbert behauptete, hierüber ein Dokument zu besitzen. Er lächelte über Sitten und Gebräuche seiner Mitbürger und liess seine bessere Art auch äusserlich erkennen. So trug er den Kinnbart französisch geschoren und den dünnen Schnurrbart an der Nase aufwärts gedreht. Den Kopf wusch er mit wohlriechenden Wässern, und seine Glatze soll darum so zart und rosig geschimmert und sich weich angefühlt haben wie ein feines samtenes Tuch. Zudem flocht Colbert französische Worte in seine Rede, wenn auch er keine grosse Auswahl hierin besass. (835)

The problem stems from Colbert's isolation in his obsession, and the consequent discrepancy between his self-image and reality. He has no contact with the real world of his servant-cum-adopted son Modlizki. Colbert is obsessed with planning his first trip to Paris. Modlizki is essential to his plans as a companion, servant and protector. For an entire year Colbert engages in ludicrously elaborate preparations for his trip in secret from his family, admitting only Modlizki to his confidence and presuming (without cause) his equal enthu-

---

[18] Francophilia was an authentic phenomenon in the 1920's which Walter Laqueur (*Weimar: A Cultural History*, pp. 38 ff.) discusses. There was a well-known man about town whose habits in reality approximated the caricatured Colbert's: "Paul Cohen Portheim, a shy man, painter, writer, author of excellent monographs on Paris and London and the *arbiter elegantiarum* of the Romanische Café, was a regular guest [at the café]. He lived in Berlin but his heart was in Paris. Every evening he would get his private weather bulletin from the French capital and would dress accordingly, rain or shin," (Laqueur, *ibid.*, p. 228).

siasm. Meanwhile the real life of which Colbert is unaware, goes on as usual, with, among other things, Modlizki regularly having Colbert's teenage daughter up to his room where he is gradually initiating her into sex.

His master's expecting the enthusiasm of a friend and equal from him becomes too much for Modlizki and resentment—unobserved by Colbert—boils within him—an inevitability (apparent only to the reader) in view of his degrading status as both quasi family member and total servant. The Paris trip plans become the last straw. When the unsuspecting Colbert finally anxiously makes the long-prepared announcement to his wife at dinner that he will be departing immediately with Modlizki on a trip to Paris, and looks pathetically to Modlizki for support, Modlizki rebels without warning, announcing that he has decided not to go along to Paris, and leaves the house for good. Colbert's entire world—a construct of his pretensions—collapses because in actuality its maintenance and functioning were dependent upon the devoted and loving servant of his imagining. Colbert had been oblivious to the hypocritical and exploitative nature of the relationship. Colbert's last words before lapsing into unconsciousness are, ironically, the first ones that show he has made contact with reality: " 'Das ist der Hauch des Umsturzes, . . .' " (848)

Hermann Hesse's story "Tragisch" (July 1924, II, 705–14) is a satire on a future when literature and regard for language have become obsolete.[19] The elderly newspaper typesetter and ex-poet, Johannes, is the last of a breed—a defender of

---

[19] Such apprehension was widespread among writers at the time. Hermand and Trommler (*Die Kultur der Weimarer Republik*) refer to it several times: "Mitte der zwanziger Jahre wurde endgültig deutlich, dass die Schriftsteller nicht nur ihre Arbeit, sondern auch ihre Position in der Gesellschaft neu einzuschätzen hatten." (p. 133) "Die Äusserungen der Ratlosigkeit über die Funktion der Künste nahmen zu dieser Zeit [1923] dramatisch zu." (p. 145)

standards of grammar and style in an era when the written word no longer has a cultural function. A special bugaboo of his is the incorrect and casually frequent use of the word "tragisch." The situation is mirrored in the contrast between the elaborately correct spoken style of Johannes and the error-filled obliviousness to style which characterizes the speech of his interlocutors at the newspaper. An irony of this portrait of an age without literature is that it appears in an issue devoted almost entirely to fiction.

Heinrich Mann's "Kobes" (March 1925, I, 235–66) creates a nightmarish world under the control of an all-pervasive, all-powerful capitalist industry. The style is reminiscent of expressionism: the dialogue consists of terse, rapid-fire, quotable statements; characters are allegories—for the middle class, for example, or the intellectual. Capitalists and capitalism—including the political system—are the primary targets of criticism, but the German self-image, idealism, intellectuals, the military, religion and the middle class are also under attack—all are controlled and exploited by the capitalist conspiracy. Culture, apart from the industry, no longer exists. The figure who represents "Geist" (characterized by an overly large head) explains, in a statement reminiscent of *Faust*: "Bin Doktor der Philosophie, der Naturwissenschaften und anderer inzwischen abgebauter Spezialitäten." (242) As in the Hesse story, culture is a thing of the past and the independent intellectual no longer has a role to play. The reigning attitude toward ideas is: ". . . was sind Ideen,—wenn nicht der sie hat, der die Macht hat?" (263) The intellectual makes a stab at usurping power from the head capitalist and cult figure, Kobes, but loses. He remains an outsider—weak, powerless, and in the end, doomed. The ruthless corporation has corrupted every person and institution in society; its power is complete. Unmitigated—as the above stories are—by a light touch, "Kobes" is totally negative in mood, nearly bereft of humor, and rather sterile in effect.

The contrast is extreme between Heinrich Mann's story and Franz Werfel's charming, funny satire on the decaying Austro-Hungarian Empire, "Das Trauerhaus" (September 1927, II, 239–83). The title refers, in an ironic reversal, to an eminent "Freudenhaus" or house of prostitution in Prague which becomes a house of mourning when its decadent owner dies on the same day on which the Austrian Crown Prince is assassinated at Sarajevo. From this central parallel many others branch out, both with the history of the Empire and with the contemporary society, making it clear that the house is meant to be a microcosm of the larger world. The parallel pokes fun at general hypocrisy and incompetence, stale traditions, manifestations of decadence and decay.

Egon Vietta's "Der Registrator" (II, 493–513), a radical departure from the above stories, appeared five years later, in October 1932. The October 1932 issue is noteworthy as well for remarks by Kayser in the "Anmerkungen" section. In an article entitled "Die Suche nach der Nation" (563–64) he examines the terms "nation" and "race" to disprove the theories of the racists and nationalist extremists. It is another example, as we have seen above—especially in the July and December 1931 and July and December 1932 issues—of Kayser's matured and insightful grasp of the theoretical foundations of political ideologies. On the subject of defining a "nation" he points to the fundamental theoretical error of the right and in so doing denies the pertinence of "metaphysical ideas" to "historical reality":

> Nichts also ist falscher als der Versuch, das Wesen einer Nation von metaphysischen Ideen herzuleiten und diese Ideen der geschichtlichen Wirklichkeit als unveränderliche Forderung gegenüberzustellen. Kein Missverständnis ist gefährlicher. Für den deutschen Nationalismus ist es aber bezeichnend. (563)

In his January 1922 essay Kayser had rejected the possibility of an extrinsic aesthetic: "Gibt es aber Gesetze für die Kunst, so sind sie allein in der Kunst selbst, nicht aber ausserhalb ihrer zu suchen" (above p. 36). Now, over a decade later (in a review of *Gehemnis des Kunstwerks* by Ferdinand Lion [Stuttgart: Deutsche Verlagsanstalt]) he rejects the possibility of an exclusively intrinsic aesthetic:

> Nichts erscheint unzeitgemässer als eine neue Philosophie der Kunst. Oder sie müsste von aussen an das Kunstwerk herantreten: von der Gesellschaft oder der zeitgeschichtlichen Situation her. Reine Kunst, deren Sinn nur aus dem eigenen Wesen abgeleitet werden kann, ist heute ebenso in ihrer geistigen wie in ihrer weltlichen Existenz bedroht. (566)

No longer does Kayser represent the "ästhetische Attitüde."[20] The times demand a revised view of art and Kayser has responded to that demand. Apparently the political and economic crises of the early twenties, as serious as they were, had not so penetrated the inherited consciousness of idealism as to revise it fundamentally.[21] This occurred rather as a process over the entire decade, culminating, it seems, in a sobriety and pragmatism, unadorned clarity and directness, a new realism. However it is described, Kayser's thinking on matters of art and politics no longer has the taint of wholesale resistance to the present which marked it in 1922. In a review which is apropos of his own new outlook (by his tacit agreement) Kayser describes the posture advocated by a French author (Jean Richard Bloch, in essays entitled *Vom Sinn unseres Jahrhunderts* [Vienna: Paul Zsolnay]): "Vor allem müssen wir das endgültige Ende des neunzehnten Jahrhunderts erkennen, seine Erinnerungen überwinden und dem sachlichen Geist unserer Zeit leben." (568)

"The pragmatic spirit of [the] times" is certainly reflected in the style of Vietta's "Der Registrator," a story which can be characterized as an example of the absurd, with surreal ele-

---

[20] See above, p. 193, n. 1.
[21] See Bermann Fischer's comment in n. 5, above p. 182.

ments. The opening section is typical of its straightforward, unadorned style:

> Jetzt lebe ich seit achtzehn Jahren in Sch. und bekleide das Amt eines Registrators. Ich habe den Globus Tausende von Kilometern bereist, bevor mich das Justizministerium in Sch. zur letzten Ruhe gebettet hat. Es besteht keine Möglichkeit, nach M. oder K. versetzt zu werden. Die Beamten fürchten den weltabgelegenen Ort. Er heisst das "Grab." Ich bin ohne Furcht nach Sch. gezogen. Ich glaubte den Ministerialräten trotzen zu können. Und hatte mich verrechnet. Es gibt unzählige Registraturen im Land, da jedoch niemand für den Posten in Sch. zu gewinnen war, musste ich, komme was wolle, bleiben. In den ersten Jahren war ich mutig um meine Versetzung eingekommen. Gesuch um Gesuch wurde mit immer neuen Gründen dem Herrn Minister vorgelegt. Ich erfuhr, dass die Gesuche, wie es in der Amtssprache lautet, bald in den Papierkorb wanderten. Ich galt als verrückt. Es war beschlossene Sache, dass ich niemals aus Sch. herausgelassen werden dürfe, das keine Registratur für meinen Geisteszustand geeignet sei. Der Minister, ein wohlwollender, aber autokratischer Kopf, schrieb mit eigener Hand in die Akten: Der Kerl soll mir vom Leibe bleiben! Der Ministerialrat kleidete es in die Worte: Sehr geehrter Herr Bunkus: Der Minister war leider nicht zu bewegen . . . Das Weitere interessiert nicht mehr.
>
> Ich wurde schliesslich vergessen.
>
> Eines Tages verbreitete sich das Gerücht: Bunkus sei der einzige geeignete Registrator für den Posten in Sch. Meine Arbeit wurde gelobt. (493)

Like the opening of a Kafka work, the matter-of-fact language emphasizes by contrast the rationally inexplicable world which it creates. The "Registrator" Bunkus is, like a Kafka protagonist, trapped by the arbitrary and apparently irrevocable decisions of an absurd and inscrutable bureaucracy. Like Kafka's "K" in *Der Prozess*, Bunkus is a hard and conscientious worker who brings a kind of guilt upon himself by single-minded devotion to his pedestrian task to the exclusion of real and giving relationships with other people (marriage, for example). As in the case of all the Kafka works the obvious story line is actually a parable for a spiritual process.

In the opening paragraph there are clues to this second

layer of meaning.[22] The Ministry which has jurisdiction over Bunkus is the Ministry of Justice. That Ministry's treatment of Bunkus is beyond his control, nor does it follow worldly laws of cause and effect. Bunkus has been assigned somewhere and must remain there against his will for an apparently unlimited extent of time. It is his "last resting place," "weltabgelegen," "das 'Grab'." There are several references to madness. The motives of death, madness, and the transcendental are repeated throughout the narrative.

Indeed madness seems to surface everywhere. It appropriately describes the farcical events which begin at a "Stammtisch" whose members, among others, are Bunkus, the mayor and a man named "Niemand." Their evening is interrupted when it is discovered that the mayor, stumbling drunkenly toward the toilet, has mistakenly taken the door to the outside where he has fallen into a manure pit. Bunkus—the town registrar respected and admired for his conscientious work and life free of burdensome responsibilities such as a family—finds himself shaken at the news that his friend the mayor has survived this experience. His disappointment shows how removed Bunkus is from his fellows. His distance from them means that it will be necessary for him to work out

[22] An essay by Vietta, "Fahrten in Lappland," which appeared in the May 1931 *NR* (I, 664–85) gives evidence for the author's inclination to conceptualize in terms of two concurrent realms: the spiritual and the worldly. The emphasis is on meaning and symbolism in the people and places he visits. The essay is built around two significant visits: to an ancient and decaying Russian Orthodox monastery, the home of the spirit; and to a flourishing iron mine, the home of modern industry. In the monastery chapel the author observes a little boy who is so intent in his concentration upon an icon that he recoils in fright when he notices that he is being watched. The author concludes: "Es gibt also auch im Leben des kleinen Kolja zwei Welten." (680) It is the word "auch" which is particularly significant. There is also an incident in which the author incurs the same kind of guilt (demonstrating a lack of feeling) in relation to Kolja as the character Bunkus does in his relationships with his fellow man.

his own salvation. That same night a drastic change occurs in Bunkus' life.

Up to that time he had sought the absolute in the form of perfect record-keeping (this too an aspect of the satire): "Meine bis ins letzte durchdachte, gepflegte und ausgearbeitete Registratur wurde vollkommen wie die Ordnung selbst." (494) The only weak point was the unpredictability of the human being—the registrar himself. In order to integrate this last possible source of unpredictability into the filing system, Bunkus creates a file called: " 'Die Meinungen, Irrtümer und Beschlüsse des Registrators Bunkus betreffend.' " (495) The realm of perfect order and predictability is his paradise. The inn and friends are the realm of disorder. The ultimate disorder represented by the mayor's unfortunate accident precipitates the upheaval in Bunkus' thinking and his life. He return to the registry, creates chaos in his files, and becomes fully aware of the impossibility of his former goal: ". . . erkannte ich zum erstenmal, dass ich der Ordnung gar nicht gewachsen war, vielmehr eine oberflächliche und scheinheilige Unordnung für gültig ausgegeben hatte. . . . Eine Sturzflut unerwarteter Beziehungen waltete in den Akten, die sich schlechterdings nicht auf eine lesbare Formel bringen liessen." (505)[23]

---

[23] Again Rothe ("Metaphysischer Realismus . . .") in his discussion of the Musil, Döblin, and Broch novels as paradigms of the modern sensibility, treats a pivotal theme—order—in a manner which sheds light on the deeper layer of meaning in "Der Registrator." "Wir leben, schrieb Musil, in einer 'Durchgangszeit,' eine 'Niedergangszeit,' die eine 'Übergangszeit' ist, in welcher sowohl eine 'sachliche Ordnung' der Dinge fehlt wie auch eine 'seelische Unordnung' der Menschheit herrscht. 'Uneigentlichkeit' ist das Wesen der Wirklichkeit solcher Zeitalter, weshalb solche Wirklichkeit abgeschafft werden muss: die 'Welt des Seinesgleichen' ist 'das bloss äusserlich Wirkliche,' nicht die 'wirkliche Wirklichkeit.' Wie konnte Europa zu einer so schlechten Wirklichkeit gelangen? Ist der 'freiwillige Glaube' an eine Ordnung

In a scene reminiscent of Kafka's *Der Prozess* two figures—one of whom is the Minister of Justice—appear in the registry and demand that Bunkus justify his conduct: "In erster Linie müssen Sie sich rechtfertigen." (507) They admonish him of the importance of fulfilling his duty and upholding the principle of order: " 'Die Faust der Ordnung ist das einzige, worauf wir uns verlassen können. In Ihre Hände, Registrator Bunkus, ist das wichtigste Amt unseres öffentlichen Lebens gegeben.' " (507) Bunkus answers "with a bad conscience": "Ich habe biz zuletzt ausgeharrt, um diese Registratur in Zucht zu halten, . . ." (507) He is told: "Jeder hat auf dem Posten zu sterben, der ihm von der menschlichen Gesellschaft angewiesen ist." (507) At this point Bunkus begins to protest, countering with his own, contrary, opinion: "Ich bin zur Überzeugung gekommen, dass auch das Chaos protegiert werden muss. Denn die Ordnung . . . garantiert nur sich selbst. . . . Sie garantiert nicht einmal sich selbst, . . ."(508) One of the visitors replies: "Anarchismus!" When they ask about a note in the files which refers to the mayor, Bunkus replies that he is dead as a result of falling into a ditch. The last word he hears from the visitors is "Mord"; Bunkus

---

'verbraucht,' meinte Musil, folgt unabwendbar ihr 'Zusammenbruch': das 'Amt' wird zum Ersatz für die verlorene religiöse Einheit." (259) In a statement which applies as well to Bunkus: "Den Protagonisten dieser Romane bleibt der Zerfall der 'Einheit,' der Verlust des 'Ganzen' einer gegliederten 'Ordnung' keineswegs verborgen. Je nach dem Grade ihrer Bewusstheit besitzen sie eine klare Erkenntnis dieses Sachverhaltes oder nur eine dumpfe Ahnung desselben, aber die Erfahrung des Mangels, den solche Ordnungslosigkeit vorstellt, und der Wunsch nach seiner Aufhebung ist bei ihnen prinzipiell der gleiche. 'Ordnung' avanciert somit zu einem Schlüsselbegriff aller drei Romane." (260) The parallel is particularly striking between Bunkus and one of Broch's characters: "Der Buchhalter im Mannheimer Zollhafen lobt und liebt die 'schöne Ordnung' seiner Bücher und Lagerlisten, der freilich das reale Durcheinander in den Schuppen nicht entspricht. . . . Hilflose Wut ist seine emotionale Antwort auf das Chaos, in das er allein nicht die erstrebte Ordnung einzuführen vermag." (264)

"sank schuldbewusst in die Knie . . ."(508) There are, in other words, two moral issues: justified and unjustified guilt. The former applies to Bunkus' (lack of) feelings about the mayor; the latter to his resistance to raising "order" to a moral imperative.

As it turns out, the entire night's experience was a dream. Nevertheless Bunkus has changed. He begins to question his complacency and the generally assumed irreproachability of his life up to this point:

> Ich bin ein Mensch geworden, der sich nicht mehr begreift.
>
> Habe ich nicht ein gesättigtes, verehrtes, ein richtiges Leben geführt? Oder war diese Korrektheit, diese unantastbare Sauberkeit wie ein Fluch in meinen Alltag gehämmert? Mir will es manchmal scheinen, als sei etwas Ungeheuerliches mit mir vorgegangen. Ich möchte mich selbst, den Registrator Bunkus, von mir wegwerfen, um solcherart gesprengt zu einem anderen Bunkus zurückzukehren—wer weiss, ob zu einem besseren, einem ausgewogeneren, wenn er nur diese vermaledeite Richtigkeit verliert. Die Menschen sind mir erschreckend wohlgesinnt, vielleicht ahnen sie, wie sehr ich von ihrem Tun und Lassen abgewichen bin. Und welcher Mensch empfände nicht die lästerliche Blasphemie seiner wohlgehegten Tage. Ich bin gedrängt, mit diesem und jenem zu sprechen, als wäre alles Wichtige versäumt, . . . (512)

Here a central theme of the modern sensibility becomes apparent—the protagonist's awareness of his alienation from himself and from others.[24]

Bunkus is moved by his new strong feelings to take bold action to break out of the pattern in which he has been trapped. In extreme agitation—in terms of superficial realism, all out of proportion to the insignificance of the occasion—he

---

[24] Rothe, ibid., p. 256, sees it as characteristic of realism *per se* since the middle ages: "Hieraus folgt die Entfremdung des Einzel-Ichs von der Wirlichkeit (und schliesslich von sich selber), oberstes Thema des Realisten qua Satirikers seit dem Verfall des christlichen Ordo."

begins writing a letter to the Minister. The discrepancy between Bunkus' exaggerated sense of the importance of his intention and its seemingly minor nature points again with Kafkaesque irony to the other level of meaning. Clearly there is more at stake than just a letter to a Minister. Bunkus explains in the letter that over the course of his eighteen years at his post he has achieved such perfect and self-perpetuating order that the job of registrar has become superfluous. He begs therefore to be released from service.

The Minister's reply has a powerful effect upon Bunkus: it makes him dizzy and escapes his comprehension. Indeed, the contrast between the Minister's letter and Bunkus' previous experience of the system is grotesque, certainly not explainable in rational terms:

> Es heisst, der Minister begreife meine Bedrückung, die unser aller Bedrückung sei. Er aber, der über den Ämtern walte, er könne nicht zulassen, dass auch der unterste Beamte im Räderwerk des Mechanismus untergehe und habe veranlasst, dass der Beamte Bunkus in die Hauptstadt des Landes berufen werde . . . Denn er wisse zu gut, dass der staatliche Apparat nur einen Sinn habe, so lange Menschen, weil und dass Menschen existieren . . . (513)

The concluding sentence of the story brings Bunkus' enigmatic reaction to his rescue: "Schliesslich schwamm mir alles vor den Augen." (513) Possibly, he is dying.[25] Perhaps he is just fainting at the absurdity of the whole thing. Certainly the conclusion does not point to any continuation in the real world. A kind of private redemption has occurred which, however, is arbitrary on its face because it ostensibly responds not to Bunkus' rejection of the untenable principle of absolute order, but to his letter about successful maintenance of that principle. Or is it meant to be a spiritual response—as myster-

[25] Cf. above quote from p. 507 about the requirement that one die at one's post.

ious as grace—to spiritual progress toward humility and the examined life—a reordering of priorities which puts the human being first?

There are no definitive answers, but many possibilities. This story would appear to exist on a different planet from the stories discussed in previous chapters. It appears to be a parable for the erring mortal who is tested, passes the test, and given his reward. But it treats these matters with profound irony, even comedy, and seems to convey the message, if any, that life is chaotic, absurd. The usual assumptions, connections, relationships between parts are not supported. It is this style, with its unexpected breaks, lack of sequence, its multiple alternatives, which puts such a great distance between "Der Registrator"—in late 1932—and the previous stories.

It is perhaps the first of the stories which we have treated up to now with a truly new sensibility, which young authors such as Süskind, Heuser, or Klaus Mann (all three wrote essays on the subject) had sought in theory but not achieved in (stylistic) practice. Marked by a sense of chaos, even madness, at the foundation of things and absurdity in the course of events, of arbitrary rewards and punishments, of human beings as both pawns and perpetrators of the absurdities, it is a bridge to the nihilistic sensibility. But it is only a bridge because the story's fundamental concerns are spiritual and the spiritual level is foreign to the stories which fall into the nihilistic category.

Chapter VI

Stories in the Nihilistic Category

The first published work of a very young writer appeared in the October 1927 *NR*. Herbert Schlüter was only twenty years old when his story "Die Kinderhochzeit" (II, 396–419) appeared.[1] It introduces a new sensibility. The tone—light-hearted, coy and a bit sarcastic—is set in the opening paragraphs:

---

[1] Herbert Schlüter, one of the several promising young authors who appeared on the scene at the S. Fischer Verlag in 1927, was born in Berlin on 16 May 1906. Along with Meisel and Heuser, Schlüter belongs to that group whose writing was cut off shortly after it began. In 1927 S. Fischer published a collection of his short stories entitled *Das späte Fest*. Of his second book, de Mendelssohn says: "Herbert Schlüters zweites Buch konnte der Verlag angesichts der allgemeinen Entwicklung um 1933 schon nicht mehr bringen, und der Dichter legte bald die Feder weg." (Peter de Mendelssohn, *S. Fischer und sein Verlag* [Frankfurt am Main: S. Fischer, 1970], p. 1102.) However, according to Kosch (Wilhelm Kosch, ed., *Handbuch der deutschen Gegenwartsliteratur*, 2nd ed. [Berne: Francke, 1949]) a novel by Schlüter—*Die Rückkehr der verlorenen Tochter*—was published in 1932. Schlüter emigrated in 1933 to France, Spain, and Italy. From 1948–49 he directed the *Literarische Revue* in Munich, and later was a literary critic and editor at a publishing house. A novel by Schlüter entitled *Nach fünf Jahren* appeared in 1947, and in 1948 a novella entitled "Im Schatten der Liebe." (*Ibid.*)

> Die Damen und Herren der Pension Finsterhaide sitzen beim Frühstück, in spärlicher Unterhaltung, aber doch angeregt, auf ernste, fast finstere Art. Sie essen; gesammelt und eifrig, sitzen sie gebeugt und picken von ihren Tellern.—
>
> Am Tische präsidiert, blass und fett, Frau Berta Brögel, Witwe seit drei Jahren nun—und seit eben der Zeit bemüht, aus einem etwas parvenümässig hergerichteten Schloss mit häufigen Gästen (das Schloss gehörte zu einem mittelgrossen Grundbesitz) eine noblere Erholungsstätte mit sympathischen Pensionären zu machen. Sie war noch nicht allzuweit damit gekommen, wie man sieht—ich denke an die Pensionäre, die in der Halle beim Frühstück sitzen. (396–97)

Frau Brögel's boarders are a group of caricatured figures with names such as Herr Dr. Tonfuss and Fräulein Wanda von Kuckucksheim. Each represents a particular type or segment of middle or upper-middle class society. The central figures are three pairs which could stand for the ages of man: the precocious children Hellmut and Mariechen whose game of marriage provides the story's title, a celebrated young actress Karola and her former boyfriend the poet Peter, and finally an octogenarian pair—Frau Regierungsrat Hippel and Herr von Trontow. All six of these characters show signs of decadence. The youngsters play at being not merely adult but aged adults, engaging in highly artificial and slightly salacious banter. Even their appearance is decadent rather than childlike. Mariechen, for example, has deep grooves at each side of her mouth which resemble wrinkles; both she and Hellmut are exceptionally pale and thin. Peter, observing them once from a distance, finds the children gnome-like. Thirteen-year-old Hellmut, who also tends to be extremely nervous, has a crush on Peter which is obviously homosexual in nature, a fact of which Hellmut and Peter are aware.

"Kindlich," "kindisch," "lüstern," "kokett" (410), "verfeinert," "ein wenig verdorben" (398) are terms used to describe Peter. He is charming, kind-hearted and dissolute. In one scene he is dancing alone to "suggestive" music wearing makeup which has been applied to his face by his friend

Wuutz with whom a homosexual bond unites him. Karola, who is still attracted to Peter, insists at one point that he take a walk with her into the woods. Once there she pulls him down to the ground next to her—a kind of sexually aggressive behavior which is new to the women characters in the *NR* stories. While women may behave seductively, they do not pull men down to the forest floor. Nor has there been, prior to this story, a sexual relationship between a woman character and a man with homosexual inclinations. The sensibility which the Schlüter story introduces is marked by a more candid and unfettered eroticism, an eroticism which is generally not connected to love.

The octogenarians are portrayed in such a way as to make them the most appealing couple. Frau Regierungsrat Hippel, in particular, displays wit and an engagingly ironic perspective on her fellow boarders and their doings. On several occasions her appearance and manner are described as "hexenhaft." Herr von Trontow, on the other hand, tends more to the gently childlike with touches of senility. Both are physically decrepit. With the exception of the children, all the characters are childish. These six central characters as well as the others engage in empty conversation and silly, pointless activity (which happens to be appropriate to the vacation setting). Not only their activities but also their relationships are devoid of strong feelings and of deeper meaning. Their interaction is superficial, as light as the language and tone. These characters, in contrast to previous stories, are not taken seriously, nor examined in depth; their psyches are not explored; their emotions are given neither weight nor significance. The caricature of society is not explored to the point of becoming satire, that is, it is not seriously critical. There is no moral or spiritual statement, no symbolism, no clue to a deeper layer of meaning. There is merely a mood of humorous decadence, a feeling that nothing which occurs is important, that human relationships are only a game. The characters are so portrayed that they appear to be drifting aimlessly, without goals or standards, or even hopes or dreams. The impression is of a cheerful nihilism.[2]

In the February 1928 issue Schlüter provides a kind of theoretical underpinning for his own stories (and by implication for the nihilistic category in general) in a manifesto entitled "Beruf und Aussicht einer Jugend." (I, 201–11) After brief comments on the works of a number of younger writers Schlüter—speaking in the first person plural as a representative of the young generation of writers—turns to his views on the existential situation of his generation. Literature, he believes, should serve as a "discussion of our existence." (207) In his review of past stages in that existence Schlüter uses a description which applies directly to "Die Kinderhochzeit" and therefore shows the connection in his mind between the young generation's experience of reality and its expression in literature: "Das Leben nahm fast kindliche Züge an. Sonderbare Einfachheit der Formen, kindische, primitiv-raffinierte Lustigkeit waren obenauf." (206) Schlüter goes on to apply to this earlier stage in the young generation's experience the very same terms used by Klaus Mann in his 1926 essay to describe a generation without ties and without a past: ". . . Voraussetzungslosigkeit, die fehlende Herkunft, . . ." ". . . ein grosses Kaspar-Hausertum." (206) These terms apply as well to the conditions portrayed in Süskind's "Raymund"—up to its conclusion—as do Schlüter's further comments on the historical situation:

> Die Kamaraderie war gross, sie war stillschweigend und unsentimental. Man fragte einander nicht erst nach den Eltern. Man hatte sie gar nicht. Man brauchte sie deshalb nicht erst abzusetzen wie es

---

[2] The concept "nihilism" is used in the non-political, non-doctrinaire sense as defined in *Webster's Third New International Dictionary* (unabridged, 1971): "A viewpoint that all traditional values and beliefs are unfounded and that all existence is consequently senseless and useless: a denial of intrinsic meaning and value in life."

etwa die aus dem Schützengraben heimgekehrte Jugend sehr aufgeregt tat. Hohe, bewahrte Beamte begannen zu verarmen, kleine Leute waren über eine illegitime Nacht vermögend geworden. Alles war ernsthaft in Frage gestellt. Wo gab es Grenzen? Wo gab es Bindungen? An die politischen glaubten dies Halbwüchsigen schon nicht mehr recht . . . (206)

Schlüter too shows the previously noted awareness of a threat to "Geist": "Die geistige Welt, in der wir zu leben meinen, beginnt sich aufzulösen." (208) The significant difference from the fears expressed by other authors is the distance implied in the phrase "in der wir zu leben meinen" which suggests that the "geistige Welt" of conventional wisdom may be an illusion. In the midst of this disintegration Schlüter holds fast to one defensible motivating force, the "Trieb nach Wahrhaftigkeit" (208), the only norm he believes worth upholding: "Wir werden aus dem Streben nach Wahrhaftigkeit gegen die Moral Partei nehmen müssen, gegen die Religionen, gegen jede Art des Glaubens." (208) He rejects the "bad conscience" which is a legacy of Judeo-Christian morality.

His generation, Schlüter explains, is skeptical of all so-called great concepts. They reject the Metaphysical, the Absolute, and an aesthetic which advocates "l'art pour l'art."[3] "Die jungen Leute glauben nicht an die objektive 'Idee,' etwa an ein in den Wolken stehendes ewiges Sternbild: Moral" (209), he writes. Where the old morality sees guilt the young generation looks for the psychological forces which motivate an act. "Es gibt wohl keinen der grossen Begriffe, der uns heute nicht gefährlich zweideutig erschiene, ja dessen Bedeutung nicht ernsthaft in Frage gestellt sei." (209)

At this point Schlüter parts company with the sensibilities expressed in the stories up to now. His rigorous re-

---

[3] For the evolution in Kayser's thinking on this point see above pp. 226–27.

jection of "eternal" verities, of traditional morality and idealism leave Schlüter and the group for which he speaks without a philosophical support system, adrift in an unexplained universe: "Es ist schwer, fast unmöglich, möchte man zuweilen fürchten, so nackt zu leben, so entblösst alles Sachlichen, Bleibenden, ohne die Sterne gleichsam." (210) Nature—"the stars"—can no longer serve as point of reference for human desires and needs. Even the temptation to create a system out of skepticism is rejected by Schlüter[4]: "Hüten wir uns ja vor jedem oberflächlichen Wunsch nach 'Ordnung,' wenn Ordnung etwas heissen soll, gegen das Vorwärtsgehen zu sein, um in Ruhe leben zu dürfen, im billigen Frieden mit sich selbst." (210)

Flexibility is called for according to Schlüter, a readiness for whatever life brings in these unpredictable times. The core of his approach is acceptance, even of what he sees as a general destructive process. The terms "Zerstörung," "Auflösung," "Abgrund" characterize his thinking. His acceptance of destruction carries Schlüter to a position beyond the anxiety for "Geist" which was inherent in the stories or expressed in the essays of other authors:

> Wir sind innerhalb völliger Zerstörung aufgewachsen, und wir meinen zu erkennen, dass die Zerstörung nicht unterbrochen werden kann. Wir wollen uns nicht sinnlos dem geistigen Prozess widersetzen. Statt dessen glauben wir gerade, dass auch Zerstörung nur ist, um zu neuem Werden zu führen. Es ist kein Fatalismus, wenn wir sehr fürchten, nach rückwärts zu sehen und uns lieber bewusst der Bewegung überlassen. Wir versuchen ja, Stellung zu finden, wir wollen uns nicht erdrücken lassen von den Trümmern, wir glauben, dass wir an einem Abgrund stehen, aber ebensosehr glauben wir auch an ein "Drüben." Wir sind nicht so töricht, schon jetzt über dieses Drüben etwas aussagen zu wollen, . . .(210)

---

[4] The same idea is expressed—after his learning experience—by the protagonist of Vietta's "Der Registrator," above pp. 230–32.

The style is noteworthy for simplification of word order, directness and pragmatism. It indicates a skepticism toward metaphor and adornment in general. The thoroughgoing skepticism extends to the political sphere. Schlüter does not represent a young generation which put its faith in revolution. The Russian revolution, on which so many had pinned their hopes for social reform, Schlüter groups with psychoanalysis as destructive forces generated by the old order to hasten its own demise.

The clash of political orders—one disintegrating, the other on the rise—is the historical context of Hans Meisel's "Hollis und noch Einer" (October 1928, II, 419–36) which is set in seventeenth-century England just prior to the Puritan revolution. Meisel is another author in his twenties whom Schlüter acknowledges with great admiration in his review of the young generation of writers, with the proviso that Meisel stands somewhat at remove from the more specific concerns of the generation.[5] "Hollis und noch Einer" is probably the most enigmatic and difficult story of all those which appeared during Kayser's editorship. It may also be the most remarkable. Deadly serious, its nihilism is of a different order from "Die Kinderhochzeit." It is predicated on a view of human nature as profoundly and totally corrupt.

A Puritan named John Hollis is arrested—for the second time—and accused of blasphemy. Six of his coreligionists have reported him to the authorities. The authority who cross-

---

[5] Meisel made his debut at S. Fischer Verlag in 1927 (along with Schlüter and Heuser) with a novel entitled *Torstenson. Entstehung einer Diktatur* which received the highest praise from Fischer's astute and sensitive editor Oskar Loerke. De Mendelssohn describes it as a powerful political allegory which had an extraordinary impact—such an accomplished work that one could hardly believe it was a first novel. The Nazi takeover put an end as well to Meisel's bright future as a writer: "Hans Meisel veröffentlichte in der *Neuen Rundschau* 1928 noch eine Novelle und verstummte ebenfalls, auch er in Amerika." (de Mendelssohn, *S. Fischer und sein Verlag*, p. 1101.)

examined in such cases was the aged Archbishop of Canterbury, William Laud, a notorious persecutor of non-conformists, who always made it his business to be present at the torture of prisoners. The most common punishment was cutting off their ears. For some unexplained reason Laud, although he is very ill and confined to bed, insists that Hollis appear before him to relate his story word for word. Laud appears to be irresistibly intrigued by Hollis and his tale. Hollis, a white-haired man of unprepossessing appearance, tells an extraordinary story of an encounter in a tavern with an ancient and mysterious man with fascinating eyes who seeks out Hollis at his table and speaks to him in a language sprinkled with Yiddish and Latin. The stranger proceeds to show Hollis and the other Puritans who have joined him a series of engravings which he purports to be selling. Hollis describes these engravings to his interlocutor Laud—who interrupts only with an occasional loaded question or urging to continue—in terms so vivid that the pictures seem to be alive. According to Hollis, he is using the words of the strange old man. The engravings, it turns out, predict the course of English history, that is, they show the coming defeat of the royalist forces by the forces of Cromwell (neither of which are named in the account) and the subsequent execution of Charles I. Not enough, the stranger goes on to tell the shocked Hollis—the other Puritans have already fled the scene—the allegedly true version of events in the Bible. First he explains why, in reality, Cain slew Abel. Drawing a picture of a lascivious first family, he attributes the murder to rivalry over Eve, who is the only woman available to the two brothers, Adam having already grown aged and impotent and caring only about his hunting dog. When the stranger goes on to assert that Jesus did not die on the cross, the numbed Hollis leaps up in horror and runs from the inn toward home. The stranger follows him into his house and proceeds to tell of a Christ who was secretly removed from the cross by friends before he died, was spirited away to the hut of an aged widow who cared for him while his wounds healed, and for whom the body of another condemned prisoner was substituted in the tomb and removed a few days later in order to prevent discovery of the substitution.

The portrait of this Christ is the heart of Meisel's story. It shows a modern anti-hero, driven by guilt for not having fulfilled his obligation, and condemned to life on earth in loneliness and alienation. His appearance altered by age, Christ returns to Jerusalem where he finds the same abuses in the temple, hears his name spoken in the streets, and encounters his former disciples who fail to recognize him. When he stops his favorite, John, to inquire whether John would be happy if he learned that the Savior were still alive, John replies: Would he then still be the Savior? Christ leaves Jerusalem and returns once more years later after an ignobly spent life. This time he comes upon a group in a cellar worshipping his image. He blushes when they call his name and turns around to face the group only to find that they have not turned toward him but are still facing the wooden portrait. In fact the worshipers are annoyed when they notice the presence of an old man who is not kneeling. Outside Christ sees Paul preaching and concludes that he would not be one who would turn the other cheek. Christ is ashamed and flees when Paul says "our Lord is in our midst." This Christ, reports Hollis, cannot die and appears everywhere in the world where war, pestilence or regicide are about to occur. He is difficult to recognize because he has white hair and because he never mentions his real name but sometimes calls himself Ahasverus. Hollis' version of the old stranger's tale continues with Christ making a pilgrimage to heaven to inquire when he may die. He finds Peter, his hands folded in concentrated prayer, who refers Christ to Mary, whom he finds in the same posture, who refers him to the young Jesus—his former self—who also cannot help and refers him yet higher to God the father, to whom the young Jesus himself is praying. The old Jesus climbs further, full of hope and love, to the greatest cloud, closes his eyes and says "I am here father." When he opens his eyes again, he finds God the father in the same posture as all the others: he too is kneeling and praying. He remains silent when Jesus asks permission to die and does not answer when Jesus asks to whom he is praying. Jesus begs to know so that he can go on for help. God says only "I am praying." God, like human beings, is in the position of a supplicant. The last portentous sentence of the story, uttered just before the mysterious stranger disappears, is "Pray for me Jonas" (Jonas is the stranger's name for Hollis).

Jesus' quest is a story of despair. Like the famous grandmother's tale in Büchner's *Woyzeck*, it says that there is no omnipotent God, no ultimate recourse, no spiritual solace, no hope, no better world beyond the vale of tears which mankind has created. Faith is an illusion. Life itself has no meaning because there is no higher justification for suffering and death. (Jesus himself was unable to accept death on the cross.) Each human being therefore is utterly and unalterably alone.

Hollis and Laud, facing each other in a kind of contest of wills, are also two men who are totally alone and isolated from their fellows. Their contest could very well be interpreted as between a Christ figure and Satan. Laud, in an unusual moment of relentment, tells Hollis to go, a free man if he will only swear not to tell anyone else his story. Hollis asks if Laud will warn the king. The archbishop's appeal for sworn silence is rejected by Hollis in the strongest terms:

> Dann solle man ihn, schrie der Mann, doch gleich hier auf der Stelle niederstossen!
>
> Das sei, erklärte froh der Erzbischof, nicht seine, des John Hollis Stimme, die so wütig tose—sondern der verschwundene Alte, der in ihn geschlüpft sei. Doch gebe es wohl Mittel, ihn von jenem zu befreien. Wenn er nicht schwören könne . . .
>
> Gelächter zur Antwort.— (436)

The story, which is based on a secret protocol recorded

by the only other witness, the archbishop's secretary, concludes with a one-paragraph summary of subsequent events. Hollis dies from exhaustion and loss of blood after only the second degree of torture. He dies blessing all those who "ended his suffering." His was the first "trial" which the archbishop himself did not attend. The six Puritans who had betrayed Hollis were imprisoned in the Tower of London. Eventually they were freed by Cromwell's forces. Archbishop Laud, and later the king were beheaded.

The deliberate ambiguity of "Hollis und noch Einer" is revealed in the dialogue quoted above. The character of Hollis, who had seemed a known quantity to the reader, turns out to be elusive, as are all the characters and events by virtue of an enigmatic style. The reader cannot know whether Hollis is supposed to be a madman, whether he actually met a mysterious stranger or whether the stranger is an invention of Hollis', whether the stranger is meant to be the aged Christ of the story, or whether Hollis himself is the Christ. There are indications for any and all of these possibilities. For example, both Hollis and the alleged stranger whose words he reports speak in a mixture of folksy elements with elaborate metaphor and in the tones of prophets. The main point, however, is unaffected: that the recalcitrant human race would not recognize the Savior if he appeared in its midst, nor would behavior be altered for his sake. He would, in fact, likely be crucified again. The opposing forces—Puritans versus the Anglicans and royalists—were equally ruthless, disregarded with equal vigor and consistency the tenets of Christianity and used it to advance their own power. The Puritan fanaticism which knew no mercy becomes vivid in a description by the old stranger of a scene in one of the engravings he is showing to Hollis and his companion. It is an example of Meisel's extraordinarily rich and controlled style, insistent rhythms, strong and sensual imagery:

> Denn es wird kommen geritten der Mann im schwarzen Eisen, der

Bart weht ihm krovatisch; und hinter ihm sehr viele Männer: über die Hügel kommen sie geritten still, eine lange, schwarze, leise klirrende Kette, da liegt Gaul an Gaul, tanzt keiner aus der Reihe, Bügel steht an Bügel, Schiene reibt an Schiene, da ruft keine Trompete, und keiner schreit zur Antwort, keiner mit dem Nachbarn spricht, nicht einmal zu den Ohren der Tiere beugen sie sich und flüstern ihnen Mut zu, nicht einmal dies, denn—sie singen. Ja, während sie die Karabiner über ihre Eisenhauben kerzengerade in den Himmel stossen, singen sie: kein Reiterlied, kein Trutzlied, doch sie singen. Und noch wenn ihre rilligen Eisen längst zwischen fremden Eisenrippen weiches Fleisch aufsuchen und erseufzend finden, singen sie; und aus den aufgesperrten, wehen Schlünden steigt der Dampf hoch über alle Schwaden eingestampfter Wiesen auf zu dem, von dem sie singen: der dies will, dieses will. (424–25)

The forces of Cromwell who sing that slaughter on the batlefield is the will of God find their equal in their ice-cold opponent, the archbishop. Although he never speaks of God, Laud uses the power of his office in a manner equivalent to the fanaticism of the Puritan forces. The archbishop's unbridled cruelty toward the non-conformists is portrayed as a consequence of a physical revulsion he feels toward them. Fifteen years earlier he had once out of curiosity attended a Bible meeting where one member of the congregation fell into a physically violent ecstasy while screaming the name of God. Laud's own reaction to the sight was uncontrollably violent—weeping, laughing, and vomiting. Since that time he has hated the non-conformists with a passion which has dictated frequent and unmitigated torture in order to silence them. Clearly the archbiship, in psychological terms, is neither balanced nor stable. In metaphysical terms he is satanic. This perverted creature—coldly reasoning yet consumed by hatred—has power of life and death over countless persons. His essence is his great age which has made him elemental, almost rock-like, amoral, pitiless. His indifference to human concerns is attributed—in powerful, original imagery—to his being less human being than dried, withered remnant of nature:

John Hollis sah den Herrn im Bett an und hielt inne, weil ein roter Hustenreiz den kissenüberdachten Kopf aufwarf und lange nicht die sonst gewohnte Farbe wiederfinden liess, die gelb war, gelb war; wohl vom allzu vielen Tabakrauchen, oder waren es die Nächte, durchgegrübelt, Menschen zu durchschauen? Die dann kamen morgens, in der Helle, hatten einen prächtigen Gang, waren alle seine Freunde; doch, und wenn sie gingen, waren sie alt wie das Leben und wussten nicht einmal, durch wen. Aber er, Laud, war so alt, wie sie alle zusammen, darum geht er auch so schwer und zittert viel, darum sind die Backen ihm so tief gehöhlt, Rinnsale, ausgewaschen durch das unsagbare Weinen der Frauen und Mütter, abgespült die Farben von dem runden Schädel ganz aus Holz. Aber kalte Kohle ist sein Auge, das dem kindischen Getrotz still hingehalten, nicht mehr Feuer fängt; denn es muss ja sein dies: dass sie weinen müssen und er sie muss weinen machen und sie immer dabei ansehen mit den nachdenkenden Augen; aber hinten, wo ihr Innen ist, sinkt Asche ab nach unten, so viel Asche, dass das ganze Herz davon bedeckt wird bis zum Hals, darum muss er so viel husten, und, wenn er ausgeht, oft stehen bleiben, steif, ein alter Strunk, der aller Rinde bar ist; oder ist er schon ein Stein? Die Tiere fürchten ihn nicht: einst erging er sich im königlichen Parke, da sass auf einem Baum ein kleines Eichhorn, lugte blank aus seinem Pelz zu ihm herab, und schon glitt es nieder, kam gesprungen und an ihm, der starr am Fleck verblieb, hoch und herauf und über seinen Hut den Rücken nieder; der Kleine, der Necker, der Windbold. War ein Husch und fort. So alt war William Laud. (422–23)

It is a remarkable set of contending forces: the amoral archbishop and the powers which he represents, against the militant Puritans with their murderous Christianity, and between both, belonging to neither, the voice of Hollis which bridles the archbishop only as long as it remains soft and meek. The story is structured as a nest of boxes: the story of Christ within the story of the old stranger within Hollis' story within the dialogue with the archbishop within the politics of England. Together and separately their import is the same: there is no reason, no justice, no goodness, no meaning in the affairs of men.

"Zerstörung durch Liebe" (August 1929, II, 234–57), Schlüter's second story, treats a different sort of meaninglessness. Emotional bonds between people, grand passions, devotion are proved to be without substance. "Zerstörung durch Liebe" is the nihilistic variant of the three stories with love as the title "character." As Süskind's title "Beginn einer Liebe" indicates, his is an affirmative story. Torberg's "Todeskampf einer Liebe" is negative. In the Schlüter story the dominant concept is destruction, a key term for the nihilistic category.

"Zerstörung durch Liebe" is more conventional than "Die Kinderhochzeit" and lacks its wry humor. Ernestine, once a famous actress and now a wealthy but lonely widow of fifty, meets—after a twenty-year separation—the poet and playwright Adolphe, the lover of her youth for whom Ernestine has sustained an all-consuming passion for twenty years. Ernestine's devotion to this love and her consequent suffering and humiliation are condemned by her cooly observant daughter, Claudia, who makes up her mind never to become a slave of passion like her mother. When the aging Adolphe does not respond to Ernestine and departs after his play has been performed (with Ernestine in the starring role), the disappointment is too great for Ernestine and she commits suicide.

The dominant mood is decadence. As in the previous two stories, aging is a theme; the physical decay of Ernestine and Adolphe is emphasized, as it was in the case of aged characters of "Die Kinderhochzeit" and "Hollis und noch Einer." There is a strong contrast—as in "Die Kinderhochzeit"—between the process of decay in the older characters and the cool indifference of the callow young characters, confident in their young bodies. As in "Hollis und noch Einer" death is a theme. It is present in the background as a sense of the inevitable conclusion to human affairs. Ernestine had actually died in spirit long before, when her existence became centered exclusively on her passion for the absent Adolphe. When she confesses her love Adolphe denies ever having been in love with her, even during their youthful affair twenty years before. Only when she confronts him with the passionate letters he wrote then does the memory of having loved her return. He is moved, not by Ernestine's devotion, but by egoistic considerations—the reminder that he was once a fiery young man. Adolphe thinks: "Wie interessant, dass er wirklich vergessen hatte. Wie man seine Träume am Morgen vergessen hat. . . . Er hat dies geschrieben, als Jüngling. Er, alt und schwammig jetzt. Dies (dass er so alt geworden ist) rührt ihn bis zu Tränen." (247) Love has neither purpose nor worth, since the passion which preoccupied Ernestine for twenty years did not even exist for Adolphe. The love which Ernestine projected all those years was lost, its object an illusion; unreceived it had no meaning.

Schlüter's style is ironic. An example is the use of romantic clichés to describe Adolphe's feelings when Ernestine reminds him of the love he once felt: "Adolphe verschlägt es den Atem. . . . Verwirrt im Herzen betrachtet er diese Zeilen." (247) The romantic phrases contradict the banality of the aging man's feeling which concern only his regret at growing old. Another device is sentence structure—the telegraphic style of incomplete sentences provides by its matter-of-factness an ironic contrast to the situations in which powerful emotions may be presumed. An example is the scene which ends in Ernestine's suicide:

> Ernestine und Adolphe unter dem flammenden Sternenhimmel. Die Luft der Verzweiflung, der Liebe, des Todes. Hinter den Büschen, über den knirschenden Kies, eilt irgendein Auto.
> Adolphe will übermorgen reisen.
>
> Adolphe ist fort, der Park leer, Ernestine allein. Ernestine im Schlafzimmer. (250)

On the level of actions the irony is most potent in the poignant scene of Ernestine's death from poison: her romantic imaginings contrast starkly with the sordid physical reality of the undignified process of dying. The final irony is that ugliness will be the last impression Ernestine leaves on Adolphe, who finds her body; Ernestine had always taken great pains about her appearance—her hair color and makeup—in order to conceal her age:

> Ernestine erinnert sich des Seligen ihres Lebens.
>
> Ausschreiten unter einem blassblauen Morgenhimmel. Von den Lüften umarmt. Man beginnt zu fliegen. Da ist die Erde. Gemacht aus Wiesen und Städten, Sand und Wasser. Da sind die Häuser. Da die Fenster. Die Strassen. Die Menschen. Der Hafen.—
>
> Ernestine, unsicher auf Händen und Füssen fortkrauchend, wird gegen den Toilettetisch geschlagen. Ein Glas fällt herunter. Scherben ritzen die tappenden Hände. Aus einer geöffneten Schachtel rieselt Puder über ihren Kopf. Ihr Haar vergilbt unter der duftenden Asche. (251)

An added, pathetic irony is that Ernestine has been completely deserted. Claudia, unaware of her mother's suicide, has left a carefree note indicating that she has left on an open-ended automobile trip with a young man. Apparently she will not, after all, escape the trap of passion. Adolphe, for his part, continues to age.

The story concludes with the following observation which introduces the fourth level of irony—philosophical irony or irony as *Weltanschauung*: "Am Fusse des ewigen Gebirges, gelagert vor den ewig verführenden Golf, in der Stadt der Welt heben jeden Morgen die Leierkästen an. Aufs neue." (251) The passions and concerns of human beings, their emotions, aging and death, the course of their lives are insignificant from the perspective of the eternal mountain and the eternal rhythm of a great city. The final ironic touch is the hurdy-gurdy which has been a *Leitmotiv* in the story—in its double meaning of music box and comment that what is being heard is the same old story over and over again.

Hermann Ungar, who contributed the satire "Colberts Reise" in 1922, is author of "Der Weinreisende" (I, 223–43) which appeared in February 1930. Although it deals, like "Colberts Reise," with a character trapped in a world of his own fantasy, "Der Weinreisende" lacks the humorous and satirical elements of the earlier story. Human nature is viewed, rather, with an attitude of unrelieved gloom. The narrator-protagonist's situation resembles that of Dostoevsky's Raskolnikov in *Crime and Punishment*, with the significant difference that there is no spiritual redemption at the end of the Ungar story. Ungar's protagonist, made desperate by his lack of money and his failures, murders a repulsive and vile example of humanity, yet he is haunted by his deed. He is disturbed by a sense of fatalism in the course of events which determined his life, but even more by the thought that events might have taken a different, more advantageous turn for him. A motto for the story could be the protagonist's thought: "Die Dinge sind voll vom qualvollen Geheimnis, in dem sich der Mensch verirrt." (228) The story is the examination of a psyche which lacks a moral sense. This lack leads to a social and moral descent from respectability to the seamy world of city back alleys, sordid poverty and criminality ending, for Ungar's protagonist, in vice as a way of life.

A young man who inherited his father's tendency toward self-delusion and ability to live in a fantasy world, drops his inherited wine sales business and seeks his fortune in a fairy-tale manner—expecting good luck to come to one who goes to the big city and dresses well. He regards himself as a cut above the normal run of humanity, believes that he deserves more than the average and has a right to forgo the usual limits and restrictions. He gambles, loses the little money he has, is not picked up by a wealthy widow as he had hoped, but by a poor prostitute who uses him for one night. The next day he decides not to use the money she has given him to pay for the flophouse room, but rather to keep it in order to force a change in his luck. When the disreputable innkeeper threatens him and bars his way, the protagonist kills him with a blow from a wine bottle and allows the innkeeper's retarded (and severely abused) daughter to be blamed and incarcerated. The protagonist remains to run the flophouse for prostitutes. He believes he is tied to the place by his fate. He spends his days drinking wine and imagining what might have been, had his expectations been fulfilled. The story is a portrait of all-pervasive corruption in a sordid world without hope, without future, without redeeming qualities.

The Ungar universe, which is not peculiarly modern, and the style, which is traditional-conventional, conveys basically the same world view as a very modern—1920's chic—story by Joachim Maass (born in 1901), another of the promising young Fischer talents of that period. The mood of "Ein ganz verbrecherischer Mensch" (July 1930, II, 61–76) is of laissez-faire egoism. These characters too are licentious and amoral in a loveless, amoral environment. Once again the setting is a city. As in "Der Weinreisende" the mode is confessional. The narrator-protagonist is the "ganz verbrecherischer Mensch" of the title—a title which could easily apply as well to the Ungar story. Here it applies not to criminality in the usual sense, but to exploitation—the nearly successful attempt by a young man with incestuous desires to force his naive younger sister to be his permanent living companion. The other characters also behave in an exploitative manner.

Motivated by jealously, the protagonist comes into conflict with his mother as well as his cronies—a bohemian group which meets every day to gossip at the "Whale Bar." One of them is a young lesbian actress who is attracted to the protagonist's sister, Thora, and attempts to seduce her. This causes a breach among the formerly inseparable cronies as the protagonist, Robbi, violently defends his first claim to his sister. Brother-sister incest and lesbian relationships have been themes in previous stories. The significant difference is that here they are not based on love—at least in the traditional sense—but on expediency, a whim of the moment. The implication is that the characters' lives are egocentric, bereft of real emotions. Nothing appears to be important other than immediate self-gratification at whatever cost. Traditional values and conventions are disregarded by these young libertines. Parents also are cast into the dustbin of outmoded tradition.[6] In his attempt to maintain his hold over Thora, Robbi does not shy from abusive language and physical threats toward his mother. Despite his best efforts Thora does return to her parents and thereby removes the object of dissension from the "Whale Bar" group which is soon reconciled and enjoying its customary empty banter.

Another group of young people—some of whom closely resemble the Maass characters—is gathered in Schlüter's third story, "Das Jahr 1923" (October 1931, II, 525–44). Like three earlier stories—Leonhard Frank's "Der Beamte" (1925), Thomas Mann's "Unordnung und frühes Leid" (1925) and W. E. Süskind's "Raymund" (1927)—it shows the social and psychological consequences of inflation. And like "Raymund," it concentrates upon the profiteers, although the victims of hardship also appear. However, Schlüter's story does not have a protagonist, but a company of characters (the narrator is one of them), several of whom play a larger role than others. The world of inherited beliefs has already disintegrated for these young characters. They are representative of the generation, described in Schlüter's essay, which considers itself to have no antecedents, and its judgmental faculty to be a *tabula rasa*. As we have seen in the Maass story and in Schlüter's essay this mentality entails rejection of parents and the heritage they represent. Two focal characters in "Das Jahr 1923"—Bettina and her younger brother Josef—have established themselves in the city (unnamed, but certainly Berlin) with money which they stole from their parents. Referring to their disassociation of themselves from parents, Bettina mockingly calls herself a "poor orphan." Some of Schlüter's characters have more or less successfully taken advantage of

---

[6] Cf. also Süskind's "Raymund," above pp. 81–82, and Schlüter's essay, above pp. 238–39.

the chaotic economic conditions, engaging in the hectic pursuit of quick pleasure or profit. Others are primarily victims of the times and are moving toward inevitable self-destruction. Bettina is an example of the former and Josef of the latter. The central fact of Josef's life is his obsessive incestuous love for his sister. Although he is a markedly talented, even brilliant thinker, Josef finds existence without his sister's love meaningless. When the beautiful, amoral Bettina taunts Josef with the fact of her affair with the confidence man Gustav, Josef commits suicide. He is an example of a series of characters in "Das Jahr 1923" who meet sad or violent ends. They are the fragile ones, who fail to thrive, in fact are destroyed by the general disorientation. In another time and place they might have been accomplished, productive individuals. Keys words indicate the trance-like state of mind of these young people: "schlafwandlerisch" (532), "traumwandlerisch" (532), "Schlafwandeln" (538), "Blendung" (541), "Zerstreutheit" (541).

The story opens with the narrator waiting for renovations to be completed on a small hotel which he appears to own. Bettina and Josef's money has been used by Gustav to renovate a nightclub which becomes an instant success. Inflation explains this building euphoria among those who are riding the crest of easy money. The narrator describes the prevailing mood: "Was das Renovieren betraf, so glaubte ich von vornherein an alles. Die ganze Stadt renovierte sich. Paläste entstanden über Nacht." (527) But the hectic activity is without foundation. It masks the essential hollowness of the economy and the people who are making quick fortunes. Appearance is everything. The elaborately decorated nightclub—Gustav calls it "Etablissement chic" (529)—which offers all of the current fads (including a "Honolulu Band") in a setting of unrelieved kitsch, could be considered a metaphor for the era. The key word to describe its effect is "empty" ("Leere," "Leerheit," 530). On opening night an impromptu master of ceremonies remarks that it has given him the sense that a new era is dawning, an era in which appearing at the opening of such a club means fun, though where things would go from there he did not know. Where it does go is downhill rapidly. The club folds the day after its grand opening, when entrepreneur Gustav is arrested for selling cocaine.

The character of Gustav is the epitome of the wheeler-dealer of the era, a shady type with the appearance of a perfect gentleman, who is forever on the make with other people's money. His characteristics are those of the epoch: "leere Augen" (530), "eine gewisse Frivolität der Mundwinkel, einen in der Zeit bedingten Zynismus." (528) There is no substance, but impressive form:

> Er hatte fabelhafte Manieren, eine ziemlich markante helle Stimme, eine wunderbare Haltung und wirkte aufregend klug. Warum, weiss ich nicht. Denn alles, was er sagte, war nicht grade blöde, und es hatte Hintergrund—aber dazu muss man nicht klug sein, nicht wahr? Es war nicht das, was er sagte, aber vielleicht die Souveränität, mit der er es sagte, die solchen Eindruck hervorrief. (529)

Gustav drives a "raspberry-cream colored" rented Cadillac.

The dark side of this desperately frivolous life is not only its inevitable collapse but the deep pessimism which it reflects and the sense of foreboding which it attempts to mask. The extravagantly decadent young people live side by side with people whose existence has been reduced to the barest necessities. The other, impoverished Berlin (also the world of "Der Beamte") is noted by the narrator:

> Wir gingen in die östlichsten Gegenden der Stadt. Wir sahen, wie zwei uniformierte Polizeibeamte einen Mann jagten und wie eine Hure einen Mann schlug, und die Leute lachten über ihn. Wir kamen an Kinos vorbei, die schon am Tage spielten und deren elektrische Klaviere auf die Strassen schollen. Wir sahen bleiche und zerlumpte Kinder, die sich um einen falschen, aus Stoffetzen gemachten Fussball schlugen. (539)

Even the bit of a natural world which survives in the city presents itself to the narrator (as he thinks of Josef's suicide) as bleak and miserable: ". . . und über den armen Kiefern [stand] ein Himmel ohne Sterne wie eine Mauer . . ." (542)

The true nature of the characters' lives is revealed in their behavior after having had to attend to the arrangements for Josef's burial: "An diesem Abend gingen wir alle aus. Man hielt uns für die übermütigste der sorglosen Jugend. Wir soffen masslos, und ich habe noch die verzweifelte Heiterkeit Irenes im Ohr, die mit einem Elias in Trance tranzte." (543) Desperation characterizes the fragile structure of defenses which they have built against the sense of living on the brink of an abyss.

"Das Jahr 1923," as the title indicates, differs from the three previous stories which also deal with the economic and social chaos of the inflationary early twenties in that it focuses primarily on the times, rather than on the fate of one or several individuals. At most it is a group portrait, but the real protagonist is a mood, a peculiar mentality inextricable from the historical situation which created it. The world is in apparently hopeless disarray and young people—who may be most attuned to their times—act and think in a manner which shows that they cannot imagine a recovery of order and meaning. Like the nihilist they are willing to exist without them.

The mood of the March 1932 issue is established in the lead essay, "Der Mensch auf der Flucht" (I, 289–300) by Carl Steuermann, which draws an apocalyptic vision of a second world war as a product of the desperate attempt of capitalism to maintain itself. Another essay, "Die Tat wider die Vernunft" (408–21) by Herbert Block, is an attack on the Nazi mentality. It exposes the dangerous illusions which lie behind its appeal to all dissatisfied groups. In his "Anmerkungen" Kayser discusses the visit of a French writer to Berlin and the impressions he took back with him to Paris of terrible poverty and misery: "Er weiss deshalb, dass der Glauben an die westliche Tradition ihm und uns nicht mehr weiter hilft. . . . In Deutschland begreift er, . . . wie viel grösser die Drohungen der Geschichte in diesem Augenblick [sind]." (429) A comparison of this statement with the sense of crisis for Germany which Kayser expressed in his March 1923 message "An die Leser" (above p. 22), shows the most striking difference to be the faith in ideals—mystical qualities of the "German soul"—as a source of salvation which was still possible in 1923 but had disappeared by the time of the even more alarming political reality of 1932.

All together this issue is an appropriate context for Jakob Schaffner's "Die Dreingabe" (377–92). Schaffner, born in 1875, did not belong to the young generation of authors represented up to now in this category. It is all the more remarkable that the statement which his story makes about the human condition should be so much in keeping with theirs, although the form in which Schaffner presents it is entirely different. "Die Dreingabe" opens a series of three stories on the theme of death. Death and aging have replaced in significance the theme of love which was prominent in previous categories.

"Die Dreingabe" is the story of the last day in the life of businessman Irwin Schaffold. His name, which is a blend of "Schaffot" and its English version, scaffold, portends the conclusion in the first sentence:

> Als der Kaufmann Irwin Schaffold, ein Mann um die fünfziger Jahre, eines Morgens aufwachte, fand er, dass es nicht so war wie sonst. Er setzte sich im Bett aufrecht und suchte zu ergründen, worin die Wolke bestand, die er plötzlich über sein Leben hängen sah; als ob man ihm die Aufgabe gerade für diesen Augenblick gestellt hätte, so gehorsam sass er da und grübelte. (377–78)

The "cloud" which Schaffold perceives remains with him as he goes about his daily routine which is marked by minor near-accidents and a general feeling of malaise, although to all intents and purposes the day seems to be a perfectly normal and pleasant one. Schaffold feels a diffuse anxiety and begins to believe he notices signs of ill luck.

The portrait of Schaffold is a humorously ironic one. He is meant to represent his class of nouveau riche, self-satisfied bourgeoisie. He is banal in mind and taste, devoted to material comforts, but guided, he believes, by a "liberal" ethical standpoint. He is a ladies' man, exaggeratedly meticulous in his personal habits, a slightly ridiculous dandy. But Schaffold is also subject to melancholy thoughts and moods, prides himself on being more refined than his colleagues, and is indeed more sensitive than ordinary to women and beauty. All told, he is also a rather touching character.

On the one hand a realistic foundation is prepared for the events to come. Irwin thinks of his father who died young of a heart attack. During a coughing fit at breakfast with his wife, and while jogging to the office Irwin's lips turn blue, and he is more out of breath than usual after his morning constitutional. But the more serious portents are not realistic: the feeling that something is waiting for him, the appearance in his office and later on the street of a shadowy apparition, and finally the sudden appearance at his side of a small coffin floating in the air. The coffin is the "Dreingabe" of the title, as it appears after Irwin has made a purchase in a jewelry store of an elegant purse for his mistress, Edith. On his way to visit Edith, Irwin suddenly finds himself in an unfamiliar lonely side street, where a cold wind is blowing and no other people are in sight. The specter appears again and seems at first to be the sexy figure of Edith, but soon it is transformed into the figure of Death—a significant juxtaposition of sex and death—which asks Irwin to step into the enlarged coffin. Here a dialogue begins between Irwin and Death which turns into conflict when Irwin refuses to step into the coffin unless Death promises to spare him suffering in exchange for Irwin's willing acquiescence. At this point the story begins to recall the classical account of the passing of a respectable "Bürger," Tolstoy's "The Death of Ivan Ilych," except for the crucial difference that Ivan Ilych dies having repented, experienced the joy of repentance, and seen a light in place of the darkness of death.

When Death refuses to bargain, Irwin for his part refuses to cooperate. He believes that the good manners and standards of liberal humanism which applied to life ought to be applicable under any circumstances. Trying to persuade Death, for whom he feels a kind of passion ("Liebessehnsucht"), Irwin draws upon his store of progressive, enlightened behavioral theory to prove that compromise is required:

> "Ein solches stures Verhalten macht nirgends einen guten Eindruck," erklärte er, indem er gereizt auf das grüne Täschchen blickte. "Man muss geschäftlich sein. Man muss sich rangieren, besonders dann, wenn man sieht, dass der Partner im Grund willig ist. Herrgott, man muss den Leuten doch die Entschlüsse erleichtern. Irgendwie muss man den Fortschritt der Psychologie auch in den äussersten Grenzposten des Lebens zu spüren bekommen, sonst hat alles keinen Sinn mehr." (389)

This proposition—". . . sonst hat alles keinen Sinn mehr"—is the key to the nihilistic posture of the story. His conditions, of course, are not met, his assumptions are not borne out. Annoyed, Irwin decides he will bargain no longer with an opponent who does not follow the rules. Irwin will withdraw from his side of the bargain and return to life. He turns toward the city, reviewing in his mind the justice of his standpoint:

> O, noch war man nicht so weit, dass man sich auf Gnade und Ungnade ergeben musste. Mangel an Gerechtigkeit und Billigkeit verstimmt. Man befand sich nicht mehr im mythischen Zeitalter, in welchem die rohe Willkür herrschte. (390)

Naturally, Irwin is proved to be wrong with his firm faith in meaning, justice, fairness, and the rule of reason over irrational and arbitrary forces. The next sensation which Irwin experiences—in complete disregard of his sensibilities—is a crude and violent blow to his chest:

> Ohne dass er etwas in seinem Rücken vernommen oder sonst gemerkt hätte, brach eine harte, grobe, knöcherne Faust von hinten in seinen Brustkorb ein, ganz einfach und wortlos, aber ungeheuer überzeugend. Ein tiefer, weher, sozusagen endgültiger Schmerz durchzog ihn. Etwas unsäglich Gemeines und Rück-

sichtsloses ging mit ihm vor, ohne allen Respekt und unter einer direkt stupiden Beiseitsetzung seiner Verdienste und gerechten Ansprüche. (391)

Here the parallel is very close to Ivan Ilych's last struggle: "Suddenly some force struck him in the chest and side, making it still harder to breathe, and he fell through the hole and there at the bottom was a light."[7] Ivan Ilych at last submits repentantly to death and is rewarded. Irwin also submits, climbs into his coffin and is grateful that he is permitted to retain his dignity rather than being kicked or shoved into the coffin. A feeling of contentment comes over him. It appears to him that he is not to be robbed entirely of his dignity and his faith in a just and merciful order of things. But the final response of the elements to this last unfounded supposition is a cold, merciless indifference:

> Erschüttert faltete er die Hände. Noch einmal konstatierte er, dass dies Verfahren zwar roh sei, aber dass es doch nicht einer gewissen Gutmütigkeit und Grösse entbehre. Dann wurde es ihm bitter im Mund. Der kalte Schweiss brach ihm aus. Ein Weinen, das noch aufkommen wollte, verkloste sich in seiner Kehle. Die hehre Gleichgültigkeit der ewigen Gesetze, die über ihn hinweg zog wie eine kalte, wild sausende Wolke, erlebte er nicht mehr, sie hätte sonst vielleicht sein Selbstgefühl noch einmal beleidigt. (392)

The differences between the Tolstoy and the Schaffner versions of dying point to the nihilism of the latter. Ivan Ilych dies in the greatest imaginable physical agony. Human suffering is neither ameliorated nor denied. But it has meaning. Life, suffering and death are given meaning by recognition of guilt, redemption, and a vision of eternity. Irwin—as deluded about the validity of his convictions and values as Ivan Ilych (who also prided himself on his "liberalism") was about his—dies

---

[7] Leo Tolstoy, *The Death of Ivan Ilych and Other Stories* (New York: New American Library, 1960), p. 154.

without insight and needless to say, without the prospect of redemption. In both stories death is the ultimate fact of life; but for Ilych death brings eternal life for the soul; Irwin's death is merely the cessation of the body's functions. There is no further meaning, nor hope, nor significance to it, nor even a minimum of dignity.

The preoccupation with death, dying and the meaninglessness of life is matched by the tenor of Kayser's comments at the time. In the May 1932 issue (I, 720) he wrote a review of *Deutscher Geist in Gefahr* by Ernst Robert Curtius, a collection of essays most of which first appeared in the *NR*. In the course of the review Kayser provides his bleak assessment of the previous decade: "Das Jahrzehnt von 1920 bis 1930 ist ein Zeitalter der Moden und Experimente, von denen nichts übrigblieb. Ein grosses Trümmerfeld des Geistes und der Politik! Die weltliche Not is unerträglich geworden, . . ." (720) The worst fears for the welfare and survival of "Geist"—expressed in previous stories and essays—were realized. The nihilistic stories portray a world without "Geist." A process of reduction has occurred to the point where the concept "Geist" is no longer relevant. The character Josef in "Das Jahr 1923" exemplifies the change. Josef is the representative of "Geist" in the story. There is no place in that society for his intellectuality. Without a role and without a purpose it is only appropriate that he end his life.

The title of Ilse Faber's story which continues the nihilistic mode is "Sterben" (I, 794–806),[8] another chronicle of the last day in the life of a protagonist. It appears in the June 1932

---

[8] Ilse Faber, who was born on 18 July 1887, lived as a writer in Weimar, and later in Berlin. She is author of the following novels: *Die silberne Kugel. Fliegerroman aus den finnischen Schären* (1930), *Herr Poehlmann reist* (1931), and *Kuckucksei rollt aus dem Nest* (1933). (Kosch, *Handbuch der deutschen Gegenwartsliteratur*.) It has not proved possible to find her name mentioned anywhere other than in the entry in Kosch.

issue, which also contains a lead essay by Hermann Heller entitled "Bürger und Bourgeois." The Heller essay sheds light on the sociological component of the nihilistic stories. "Die Dreingabe" and "Sterben" in particular, but also "Das Jahr 1923," "Der Weinreisende," and "Ein ganz verbrecherischer Mensch" show the decline, decay, or "death" of the bourgeois class as represented by the central characters. Heller's essay begins:

> Dass es mit dem "Bürgertum" zu Ende geht, ist eine der wenigen Ansichten, in der die öffentliche Meinung nicht nur Deutschlands durchaus einig zu sein scheint. Bolschewisten wie Fascisten verkünden in apokalyptischen Visionen, dass das Reich nahe und der Tod aller bourgeoisen Lebensformen besiegelt sei; laut läuten sie die Sterbeglocken des Bürgers.
>
> Und geben nicht alle Zeichen der Zeit diesen Propheten recht? Nicht nur der eigentliche Mittelstand, sondern zahllose alte und neue Grossbürger sind durch den Weltkrieg, die Inflation und die Weltwirtschaftskrise ökonomisch proletarisiert worden. Die Zersetzung der geistigen Gehalte und der politischen Formen hat aber grosse Teile des deutschen Bürgertums ausserdem noch anarchisiert. (721)

The sense of the times is that the death knell of the bourgeois class has been sounded—both of its economic and its intellectual, moral and spiritual foundations, its entire value system. If this is the conventional wisdom, it is inevitable that it would influence literature. The preoccupations of the nihilist category are probably the consequence not only of a private state of mind but also of the consciousness that an entire class and its system of values has undergone a process of dissolution. Most affected are the real or pseudo representatives of "Geist" (or those normally destined to be so by their heritage), but also the small businessman (such as wine and silk merchants) and in the Faber story, the prosperous but socially reactionary farmer whose rapid physical breakdown contrasts strikingly with the vigor of a group of modern, chic, and urbane young characters. The class component of the protagonist's situation is apparent in the opening sentences:

> Matthias Düvenkloth löste sich eine Fahrkarte zweiter Klasse. Das entsprach durchaus seinen Verhältnissen—seiner Vermögenslage nach hätte er sich auch nach dem Krieg auf die erste Fahrklasse beschränken können—widersprach aber gänzlich seinen Gewohnheiten. (794)

Clearly we have to do with the type of the prosperous but frugal, conservative northern German, unaccustomed to self-indulgence. Düvenkloth, a heavy, clumsy, peasantlike man, is returning home to his farm after a business trip. He does not feel well. In particular, he is plagued by exhaustion and a terrible thirst. He only half hears the good-natured taunts which a sophisticated young woman and her gentleman companions in the same compartment make about the crude appearance of their fellow traveler. Once he has alighted at his station, Düvenkloth—driven by his habitual frugality—walks the long distance to his farm rather than take a taxi. On the way his companions from the train drive by and offer Düvenkloth a ride, but he refuses. By the time he arrives home he is barely able to stand, but because the farmhands are needed elsewhere the "master" forces himself to take the scythe and mow the fields. In the process Düvenkloth wounds his hand, and the wound does not stop bleeding. The continually bleeding wound is the first dramatic sign of his inexorable physical disintegration. From then on one further symptom of illness follows another until Düvenkloth becomes incapacitated and must take to his bed. These symptoms and the reaction of the low-German-speaking servants who live in a feudal relationship with their master are described in naturalistic detail. The illness takes on a clinical accuracy of detail until it is finally named: uremic poisoning. Prior to that point the servants' main interest is in the master's rumored loss of sexual capacity. When he hears of the rumor, Düvenkloth takes one of the servant girls to bed with him in order to prove himself, but naturally in his condition does nothing but fall asleep. This fact gives rise to further discussion among the servants. As in "Die Dreingabe" sex and death are close partners—bound by the community of the flesh in its needs and limitations. Love, as a romantic ideal, is absent, its place taken by elemental drives which are enjoined only by the finality of death.

"Doktor Klopfleisch" is called to administer an injection, and is followed later by the local practitioner of herbal medicine. In her conversation with the by now rapidly fading Düvenkloth, we learn that he had made love to her and left her to be deserted in revenge by her husband. Düvenkloth's reaction to her reminder of their past relationship is the same as the reaction of Adolphe in Schlüter's "Zerstörung durch Liebe": "Das habe ich alles vergessen." (804) To all intents and purposes his feeling for her never existed, since it is not even preserved in his memory.[9] Before the fact of the body the past has no meaning.

Düvenkloth reviews his meagre past apparently without emotion:

> Einmal kam ihm noch das Bewusstsein seines früheren Ichs zurück. Er lag lächelned in den Kissen, schabte mit der gesunden Hand über die langen, weissen Bartstoppeln, die seine aufgeschwemmte Haut getrieben hatte, und überdachte seines Lebens kümmerlichen Inhalt. Er schaute so weit zurück, dass ihm sogar lateinische Vokabeln über die Lippen kamen. Das war von damals, als er das Gymnasium besucht hatte. Da sollte aus ihm ja wohl ein Doktor werden . . . Aber dann starb der Bruder, und er kam auf den Hof. Das Einjährige hatte er gerade geschafft.
>
> Die Ärmlichkeit seiner Erlebnisse zwang ihn zum Grübeln. (805)

This is most likely the first occasion Düvenkloth has had to examine his life. His being unaccustomed to elaborate thought processes, to contemplation, self-analysis and articulation puts realistic limitations on the autobiographical process.

---

[9] This is an important contrast with the saving power of the living force of memory in such affirmative stories as Schickele's "Tulpen" (above pp. 48–49) and von der Vring's "Aube" (above pp. 107–15).

Nevertheless these few sentences which sum up a life of sixty years or so are indicative of the nihilistic perspective. A long life, successful in terms of its own standards, full of back-breaking labor and dealings with people (in emotional isolation from them) can be summarized in a brief, poignant paragraph. There is no apparent purpose to Düvenkloth's having lived. His end is without dignity, strong emotions on the part of others, guilt or regret.

His body and face have become hideously swollen and distorted. When his young companions from the train—apparently desirous of looking him up—drop by and look in the window, the young woman screams with horror and runs away—an effect which Düvenkloth enjoyed creating as a bit of revenge upon those alien creatures: "Der Bauer grinste hämisch." (805) To this process of dying—unmitigated by the usual palliatives—the traditional religious or moral categories are irrelevant. Dying has become the paramount fact of Düvenkloth's existence, its most significant event.

The conclusion—in a naturalistic yet lyrical series of images—creates a breathlessly still atmosphere in which Death is present (although not as a specter). It is as if all the creatures and the objects of daily life momentarily react to the presence of Death and by their disquiet register its passing through—a moment which touches upon the mystical. But once Death has passed through it leaves behind an unsightly, decaying mass which hygiene dictates must be removed after three days:

> Dann wurde das Schweigen bedrückend—die Stunde stand still. Still wie die Wolke, die herrschsüchtig über dem Hoftor aufgestiegen war.
>
> Wind fächelte, blähte die bleichen Gardinen zu gespenstischem Leben auf. Die Katze sprang mit gesträubtem Fell vom Fensterbrett ab, verschwand ohne Laut.
>
> Die grossen, blauen Schwalben begaben sich auf Jagd; sie schwirrten mit schneidendem Flügelschlag vorbei.
>
> Eine Ente patschte durch die Gosse . . .
>
> Wo steckte das Gesinde? Lachen und Zuruf blieben aus und das hölzerne Kappern der Pantoffel.

Klirrte eine Kette im Stall? . . . Murmelte es vor der Tür? . . .
Flüstern ging um. Und Grauen quoll auf . . . versickerte dumpf in Stöhnen und fiebrige Schauer.

Der Arzt fand den Kranken in tiefer Bewusstlosigkeit. Trotzdem aber schrie er laut vor Schmerz, als ihm die Einspritzung gemacht wurde.

Dann lag er und liess leise seine letzten Atemzüge über den aufgetriebenen Leib wehen.

Als die Sonne in das Meer tauchte, fiel sein Kiefer mit hörbarem Geräusch herab.

Nach den üblichen drei Tagen wurde der Bauer begraben. (806)

The third in the series on death is "Der Tod des Achilleus" (January 1933, I, 65–81) by Willy Seidel, born in 1887, another of the authors in this category who do not belong to the young generation. Several of Kayser's remarks in this issue indicate his state of deep discouragement, even hopelessness. In a piece entitled "Kulturreaktion" (in "Anmerkungen," 137–38) Kayser criticizes Ludwig Klages' "Geist" versus "Seele" ideology on the occasion of Klages' sixtieth birthday. In the course of his discussion Kayser formulates the following damning judgments on the times: "Kurz vor Anbruch der Katastrophe, in deren letztem Akt wir zu stehen scheinen, . . ." and ". . . die Mitte unseres geistig-seelischen Krankheitszustandes . . ." (138) Although the Seidel story is the recreation of an ancient Greek myth in imitation of Homeric style, its sensibility is completely in keeping with Kayser's assessment of conditions at the beginning of 1933. "Der Tod des Achilleus" is separated from the other nihilistic stories by its artificial language marked by frequent archaisms. An example of this stylistic *tour de force* is the description of Achilles' death on the battlefield, as observed from a superior vantage point by his soul which has already departed the dying body:

Halb zusammengekrümmt lag dieser Mann. Aus dem grünen Leibrock, der unter dem Panzer hervorquoll, ragten die Schenkel matt geöffnet mit den Beinschienen aus Zinn. Brust und

Kopf waren unter dem Schild; wie ein kleiner Kosmos glänzte dessen Figurengewimmel zu ihm herauf: die grosse Kunst des Hephaistos. Widerwillig riss er seinen Blick los von den silbernen Abbildern des Lebens und führte ihn jenen riesigen Arm entlang, den Arm voll dräuender Muskeln, bis zu der machtlosen Faust, die noch den Schwertgriff hielt . . . Kaum konnte der's ertragen zu sehn, wie sich das Blut aus der Ferse dort im Staub verbreitete wie ein zerfranster Fächer. Und ein letztes Zucken durchlief auch den mächtigen Körper drunten; der Schild hob sich noch einmal, — wandte, erneut von einem Sonnenblitz gestreift, sein mächtig funkelndes Rad zur Seite, diesen Kranz von erlesenem Zierrat, und klappte um: da sah Achilleus, und ihn grauste, die eigne ekelverzerrte Lippe und den tiefen unversöhnlichen Grimm der Falte, die wie ein Schnitt aus der niederen breiten Stirn in den Nasenrücken sinkend unter der goldenen Hülse des Brauenschutzes, die wie ein Stachel wegstand vom verschobenen Helm . . . Er sah, wie sein Kehlkopf sich blähte oberhalb des Stahlrandes der Rüstung; seine gekrümmten Kniee flogen zueinander, streckten sich. Und während dies geschah, stieg ein hohles Seufzen aus dem Hals des Mannes; es war das letzte. Es umhüllte den Darüberschwebenden wie ein Flammenmantel. (67)

Death, as in the previous stories, is an ugly process[10]: not a glorified hero but a muscle-bound body capped by a brutal visage with a last expression of disgust. As in "Die Dreingabe" and "Sterben" (as well as Tolstoy's classic version), the mind (or soul) of the dying man unsparingly observes the last moments of the death process—the gradual loss of sensation and the body's last signs of life. In all these stories the reaction of the observer is similar. It is one which defies the conventional euphemisms and attempts by religious usage to sanctify death and dying.[11] Shock, resentment, anger, curiosity are the responses of the three protagonists to the final insult to their

---

[10] Its portrayal in the nihilistic category has something in common with the late medieval apocalyptic mood and emphasis on death manifested in hideous decay of the body as *memento mori*. The obvious difference is that the image of death in the nihilistic category is no longer a function of faith.

[11] For Kayser's earlier glorification of death in a 1922 essay see above p. 194.

bodies. Of the soul of Achilles: "Nur noch diese Gefühle beherrschten ihn: Zorn und Neugier und äusserstes Erstaunen." (67)

The fact that Achilles' story is told from the viewpoint of this still extant soul does not indicate a hopeful attitude. During a transitional state on earth before its final departure to Hades, the soul of Achilles is subjected to intense suffering; death has not brought peace. His mother, the goddess Thetis, emerges from the sea to mourn her son and view his body, but she cannot sense the presence of his soul: "Wiederum war sie taub und blind für die Qual des wahren Sohnes, der so Unnennbares litt." (72) His unquenchable thirst for life drives Achilles' soul to drink the blood of the animals sacrificed for his cremation. He sees his beautiful young mistress and is overcome by regret at having to depart from life. "Es war schwer, von diesem allen zu scheiden. Vom Sonnenlicht zu scheiden. Es ging nicht an. Es war zu früh." (73) Once his body has been consumed by the flames, the inevitable moment of departure comes much in the same manner in which it came to Irwin Schaffold (and to Ivan Ilych)—with a sudden, painful blow: "Und auf einmal, nach einem kurzen Schmerz, nach einem grausamen Schlag, war nichts mehr da . . ." (74) Loneliness and despair follow.

In Hades Achilles' ghost meets his best friend Patroklos and from Patroklos he learns the ways of the world of shades. The victims of Achilles' sword in life—many of them children when he killed them—still bear the wounds he gave them. Their hideously maimed, disfigured, torn bodies inhabit Hades in the same state they were in at the time of their deaths. There is no transfiguration after death. But they have no memory of Achilles, in fact of anything at all in life. Achilles' shocked reaction is to question the meaning of his deeds, of action *per se* (by implication, of life itself): "Was—ist—dann—Tat?" (78) Only Achilles and Patroklos still remember life. Each tells the other stories of treachery which the other had not known about, of deception and murder of which each had been ignorant in life. Even after death there is a desire to inflict pain. The name of Phoebus as the source of light and the author of the treachery fatal to them both is more than either Achilles or Patroklos can bear to hear or think about. They turn to the only cure for the torture of memory of the sun and light, to the panacea which the other inhabitants of Hades crowd each other to reach, a drink from the water which erases all memory. With it the past, life and all that it seemed to signify has been obliterated. It is, as in the case of forgotten love in two previous stories, as if it all had never existed. As the previous nihilistic stories indicated, what we believe and remember is wrong and the truth is only a source of torture. The truth about their isolation, their fruitless efforts, their illusory ideals, their meaningless lives is too harsh to be borne by human beings. This insight brings them to the edge of an abyss.

The last of the stories, Joachim Maass' "Fräulein Ursula oder das Frühjahr in Paris" (February 1933, I, 221–40) treats another kind of death—the "death of the heart" in a loveless world. Kayser, in a review of a book called *Der Bürger und die Liebe* (Paris: Gallimard) by Emanuel Berl, presents the author's assessment of the treatment of love in contemporary literature as a reflection of the changed attitudes toward love among the bourgeoisie:

> In der Literatur ist Liebe fast nur noch Sexualität. Noch nie war soviel von ihr die Rede, noch nie herrschte ein solcher erotischer Pessimismus. So hat der Bürger die Liebe als seine edelste Zuflucht verloren. Das ist, nach dem Glauben dieses Buches, das letzte Geheimnis der bürgerlichen Katastrophe. (283)

From this point of view, therefore, the toppling of romantic love from its pedestal in literature is coincident with the toppling of the values of the bourgeois class and consequent loss of its former secure position. This is one possible, more restrictive, interpretation of the lovelessness which characterizes the nihilistic stories. A broader possibility is to view it as indicative of a pervasive sense of despair which is not confined to the consciousness of a threatened class. A story such as "Hollis und noch Einer" as well as the three "death" stories obviously transcend particular class associations and mark a more profound agony.

"Fräulein Ursula . . ." has to do with the kind of disoriented young 1920's types who people "Die Kinderhochzeit," "Ein ganz verbrecherischer Mensch," and "Das Jahr 1923." They are refugees from their dislocated class and the value-laden older generation. Their talk and their relationships are shallow, without real communication or contact. The dialogue is ironic light comedy. In this story nihilism is propelled by style beyond issues of class to a world view. The twenty-page story is divided, in imitation of a novel, into six titled chapters: "Ankunft," "Spaziergang," "Es unverdient gut haben," "Spaziergang," "Wer liebt, wird gequält," and "Abfahrt." The titles reveal several levels of irony: self-irony on the part of an author who pretentiously divides a twenty-page short story into six titled chapters; irony of the story itself, not only because there are chapter titles but because at least four of them seem so banal as to be useless—mere excuses for titles—and the two with more content stand in the relationship of non-sequiturs to the first four. Implied is an ironic approach to literature *per se* and beyond that, an ironic world view. Life—or at least the segment contained in these six chapters—seems to be a banal, redundant, pointless process of coming and going. The two statements which have content indicate that the one-third portion of life which is subject to interpretation is intrinsically negative, a matter of undeserved good fortune or well-earned misfortune.

The several young characters who meet, walk, and talk in the sleazy bohemian side of Paris (inhabited, it seems, primarily by impoverished young German expatriot artists) address one another—even among friends—by "Sie." The familiar "du" form would breach the tacitly accepted emotional isolation of each from the other. Even erotic encounters are calculated and distant. The first-person narrator speaks only German and cannot communicate with the character who speaks only French—which leads to a certain amount of talk among the bilingual characters that inevitably isolates those two.

The narrator, a young man called only "M.," has come by train from Germany to Paris for a brief visit with his friend Cecil before continuing on to Portugal, which is his ultimate destination. Cecil and his girlfriend Ursula meet M. at the station and bring him to the shabby rooming house where they live—Cecil in a room of his own, Ursula in two rooms which she shares with a young German woman artist, Fräulein Brommel—whom the narrator calls "das Persönchen" because of the coldness of her manner—and Fräulein Brommel's very young French boyfriend (who speaks no German).

Ursula is the central character. She is the character to which the most descriptive effort is devoted. Contrary to the standard conventions for creating women characters, neither her body nor her facial features are described, nor is it said that she is (or is not) pretty. The only remark on a facial feature is that she bears a scar which extends from eyebrow to hairline. This flaw is indicative of Ursula and of the entire physical environment as well. For example, when Ursula dresses up she wears silk trousers which have a run. Her person is created from a series of several attributes—used like building blocks—which are repeated with some variation until we have a portrait of a sensual, phlegmatic, somewhat slovenly young woman, without money, without direction, and without qualities of personality, appearance, character, energy or intelligence which might raise her above the norm or promise a brighter future.

The descriptive style can perhaps best be characterized with that well-worn attribute "Neue Sachlichkeit." It is sober and unadorned. Like a camera, the narrator's eye registers and records what it perceives—persons, objects, colors and textures, his own and other characters' behavior—without judgment upon merits or demerits. (The effect of objectivity, or neutrality, is misleading, of course, because just as the photographer does, the author applies a process of selection and ordering which determines the outcome.)

Ursula's manner of speaking is more important for her characterization than what she says: "mit starkem R-Rollen, aber etwas schläfriger Stimme," (222) "mit ihrer etwas schläfrigen, doch stark skelettierten Sprache," (223) "schläfrige, aber konsonantenschwere Stimme," (228) "mit ihrer etwas schwerfälligen Stimme," (230) "sagte sie konsonantenschwer und gleichgültig," (231) "schläfrig und konsonantenschwer," (237) "mit ihrer etwas schläfrigen, aber stark skelettierten Sprache." (239) Ursula says very little and what she says is without substance. Its very insubstantiality stands for her life situation and lack of commitment (as well as that of her fellows). For example, Ursula supports her suggestion that she, Cecil and M. visit Sacre Coeur in the evening with the recommendation: "Es ist so komisch, so raufzusteigen und runterzugucken." (229) Her posture, movements, gestures and clothes are the other elements which work to compose her total portrait. Generally, she is supine on a chaise longue. Often she stretches, revealing bare skin beneath a thin blouse. She tends to look the narrator straight in the eye. The description of her at their first meeting underscores the vast distance which separates the methods of drawing women characters in this story from the stereotypes of the stories in previous categories: "Sie stand in kurzem Jäckchen und engem Rock gegen einen geschlossenen Kiosk gelehnt, sie lachte unter einem Filzhelmchen hervor, ihr Gesicht war mit Härchen und Puder beflaumt wie ein Pfirsich, sie streckte mir lachend die Hand hin und sah mir ins Gesicht und sagte: 'Guten Abend!' " (222) Instead of operating with preconceived notions of womanhood or ideals of feminine beauty or the conventional image of the seductress, the narrator merely reports what he sees. Only belatedly does the reader see Ursula's effect on the narrator when he begins to tease her and to establish physical contact, carrying out what is obviously an emotionless and well-worn strategy to arouse her.

Not only does Ursula defy the preconceived notion of romantic Paris in springtime, but so does the city itself when viewed through the lens of Maass' "Neue Sachlichkeit." Its cafés—at least those frequented by the narrator and his impecunious companions—are dingy, bare, poorly-lit and characterized in particular by marble table tops inevitably wet with puddles left by the dirty cloths of surly waiters. The food is often indigestible. Paris in springtime is not a city enhanced by a magical aura: "Wir gingen über Pont Neuf, das Seinewasser trieb schlammgelb, der Eiffelturm stand im graublauen Dunst und schräg vor uns lag Notre-Dame mit den abgebrochenen Türmen." (227) Its street scenes slip past as if in a film, viewed from a walking pace or a moving vehicle:

> Gleich links vom Boulevard verengten und verwinkelten und verschatteten sich die Strassen zu Gassen mit seltenen, schräg einfallenden Sonnenstrahlen und zuweilen kulissenhaft vorgebauten Häusern; in den alten Fronthäusern sassen die Schaufenster flach in braunen Holzwandungen mit geschwungenen Goldaufschriften, hinter den Scheiben baumelten in Marmorauslagen Fleischstücke an Haken, aus den offenen Türen wuchsen die Berge Bohnen, Artischocken und Kartoffeln und wechselten mit Bücherständen, dann wieder kamen in der Kühle hinter den Scheiben alte Möbel, Uhren und Porzellane und Kupferstiche auf schönem, körnigem Papier und altertümliche Erdkarten mit bunten Wappen und Windrosen. An einer langen, hohen Lattenwand dankten auf gelben, roten und grünen Plakaten die Deputierten den Wählern für ihre Stimmen und gelobten zum Lohne Freiheit, Wirtschaftsaufstieg, la gloire de la nation, Humanität und Arbeit. (227)

One sight fulfills romantic expectations—Place de la Concorde at night. The narrator admits: "Das ist nun wirklich märchenhaft!" (231) That experience is part of the chapter "Es unverdient gut haben," the title of which is a remark by Cecil in the last scene of the previous chapter on the occasion of enjoying an especially good meal with M. The undeserved good fortune is on a very modest scale. On either side of that chapter is one titled "Spaziergang." The first is marked, in the next to the last scene, by the narrator's warning the good-natured Cecil—who has come to Paris on Ursula's account—against Cecil's intention to ask Ursula to accompany him to Berlin. The second "Spaziergang" brings the outcome of that issue, again in the next-to-the-last scene. Cecil has indeed asked Ursula to come with him and she has refused. This symmetrical pattern is an example of the meticulous, highly organized, almost rigid structuring of the story—an apparent contradiction to the casual, seemingly aimless course of events and relationships. Perhaps form provides the substance which is lacking in the nihilistic sense of the human condition. Perhaps in this particular historical situation form provides a framework, a support, an article of faith when all others have been found unacceptable.

The author cuts almost cruelly through potential sources of romantic illusion and exposes sordid reality. An example is the narrator's simile comparing a pathetic, tawdry light fixture to a sausage skin: "Wir stiegen zum Appartement 27 empor. Die Birne unter der Decke war mit einem roten Schal umwickelt, er hing wie eine Wurstpelle herunter und entliess einen grellen Lichtkegel in den rötlichen Schummer ringsum." (231) The sleazy light bulb exemplifies the sleazy rooming house and the sleazy treatment characters receive at each other's hands. The chapter "Wer liebt, wird gequält" illustrates the casually cruel exploitations of the caring member of each of the couples. Ursula treats Cecil with shabby disregard; the narrator uses Ursula; "das Persönchen" orders her young lover around as if he were her slave. In each case the abused party accepts the relationship because he or she is emotionally dependent. Ursula's self-defense typifies the lack of seriousness, responsibility and a sense of obligation which characterizes attitudes and behavior among the couples. "Ich kann doch nichts dafür, dass er verliebt ist" (237), she remarks about Cecil just before sleeping on the chaise longue with the narrator. The title "Wer liebt, wird gequält" is a remark by "das Persönchen" in response to the narrator's calling her a "beast" for her treatment of her slavishly devoted boyfriend. Finally, when Cecil—the only member of the group who has behaved with decency—leaves the room, the young Frenchman whom Cecil had often defended, as well as the two women immediately begin to make fun of Cecil. The "Männerfreundschaft" between the narrator and Cecil is the only relationship which seems more solid (even though Cecil knows that M. slept with Ursula the night before Cecil's departure for Berlin). M. brings Cecil to the train and they arrange to meet each other in the fall. That evening Ursula accompanies M. to the train for his departure to Portugal.

This concluding scene speaks for the whole story. Ursula, destitute and forsaken, says: "Ich weiss gar nicht, was ich tun soll." (239) The narrator, heading off alone to good times and greener pastures (a fact he had made clear to the little group of bohemians), does not allow himself to be drawn into a serious conversation. He has always spoken to her in the clichés of a superior seducer to an inferior, childish object of seduction, and so continuing to maintain the superficial, paternal tone he responds: "Ja, aber, Ursula, . . . was sollte es denn zu tun geben auf dieser Erde?" (239) When Ursula pathetically protests: "Ich weiss gar nicht, wo ich hingehöre" (239), he reminds her to take possession of the blue drinking glass that was in his room—a standing joke of his about the particular desirability of that glass. Finally, commenting in his detached, offhand manner on the giant locomotive on the track next to them, the narrator says: "Südexpress wär' mir lieber gewesen." Ursula's response—"Ich finde diesen schon ein Märchen"—is followed by the narrator's comment: "sagte Fräulein Ursula ehrlich." (240) It is the first and only time the term or the concept "honest" appears. The narrator—were it not for whom Ursula might have gone with Cecil to Berlin—gives her money for the taxi fare to the rooming house and a goodbye kiss. She leaves without looking back. By revealing honestly her simplicity and by not looking back Ursula has shown unexpected dignity. She is a victim, a pathetic figure whose plight—to know neither what one ought to do nor where one belongs—is a representative one for the nihilistic category.

The nihilistic sensibility in its various forms is clustered in the later years of Kayser's editorship. The first story appeared in 1927. The very last two stories under Kayser's aegis are nihilistic ones. The heavy representation of young authors shows them perhaps to be particularly attuned to a mood of the times. But the scattering of nihilistic stories across a gamut of age groups and styles shows them not to be purely a product of a single generation or a peculiar aesthetic imagination. These stories ought to be seen not merely as expressions of class consciousness under attack—awareness by representatives of a doomed bourgeois culture of its demise—but more importantly of a more profound, if diffuse feeling expressed in Herbert Schlüter's image of facing an abyss and not knowing what is to come on the other side. The nihilistic stories are products of the inheritance of deep postwar disillusionment compounded by an even more deeply disturbing historical evolution since then. That which was most feared had indeed already come to pass. They are products of an historical constellation in which a society plummeting toward destruction appeared neither susceptible nor worthy of rescue.

Conclusion

The stories in the *Neue Rundschau* show a significant evolution between 1922 and 1933. Over the course of these critical years which encompass the prime and the decay of the Weimar Republic changes have taken place in dominant concerns and emphasis as revealed in themes, treatment of themes, and views of the human condition. Broadly speaking, it has been a progression from idealism to realism, from love to lovelessness as well as to preoccupation with corruption and death. Values have first faltered, then disappeared. Traditional concern with nature as an aspect of human experience, with women as peculiar beings, and with the role of "Geist" in society fade in favor of a pervasive nihilism. Within the limitations imposed by the genre short story, by the selection process of editor and publisher, by traditions and trends, coincidences of availability of authors and stories, a portrait of the epoch has emerged. It is a portrait of loss of illusions and disintegration of confidence, but also of a growth of objectivity and a turn toward dispassionate observation.

Reviewing the spectrum of literary strategies represented in the seventy-three stories, we arrive at a sense of the contradictions of the epoch. Initially, philosophical dualism is a dominant factor, pitting an amorphous concept called "life" or "the soul" against a factor considered colder and more mechanical, whether it be called "mind," "reason," "science," or "the machine." This dualism is buttressed by various theories in currency at the time, such as those of Ludwig Klages, whose main work is *Der Geist als Widersacher der Seele* (1929–32). This cast of mind also permeates the early contributions of *Neue Rundschau* editor Rudolf Kayser. It is an aspect of philosophical idealism which proposes the construct of mutually exclusive realms: the pristine ideal and the faulted worldly. Obviously, to such a world view political reality is distasteful, foreign, and irrelevant to what is most important.

In the aesthetic realm the concomitant to this view are stories whose hallmark is a rhapsodic and unfettered style consequent on the denial of the strictures of form. Kayser expresses such an aesthetic in his maiden essay as editor in January 1922. Art, he maintains there, is not to be bound or subject to rules outside itself—possibly to none at all—in order to give unrestricted scope to "genius." Indeed, the early stories are marked as well by the protagonist who, if not necessarily a genius, is always an exceptional individual and a law unto himself, unrestrained by bourgeois standards. Here the influence of Nietzsche is particularly apparent. The protagonist may or may not be a high achiever, but he is the center and focus of each story's universe. His worth and significance as an individual are unquestioned, as are the worth and significance of such categories as, for example, love and memory. The main conflict is resolved, in general, by the protagonist's searching his soul to arrive at insight. The influence of Freudian concepts is usually apparent in this process. In the case of stories which can be ranked as affirmative, the protagonist's moment of insight marks not only a resolution of the primary conflict, but also the achievement of a higher state of being in the spiritual sense. The general tenor is one of reconciliation and redemption.

Showing the dark side of this process, contemporary negative stories recount a movement toward insight which leads to disillusionment, loss, or deprivation. In both categories the transcendental plays a large role. Toward the end of the twenties a number of the negative stories, hand in hand with Kayser's writings and other essays in the *Neue Rundschau*, reveal an increasing apprehension about the fate of "Geist" in German society, that is the fate of enlightened reason as a cultural force. Kayser, Ernst Robert Curtius, Heinrich Mann and like-minded thinkers observe correctly that "Geist" is under attack by the benighted right wing, in particular the Nazis. "Geist" in the sense which its defenders viewed it is thought, however, to have been doomed as well by certain dynamics of the contemporary society such as the growth of mass culture and the extinction of the leading role of the well-to-do bourgeois elite as bearers of culture. By the late twenties Kayser has moved away from the philosophy of dualism, from his early rhapsodic tone and toward a precision, clarity and sobriety of thought and style which is accompanied by a new obeisance to form in art and the possibility of an extrinsic aesthetic which relates art to the social context.

The tensions of a society in transition are particularly evident within the boundaries of a single story, W. E. Süskind's "Raymund," published in the *Neue Rundschau* in April 1927. A portrait of the rootless young generation of the twenties, with their fashions and fads, their fast living, superficiality, and lack of direction, "Raymund" concludes, however, with the protagonist's vision of union with an organic essence of life and his faith in the permanence and rightness of things. The concluding redemptive vision is essentially ideologically regressive, folkish and completely out of keeping with the "new sobriety" and modernism in tone and style of the rest of the story. This contradiction, in different form, is apparent as well in a key essay by Klaus Mann, "Fragment von der Jugend," which appeared in the *Neue Rundschau* in 1926. There a gesture of rejection of the past, the older generation and its values, is combined with harking back for inspiration and guidance to the ecstatic visions of an even earlier generation. Perhaps the term "insecurity" best characterizes the middle period. The stories in the negative category reveal insecurity and a posture of rejection, protest or denial, ending in defeat. The negative and affirmative groups largely overlap in time except for a disjunction which indicates a certain progression in mood: the body of negative stories begins later and continues later than does the body of affirmative stories.

Finally, perhaps inevitably, the concluding vision—in time and logic—is a nihilistic one. All traditional purveyors of meaning—values, hopes, love, memory—are no longer valid in these stories which include the last ones to appear under Kayser's aegis. Love, for example, no longer exists; even as a figment it appears only in one story and acts there as a vehicle for a character's destruction. Memory, a saving force in earlier stories, proves treacherous in the nihilistic ones; it is a device which proves by its dysfunction that the past is meaningless. Such hopeful themes as love and memory have been annulled by a posture of obliviousness, resignation, and indifference. An atmosphere of corruption and decadence pervades these stories. New themes and preoccupations are aging, decay, and death. The transcendental realm is not a concern. Where the concept of the transcendental appears it is denied the substantiality with which idealism had endowed it, and exposed as merely a construct of the human imagination and a sordid extension of the secular world. Literature and art in general are no longer themes as they were in previous categories. The mood is one of acceptance of the inevitable. Life has no meaning beyond the moment, nor is it governed by a moral code or the sacred values of tradition. One of the most sacred values jettisoned in the nihilistic stories is that of the uniqueness and worth (and potential immortality) of the individual. As the nihilistic category becomes dominant, editor Kayser's political realism is growing. His articles in the *Neue Rundschau* become more pointed, astute, and hard-hitting. His development in this respect points to the positive aspect of the nihilistic mentality represented in the stories: it has stripped away the fabric of idealism and illusion to present as objective and unadorned a portrait as possible of the human condition.

It appears that there is a lag between major social and political upheavals and their reflection in literature. Their effects must be digested, reworked, cast into terms of literary discourse. Within the confines of one journal we have seen an epochal leap of consciousness. Over the course of eleven plus years there occurred a change in outlook and sensibility so great that entire generations seem to have passed between beginning and end. The evolution in the *Neue Rundschau* stories and in editor Kayser's attitudes would seem to indicate that the real change to the expression of a characteristic modern hopelessness occurred not directly post-World War I, but rather only when the shock of that war and its aftermath had not proved to lead to productive renewal after all, when it became obvious that the war had not meant even a delayed "cleansing" and new beginning as many had hoped, but rather proved to have no meaning beyond its destructive self. Contrary to hopes neither true recovery ensued, nor reform, nor widespread betterment, nor general prosperity, nor security, nor justice, nor domestic tranquility.

Appendix

Alphabetical List of Authors with Stories and Dates

von Boetticher, Hermann (1887–1941)
  Die aussätzige Magd (1924)
Brod, Max (1884–1968)
  Beschneite Spinnweben (1926)
Faber, Ilse (1887–?)
  Sterben (1932)
Flake, Otto (1880–1963)
  Die zweite Jugend (1924)
  Der Selfmademan (1931)
Frank, Bruno (1887–1945)
  Der Magier (1929)
Frank, Leonhard (1882–1961)
  Der Beamte (1925)
Hesse, Hermann (1877–1962)
  Üble Aufnahme (1925)
  Tragisch (1924)
Heuser, Kurt (1903–1975)
  Sterben auf einer Pflanzung (1928)
  Elfenbein für Felicitas (1927)
  Wiederkehr der Amazonen (1928)
  Ein Feldzug gegen England (1930)

Hirschfeld, Georg (1873–1942)
  Die Insel des Verbrennens (1923)
Hoeflich, Eugen (later name changed to
  Moscheh Ya'akov Ben-gavriêl) (1891–1965)
  Der Meister (1923)
Kafka, Franz (1883–1924)
  Ein Hungerkünstler (1922)
Kayser, Rudolf (1889–1964)
  Die Begegnung in Padua (1924)
Kesten, Hermann (1900–?)
  Emilie (1929)
Kolb, Annette (1875–1967)
  Spitzbögen (1925)
  Geraldine oder die Geschichte einer Operation (1923)
Lehmann, Wilhelm (1882–1968)
  Verführerin, Trösterin (1928)
Lichnowsky, Mechtilde (1879–1958)
  Das Rendezvous im Zoo (1927)
Lübbe, Axel (1880–1963)
  Hugo von Brandenburg (1927)
  Der Rettungsversuch (1929)
Maas, Joachum (1901–?)
  Ein ganz verbrecherischer Mensch (1930)
  Fräulein Ursula oder das Frühjahr in Paris (1933)
Mann, Heinrich (1871–1950)
  Kobes (1925)
Mann, Thomas (1875–1955)
  Unordnung und frühes Leid (1925)
Meisel, Hans (1900–?)
  Hollis und noch Einer (1928)
Musil, Robert (1880–1942)
  Die Amsel (1928)
Ponten, Josef (1883–1940)
  Das grosse Asien oder: Wiedersehen mit Charlotte (1924)

Unterredung im Grase (1922)
Das Autodafé (1922)
Frau im Süden (1925)

Regler, Gustav (1898–1963)
Ein Lamm hat sich verlaufen (1931)

Reisiger, Hans (1884–1968)
Not und Verklärung (1928)
Stehe auf und wandle (1926)

Roth, Joseph (1894–1939)
Der stumme Prophet (1929)

Schaeffer, Albrecht (1885–1950)
Das Gitter (1922)
Meleagros und Atalante (1928)
Die silberne Saite (1930)
Der Major (1931)

Schaffner, Jakob (1875–1944)
Die Dreingabe (1932)

Schickele, René (1883–1940)
Tulpen (1923)
Die Gletscherspalte (1925)

Schlüter, Herbert (1906–?)
Die Kinderhochzeit (1927)
Zerstörung durch Liebe (1929)
Das Jahr 1923 (1931)

Schmidtbonn, Wilhelm (1876–1952)
Die verwegenen Girlanden (1928)
Die zwei Indianer (1926)
Der Vater (1932)

Schnitzler, Arthur (1862–1931)
Fräulein Else (1924)

Seidel, Willy (1887–1934)
Der Tod des Achilleus (1933)

Strauss, Ludwig (1892–1953)
Gertrud und Bianca (1931)

Stucken, Eduard (1865–1936)
König Pfauhahn (1931)
Süskind, W. E. (1901–1970)
Raymund (1927)
Beginn einer Liebe (1930)
Das Leben zu dritt (1931)
Torberg, Friedrich (1908–?)
Todeskampf einer Liebe (1930)
Trebitsch, Siegfried (1869–1956)
Der Geheilte (1926)
Ulitz, Arnold (1888–1971)
Boykott (1930)
Ullmann, Regina (1884–1961)
Die Barockkirche (1923)
Ungar, Hermann (1893–1929)
Colberts Reise (1922)
Der Weinreisende (1930)
Vietta, Egon (pseudonym for Egon Fritz) (1903–1959)
Der Registrator (1932)
von der Vring, Georg (1889–1968)
Aube (1930)
Wassermann, Jakob (1873–1934)
Das Gold von Caxamalca (1923)
Weiss, Ernst (1884–1940)
Marengo oder das Leben ohne Illusionen (1926)
Werfel, Franz (1890–1945)
Carbrinowitsch. Ein Tagebuch aus dem Jahre 1915 (1923)
Das Trauerhaus (1927)
Winder, Ludwig (1889–1946)
Turnlehrer Pravda (1923)
Zweig, Stefan (1881–1942)
Phantastische Nacht (1922)
Rahel rechtet mit Gott (1927)

Selected Bibliography

1. *Die Neue Rundschau* and Weimar Culture

Bermann Fischer, Gottfried. *Bedroht-Bewahrt: Weg eines Verlegers*. Frankfurt am Main: S. Fischer, 1967.

Bracher, Karl Dietrich. *Die Auflösung der Weimarer Republik*. 5th ed. Villingen/ Schwarzwald: Ring, 1971.

Buchheim, Karl. *Die Weimarer Republik. Das Deutsche Reich ohne Kaiser*. 3rd ed. Munich: Kösel, 1970.

Bullivant, Keith, ed. *Culture and Society in the Weimar Republic*. Manchester: Manchester Univ. Press, 1977.

Diwald, Hellmut. "Literatur und Zeitgeist in der Weimarer Republik." In *Zeitgeist der Weimarer Republik*. Ed. Hans Joachim Schoeps. Stuttgart: Ernst Klett, 1968, pp. 203–260.

Eschenburg, Theodor. *Die improvisierte Demokratie. Gesammelte Aufsätze zur Weimarer Republik*. Munich: R. Piper, 1963.

Frenzel, Ivo. "Utopia and Apocalypse in German Literature." *Social Research*, 39, No. 2 (Summer 1972), 306–21.

Friedrich, Otto. *Before the Deluge: A Portrait of Berlin in the 1920's*. New York: Harper & Row, 1972.

Gay, Peter. *Weimar Culture: The Outsider as Insider*. New York: Harper & Row, 1968.

Grimm, Reinhold and Jost Hermand, eds. *Die sogenannten zwanziger Jahre. First Wisconsin Workshop*. Bad Homburg: Gehlen, 1970.

Grothe, Wolfgang. "Die Neue Rundschau des Verlages S. Fischer: Ein Beitrag zur Publizistik und Literaturgeschichte der Jahre von 1890 bis 1925." *Archiv für Geschichte des Buchwesens*, 4 (1963), cols. 809–996.

Hermand, Jost and Frank Trommler. *Die Kultur der Weimarer Republik*. Munich: Nymphenburg, 1978.

Kurucz, Jenö. *Struktur und Funktion der Intelligenz während der Weimarer Republik*. Spich Bez. Köln: Grote, 1967.

Laqueur, Walter. *Weimar: A Cultural History 1918–1933*. New York: G. P. Putnam's Sons, 1974.

Lethen, Helmut. *Neue Sachlichkeit 1924–1932: Studien zur Literatur des 'Weissen Sozialismus.'* Stuttgart: Metzler, 1970.

Mendelssohn, Peter de. *S. Fischer und sein Verlag*. Frankfurt am Main: S. Fischer, 1970.

Pachter, Henry M. "The Intellectuals and the State of Weimar." *Social Research*, 39, No. 2 (Summer 1972), 228–53.

Pross, Harry. *Literatur und Politik. Geschichte und Programme der politisch-literarischen Zeitschriften im deutschen Sprachgebiet seit 1870*. Olten and Freiburg im Breisgau: Walter, 1963.

Romoser, George K. "Introduction." *Social Research*, 39, No. 2 (Summer 1972), 207–12.

Rothe, Wolfgang. "Metaphysischer Realismus. Literarische Aussenseiter zwischen Links und Rechts." In *Die deutsche Literatur in der Weimarer Republik*. Ed. Wolfgang Rothe. Stuttgart: Reclam, 1974, pp. 255–80.

Sauer, Wolfgang. "Weimar Culture: Experiment in Modernism." *Social Research*, 39, No. 2 (Summer 1972), 254–84.

Schäfer, Hans Dieter. "Naturdichtung und Neue Sachlichkeit." In *Die deutsche Literatur in der Weimarer Republik*. Ed. Wolfgang Rothe. Stuttgart: Reclam, 1974, pp. 359–81.

Schlawe, Fritz. *Literarische Zeitschriften 1910–1933*. 2nd ed. Sammlung Metzler, 24. Stuttgart: Metzler, 1973.

Schulz, Gerhard. *Deutschland seit dem Ersten Weltkrieg 1918–1945*. Göttingen: Vandenhoeck & Ruprecht, 1976.

Schwarz, Falk. "Die gelenkte Literatur. Die 'Neue Rundschau' im Konflikt mit den Kontrollstellen des NS-Staates und der national-sozialistischen 'Bewegung.' " In *Die deutsche Literatur im Dritten Reich*. Eds. Horst Denkler and Karl Prümm. Stuttgart: Reclam, 1976, pp. 66–82.

———. "Literarisches Zeitgespräch im Dritten Reich: dargestellt an der Zeitschrift 'Neue Rundschau.' " *Archiv für Geschichte des Buchwesens*, 12 (1971–72), cols. 1282–1483.

Solmsen, Friedrich and Lieselotte Solmsen. Private interview on their memories of Weimar culture. Chapel Hill, N.C. May 1979.

Sontheimer, Kurt. *Antidemokratisches Denken in der Weimarer Republik*. Munich: Nymphenburg, 1962.

———. "Weimar—ein deutsches Kaleidoskop." In *Die deutsche Literatur in der Weimarer Republik*. Ed. Wolfgang Rothe. Stuttgart: Reclam, 1974, pp. 9–18.

Stappenbacher, Susi. "Die deutschen literarischen Zeitschriften in den Jahren 1918–1925 als Ausdruck geistiger Strömungen der Zeit." Diss. Erlangen-Nürnberg 1961.

Stern, Guy. *War, Weimar, and Literature: The Story of the 'Neue Merkur' 1914–1925*. University Park and London: Pennsylvania State Univ. Press, 1971.

Wendler, Wolfgang. "Die Einschätzung der Gegenwart im deutschen Zeitroman." In *Die deutsche Literatur in der Weimarer Republik*. Ed. Wolfgang Rothe. Stuttgart: Reclam, 1974, pp. 169–94.

Willett, John. *Art and Politics in the Weimar Period. The New Sobriety, 1917–1933*. New York: Pantheon Books, 1978.

Zuckmayer, Carl. *Als wär's ein Stück von mir: Erinnerungen*. Frankfurt am Main: Fischer Bücherei, 1969.

II. Principles of Criticism and General Literary Reference Works

Abrams, M. H. *A Glossary of Literary Terms*. 3rd ed. New York: Holt, Rinehart and Winston, 1971.

Alker, Ernst. *Profile und Gestalten der deutschen Literatur nach 1914*. Ed. by Eugen Thurnher. Stuttgart: Alfred Kröner, 1977.

Berger, Bruno and Heinz Rupp, eds. *Deutsches Literatur-Lexikon*. 3rd ed. Berne and Munich: Francke, 1968.

Braak, Ivo. *Poetik in Stichworten: Literaturwissenschaftliche Grundbegriffe*. 4th ed. Kiel: Ferdinand Hirt, 1972.

Falk, Eugene H. *Types of Thematic Structure: The Nature and Function of Motifs in Gide, Camus, and Satre*. Chicago and London: Univ. of Chicago Press, 1967.

Frenzel, Herbert A. and Elisabeth Frenzel. *Daten deutscher Dichtung: Chronologischer Abriss der deutschen Literaturgeschichte*. 5th ed. Munich: Deutscher Taschenbuch Verlag, 1969.

Holman, C. Hugh. *A Handbook to Literature*. 3rd ed. New York: Bobbs-Merrill, 1972.

Ingarden, Roman. *The Literary Work of Art: An Investigation on the Borderlines of Ontology, Logic, and the Theory of Literature*. [1931]. Trans., with an intro. by George G. Grabowicz. Evanston: Northwestern Univ. Press, 1973.

Kayser, Wolfgang. *Das sprachliche Kunstwerk*. 5th ed. Berne and Munich: Francke, 1959.

Kosch, Wilhelm, ed. *Deutsches Literatur-Lexikon*. 2nd ed, Berne: Francke, 1949.

Kunisch, Hermann, ed. *Handbuch der deutschen Gegenwartsliteratur*. 2nd ed. Munich: Nymphenburg, 1970.

Lemon, Lee T. and Marion J. Reis, trans. *Russian Formalist Criticism: Four Essays*. Regents Critics Series. Lincoln: Univ. of Nebraska Press, 1965.

Lennartz, Franz. *Deutsche Dichter und Schriftsteller unserer Zeit*. 10th ed. Stuttgart: Alfred Kröner, 1969.

Schuder, Werner, ed. *Kürschners Deutscher Literatur-Kalendar. Nekrolog 1936–70*. Berlin, New York: Walter de Gruyter, 1973.

Thomson, Philip. *The Grotesque*. The Critical Idiom, 24. Ed. John D. Jump. London: Methuen & Co Ltd, 1972.

Wellek, René. *Concepts of Criticism*. New Haven and London: Yale Univ. Press, 1963.

Wellek, René and Austin Warren. *Theory of Literature*. 3rd ed. New York: Harcourt, Brace & World, 1956.

Wilpert, Gero von. *Deutsches Dichterlexikon*. Stuttgart: Alfred Kröner, 1963.

Index

studia humanitatis

PUBLISHED VOLUMES

Louis Marcello La Favia, *Benvenuto Rambaldi da Imola: Dantista*. xii–188 pp. US $9.25.

John O'Connor, *Balzac's Soluble Fish*. xii–252 pp. US $14.25.

Carlos García, *La desordenada codicia*, edición crítica de Giulio Massano. xii–220 pp. US $11.50.

Everett W. Hesse, *Interpretando la Comedia*. xii–184 pp. US $10.00.

Lewis Kamm, *The Object in Zola's* Rougon-Macquart. xii–160 pp. US $9.25.

Ann Bugliani, *Women and the Feminine Principle in the Works of Paul Claudel*. xii–144 pp. US $9.25.

Charlotte Frankel Gerrard, *Montherlant and Suicide*. xvi–72 pp. US $5.00.

The Two Hesperias. Literary Studies in Honor of Joseph G. Fucilla. Edited by Americo Bugliani. xx–372 pp. US $30.00.

Jean J. Smoot, *A Comparison of Plays by John M. Synge and Federico García Lorca: The Poets and Time*. xiii–220 pp. US $13.00.

Laclos. Critical Approaches to Les Liaisons dangereuses. Ed. Lloyd R. Free. xii–300 pp. US $17.00.

Julia Conaway Bondanella, *Petrarch's Visions and their Renaissance Analogues*. xii–120 pp. US $7.00.

Vincenzo Tripodi, *Studi su Foscolo e Stern*. xii–216 pp. US $13.00.

GENARO J. PÉREZ, *Formalist Elements in the Novels of Juan Goytisolo.* xii–216 pp. US $12.50.

SARA MARIA ADLER, *Calvino: The Writer as Fablemaker.* xviii–164 pp. US $11.50.

LOPE DE VEGA, *El amor enamorado,* critical edition of John B. Wooldridge, Jr. xvi–236 pp. US $13.00.

NANCY DERSOFI, *Arcadia and the Stage: A Study of the Theater of Angelo Beolco* (called *Ruzante*). xii–180 pp. US $10.00

JOHN A. FREY, *The Aesthetics of the* ROUGON-MACQUART. xvi–356 pp. US $20.00.

CHESTER W. OBUCHOWSKI, *Mars on Trial: War as Seen by French Writers of the Twentieth Century.* xiv–320 pp. US $20.00.

JEREMY T. MEDINA, *Spanish Realism: Theory and Practice of a Concept in the Nineteenth Century.* xviii–374 pp. US $17.50.

MAUDA BREGOLI-RUSSO, *Boiardo Lirico.* viii–204 pp. US $11.00.

ROBERT H. MILLER, ed. *Sir John Harington: A Supplie or Addicion to the Catalogue of Bishops to the Yeare 1608.* xii–214 pp. US $13.50.

NICOLÁS E. ÁLVAREZ, *La obra literaria de Jorge Mañach.* vii–279 pp. US $13.00.

MARIO ASTE, *La narrativa di Luigi Pirandello: Dalle novelle al romanzo Uno, Nessuno, e Centomila.* xvi–200 pp. US $11.00.

MECHTHILD CRANSTON, *Orion Resurgent: René Char, Poet of Presence.* xxiv–376 pp. US $22.50.

FRANK A. DOMÍNGUEZ, *The Medieval Argonautica.* viii–122 pp. US $10.50.

EVERETT HESSE, *New Perspectives on Comedia Criticism.* xix–174 pp. US $14.00.

ANTHONY A. CICCONE, *The Comedy of Language: Four Farces by Molière.* xii–144 $12.00.

ANTONIO PLANELLS, *Cortázar: Metafísica y erotismo.* xvi–220 pp. US $10.00.

MARY LEE BRETZ, *La evolución novelística de Pío Baroja.* viii–476 pp. US $22.50.

Romance Literary Studies: Homage to Harvey L. Johnson, ed. Marie A. Wellington and Martha O'Nan. xxxvii–185 pp. US $15.00.

GEORGE E. MCSPADDEN, *Don Quijote and the Spanish Prologues,* volume I. vi–114 pp. US $17.00.

Studies in Honor of Gerald E. Wade, edited by Sylvia Bowman, Bruno M. Damiani, Janet W. Díaz, E. Michael Gerli, Everett Hesse, John E. Keller, Luis Leal and Russell P. Sebold. xii–244 pp. US $20.00.

LOIS ANN RUSSELL, *Robert Challe: A Utopian Voice in the Early Enlightenment*. xiii–164 pp. US $12.50.

CRAIG WALLACE BARROW, *Montage in James Joyce's* ULYSSES. xiii–218 pp. US $16.50.

MARIA ELISA CIAVARELLI, *La fuerza de la sangre en la literatura del Siglo de Oro*. xii–274 pp. US $17.00.

JUAN MARÍA COROMINAS, *Castiglione y La Araucana: Estudio de una Influencia*. viii–139 pp. US $14.00.

KENNETH BROWN, *Anastasio Pantaleón de Ribera (1600–1629) Ingenioso Miembro de la República Literaria Española*. xix–420 pp. US $18.50.

JOHN STEVEN GEARY, *Formulaic Diction in the* Poema de Fernán González *and the* Mocedades de Rodrigo. xv–180 pp. US $15.50.

HARRIET K. GREIF, *Historia de nacimientos: The Poetry of Emilio Prados*. xi–399 pp. US $18.00.

El cancionero del Bachiller Jhoan López, edición crítica de Rosalind Gabin. lvi–362 pp. US $30.00

VICTOR STRANDBERG, *Religious Psychology in American Literature*. xi–237 pp. US $17.50

M. AMELIA KLENKE, O.P., *Chrétien de Troyes and "Le Conte del Graal": A Study of Sources and Symbolism*.xvii–88 pp. US $11.50

MARINA SCORDILIS BROWNLEE, *The Poetics of Literary Theory: Lope de Vega's* Novelas a Marcia Leonarda *and Their Cervantine Context*. x–182 pp. US $16.50

NATALIE NESBITT WOODLAND, *The Satirical Edge of Truth in "The Ring and the Book."* ix–166 pp. US $17.00

JOSEPH BARBARINO, *The Latin Intervocalic Stops: A Quantitative and Comparative Study*. xi–153 pp. US $16.50

EVERETT W. HESSE, *Essays on Spanish Letters of the Golden Age*. xii–208 pp. US $16.50

SANDRA GERHARD, "Don Quijote" *and the Shelton Translation: A Stylistic Analysis*. viii–166 pp. US $16.00.

VALERIE D. GREENBERG, *Literature and Sensibilities in the Weimar Era: Short Stories in the "Neue Rundschau."* Preface by Eugene H. Falk. xiii–289 pp. US $18.00.

FORTHCOMING PUBLICATIONS

HELMUT HATZFELD, *Essais sur la littérature flamboyante.*

NANCY D'ANTUONO, *Boccaccio's novelle in Lope's theatre.*

Novelistas femeninas de la postguerra española, ed. Janet W. Díaz.

La Discontenta and La Pythia, edition with introduction and notes by Nicholas A. De Mara.

PERO LÓPEZ DE AYALA, *Crónica del Rey Don Pedro I*, edición crítica de Heanon y Constance Wilkins.

ALBERT H. LE MAY, *The Experimental Verse Theater of Valle-Inclán.*

DENNIS M. KRATZ, *Mocking Epic.*

CALDERÓN DE LA BARCA, *The Prodigal Magician*, translated and edited by Bruce W. Wardropper.

JAMES DONALD FOGELQUIST, *El Amadís y el género de la historia fingida.*

HELÍ HERNÁNDEZ, *Antecedentes italianos de la novela picaresca española: estudio lingüístico-literario.*

BIRUTÉ CIPLIJAUSKAITÉ, *Los noventayochistas y la historia.*

FERNANDO RIELO, *Teoría del Quijote.*

ALONSO ORTIZ, *Diálogo sobre la educación del Príncipe Don Juan, hijo de los Reyes Católicos.* Introducción y versión de Giovanni Maria Bertini.

EGLA MORALES BLOUIN, *El ciervo y la fuente: mito y folklore del agua en la lírica tradicional.*

ANDREA PERRUCCI, *Shepherds' Song (La Cantata dei Pastori).* English version by Miriam and Nello D'Aponte.

GALEOTTO DEL CARRETTO, *Li sei contenti e La Sofonisba*, edizione e commento di Mauda Bregoli Russo.

EDITH MARIA TOEGEL, *Emily Dickenson and Annette von Droste-Hülshoff: Poets as Women.*

MARY JO MURATORE, *The Evolution of the Cornelian Heroine.*